D0458405

THE
CONSERVATIVE ASSAULT
ON THE CONSTITUTION

Erwin Chemerinsky

SIMON & SCHUSTER
New York   London   Toronto   Sydney

 Simon & Schuster
1230 Avenue of the Americas
New York, NY 10020

First Simon & Schuster hardcover edition September 2010

SIMON & SCHUSTER and colophon are registered trademarks
of Simon & Schuster, Inc.

For information about special discounts for bulk purchases,
please contact Simon & Schuster Special Sales at
1-866-506-1949 or business@simonandschuster.com.

The Simon & Schuster Speakers Bureau can bring authors
to your live event. For more information or to book an event,
contact the Simon & Schuster Speakers Bureau at
1-866-248-3049 or visit our website at www.simonspeakers.com.

Designed by Renata Di Biase

Manufactured in the United States of America

10   9   8   7   6   5   4   3   2   1

Library of Congress Cataloging-in-Publication Data
Chemerinsky, Erwin.
    The conservative assault on the constitution / Erwin Chemerinsky. —
1st ed.
        p.   cm.
Includes bibliographical references and index.
ISBN-13: 978-1-4165-7468-2
ISBN-10: 1-4165-7468-9
ISBN-13: 978-1-4516-0635-5 (ebook)
1. Constitutional law—United States.   I. Title.
KF4550.C426 2010
342.73—dc22

                                                    2010027864

To my wife, Catherine.
Her support and encouragement made this book possible;
her love makes every day a joy.

CONTENTS

The Constitution Touches Everyone

My former client Leandro Andrade is serving a sentence of life in prison with no possibility of parole for fifty years for stealing $153 worth of videotapes from Kmart stores in Southern California. He received this sentence under California's "three-strikes" law even though he had never committed a violent felony. No one in the history of the United States ever had been sentenced to life in prison—which is effectively what Andrade's sentence amounts to—for shoplifting before California adopted its three-strikes law. The Eighth Amendment to the Constitution prohibits "cruel and unusual punishment." Surely life in prison for shoplifting is cruel and it ought to be unusual.

Yet, as I stood before the United States Supreme Court justices on a Tuesday morning in November 2002 to argue that Andrade's sentence was unconstitutional, I knew that the odds were against me. Chief Justice William Rehnquist and Justices Antonin Scalia and Clarence Thomas already were on record expressing the view that the length of a person's sentence never could be challenged under the cruel and unusual punishment clause of the Eighth Amendment. Nothing that I could say could change their minds.

I was confident that I would get the votes of the more liberal justices—John Paul Stevens, David Souter, Ruth Bader Ginsburg, and Stephen Breyer—because each had previously expressed great concern about the constitutionality of life sentences for shoplifting under California's three-strikes law. But that meant to prevail I would need to get the vote of either Sandra Day O'Connor or Anthony Kennedy. Both of these justices were appointed by

President Ronald Reagan and they were far more likely to side with the conservatives than with the liberals, especially in cases involving criminal defendants.

As I wrote the brief for the Supreme Court and prepared for the oral argument, I thought that I could not have a stronger set of facts for arguing that a sentence was unconstitutional. Almost seven years to the day before my argument in the Supreme Court, on November 4, 1995, Leandro Andrade—a nine-year army veteran and father of three—was caught shoplifting five children's videotapes (*Snow White, Casper, The Fox and the Hound, The Pebble and the Penguin,* and *Batman Forever*), worth a total of $84.70, from a Kmart store in Ontario, California. The store's loss prevention officer observed Andrade's actions and Andrade was stopped, the videotapes confiscated, and he was arrested for shoplifting.

Just two weeks later, on November 18, Andrade went to a different Kmart, in Montclair, California, and was caught shoplifting four children's videotapes (*Free Willy 2, Cinderella, The Santa Clause,* and *Little Women*) worth $68.84. Again Andrade was observed on store video cameras, he was stopped by security officers, the videotapes were confiscated, and Andrade was arrested for shoplifting.

Andrade's reason for stealing the videotapes never was clear. He maintained that the videos were to be gifts for his nieces and nephews. The state contended that he meant to sell them and buy drugs. Andrade had become a heroin addict while serving in the army and had long struggled with addiction.

I never asked him why he stole the videotapes. At trial, before a jury, it might matter in making him seem more sympathetic. But I became his lawyer on appeal, in the federal court of appeals and then the Supreme Court, where the issue was solely about whether his sentence was constitutional. Besides, the reason for his crimes doesn't matter under the law. Stealing $153 worth of videotapes generally is regarded as the crime of "petty theft," a misdemeanor under California law. Petty theft is defined as stealing $400 or less of money or merchandise and is punishable by a fine or a jail sentence of six months or less. A person who gets caught shoplifting twice in California faces a maximum sentence of one year in jail, six months for each crime.

California law, however, provides that petty theft can be charged as a felony if the defendant has previously been convicted of a property crime. This is titled the offense of "petty theft with a prior." When someone with a prior property conviction gets caught shoplifting, the district attorney's office in that county decides whether to charge the person with the misdemeanor of petty theft or with the felony of petty theft with a prior.

When Andrade got out of the army he committed a series of relatively minor property crimes, including some other shoplifting. His most serious offenses were in 1983, twelve years before he was caught stealing from the Kmart stores, when he committed three residential burglaries on the same day. He was unarmed and nobody was home at any of the houses when he broke into them. He was caught and convicted of the burglaries. He was sentenced to two and a half years in prison, which he served. Unfortunately, the time in prison did not cure his heroin addiction; drug treatment programs are lacking in California's prisons and prisons across the country.

Because of those three residential burglaries that occurred more than a decade earlier, Andrade's stealing of the videotapes from the Kmarts was charged as the crime of petty theft with a prior. Ironically, if Andrade's prior crimes had been rape and murder, his maximum sentence for stealing the videotapes would have been one year in jail; "petty theft with a prior" requires that the previous conviction be for a *property* offense.

Petty theft with a prior in California is punishable by three years in prison. The way California's sentencing structure works, two counts of petty theft with a prior is punishable by a maximum of three years and eight months in prison. If that had been his sentence, he would have received a significant punishment for stealing $153 worth of videotapes.

But in 1994 California voters passed an initiative and adopted a law called "three strikes and you're out." The three-strikes law in California requires that the first two felonies be serious or violent felonies, but the third strike can be any felony; it need not be a serious or violent one. About half the states in the country have three-strikes laws, but California is alone in not requiring that the third strike be a serious or violent crime. The campaign for the initiative focused on how a young girl, Polly Klaas, had been kidnapped and murdered by Richard Allen Davis, a man who was free on probation despite several prior convictions for violent crimes. All of the publicity surrounding the initiative emphasized the need to keep violent criminals locked up. None of the newspaper editorials about the initiative or the mailings sent to voters about it mentioned the possibility that it could be applied when the third strike was a minor offense such as shoplifting or possession of a small amount of drugs. There is no indication that California's voters realized this aspect of the initiative.

Because Andrade was convicted of two counts of petty theft with a prior, he was sentenced under the California three-strikes law to two sentences of twenty-five years to life to run consecutively. His sentence, properly phrased, is an indeterminate life sentence with no possibility of parole for fifty years. He was convicted in 1996 when he was thirty-seven years old. By the time he is eligible for parole in the year 2046 he will be eighty-seven years old.

Andrade is not unique in California. At the time I argued his case in 2002, there were 344 individuals serving sentences of twenty-five to life or more for petty theft with a prior under California's three-strikes law. More than six hundred others were serving life sentences for being caught with small quantities of drugs.

It was a matter of circumstances that led to Andrade being sentenced to a minimum of fifty years in prison for shoplifting. Had he been caught shoplifting in San Francisco or Los Angeles or San Diego, the district attorney's office would not have charged him under the three-strikes law. Those offices have the policy of not using that law when the last crime is petty theft. It was up to the prosecutor to decide what to charge, and Andrade had the misfortune of doing his shoplifting in a county, San Bernardino, where the district attorney's policy was to seek the maximum penalty, even when it meant life in prison for shoplifting. Also, Andrade's ethnicity—he is Latino—may have mattered. Studies show that African-Americans and Latinos are more likely to be charged under the three-strikes law, even when whites have committed the same offense and have the same prior criminal history.

The jury that convicted Andrade of shoplifting had no idea what his sentence would be. The only issue before them was whether Andrade stole the videotapes. A week before the Supreme Court heard Andrade's case, Dan Rather on *60 Minutes II* broadcast a segment on the case and found some of the jurors who had convicted Andrade. They expressed shock and dismay when they learned of the punishment imposed. Rather went to the prison where Andrade was incarcerated and spoke with him on camera. Andrade was very articulate in expressing regret for his crime and bewilderment and outrage that he was serving a life sentence for shoplifting.

After Andrade was convicted and sentenced, his lawyer appealed to the California Court of Appeal, but it rejected his claim that his sentence was cruel and unusual punishment. He sought review in the California Supreme Court, but it denied review, as it has done in every case where an individual has argued that his or her life sentence under the three-strikes law is cruel and unusual punishment.

On his own, Andrade filed a lawsuit—called a petition for a writ of habeas corpus—in federal court to have his sentence declared unconstitutional. Habeas corpus allows a convicted person to seek relief in federal court on the ground that the U.S. Constitution has been violated. Andrade had a lawyer for his appeals in the California court system, but there is no right to a lawyer on habeas corpus in federal court. The federal court dismissed Andrade's petition. On his own, Andrade filed an appeal in the federal court of appeals.

Through a coincidence, I was asked to represent Andrade there. The staff attorneys who work in the federal court of appeals can identify cases in which attorneys should be appointed to represent individuals who do not have lawyers. There are cases with complex or important issues where the judges and the court staff think that the court would benefit from a lawyer's briefing and arguing the matter. Lawyers in various regions of the state help to find volunteer attorneys for these cases. I have been asked many times to handle these "pro bono" appeals and always have accepted. The rules of professional conduct for lawyers are clear that attorneys should refuse such court appointments only under extraordinary circumstances.

A former student of mine, Peter Afrasiabi, was helping to find volunteer attorneys to handle cases coming from Southern California. About a year earlier, I had mentioned to Peter that I was seeking U.S. Supreme Court review on behalf of a man, Stanley Durden, who had received a life sentence with no possibility of parole for twenty-five years for stealing an umbrella and two bottles of liquor worth forty-three dollars from a supermarket on a cold, rainy night. Durden, like Andrade, received this sentence under the three-strikes law even though he had never committed a violent felony. The lawyer representing Durden became ill and asked if I would prepare the petition for Supreme Court review in his case. I did so, but the Supreme Court refused to hear the matter. Durden remains in prison serving his twenty-five-year sentence for shoplifting. When Peter was asked by the staff attorney at the federal court of appeals to find a lawyer for Andrade, he immediately thought of me.

I argued Andrade's case in the federal court of appeals in San Francisco in May 2001. Six months later, the court ruled in my favor by a 2–1 margin and held that Andrade's sentence was cruel and unusual punishment. Andrade told me of the jubilation that he and others in the prison felt when they heard of the ruling. I remember my elation the day the decision came down and knew that it gave tremendous hope to the families of the many people serving life sentences for minor crimes under the three-strikes law. Some of these family members contacted me to see if I would handle the appeals of their loved ones. As a full-time law professor, I can accept only a limited number of cases. Because I almost always handle cases pro bono, without any charge, I receive hundreds of requests to take matters. In choosing a few a year,

I generally focus on the chance for the case to make a difference in the law. Sometimes, though, I am moved by the underlying human story. I took one of these cases, agreeing to handle the appeal in federal court of Jeffrey Rico, a young man in his twenties whose third strike was stealing a television set worth $128 from a department store. His mother called me several times and I was very affected by her story and the senselessness of having a man spend a quarter of a century in prison for theft of a cheap television.

Soon after the court decided Andrade's case, a staff attorney at the federal court of appeals called and said that the court wanted to appoint me to represent two other individuals, Ernest Bray and Richard Brown, who were each serving twenty-five to life for shoplifting small amounts of merchandise. I immediately accepted the appointment. What made their cases different from Andrade's was the seriousness of their prior offenses; they had earlier committed violent crimes, though each of their last offenses was shoplifting. The court of appeals asked for expedited briefing and argument, hearing the cases in December 2001, just six weeks after its decision in Andrade. The court of appeals ruled for Bray and Brown, concluding that it was inherently cruel and unusual punishment to sentence a person to prison for life for shoplifting, no matter the nature of the prior offenses.

To my dismay, the state of California sought review in the U.S. Supreme Court in Andrade's case and it was granted in April 2002. The attorney general of California, Bill Lockyer, did not have to seek Supreme Court review; states choose not to seek Supreme Court review in hundreds of cases a year. I was hopeful that as a fairly liberal Democrat he would not want to defend life imprisonment for shoplifting. But Lockyer was contemplating a run for governor, and being seen as soft on crime is never politically advantageous.

The briefs in the Andrade case were written during the summer of 2002. Since I had won in the court of appeals, the state of California filed its brief first; I then wrote and filed mine. In the U.S. Supreme Court, the briefs are no more than fifty pages, presenting the justices with a summary of the facts in the case and a detailed presentation of the legal arguments. My brief went through dozens of drafts as I solicited comments from experienced lawyers and worked to refine both the writing and the analysis. I worked on it constantly, at home, at the office, on airplanes, in hotel rooms as I traveled. The state then filed a shorter reply brief. Approximately a dozen organizations filed briefs in the Supreme Court in the case, roughly the same number for each side of the litigation. Sometimes such briefs, commonly called amicus curiae ("friend of the court") briefs, present arguments not in the briefs of the parties; more commonly they are a chance for interested organizations to present their views to the court.

The oral arguments were scheduled for the first Tuesday in November 2002. The same day that I argued Andrade's case, the Supreme Court heard oral argument in another case coming from California regarding the three-strikes law. Gary Ewing went into a pro shop and stole three golf clubs worth a total of $1,200. I am not a golfer and was astounded to learn that golf clubs could be worth that much. Ewing put the clubs down his pants and tried to walk out of the store. He was caught and charged with grand theft. Because of his prior convictions, he was sentenced to life in prison with no possibility of parole for twenty-five years. Ewing's case was different from Andrade's in that Ewing had a prior conviction for a violent offense and also Ewing's theft of the golf clubs was grand theft since it was for more than $400, while Andrade's crime was petty theft. Ewing had been diagnosed with AIDS and was in poor health by the time the Supreme Court heard his case.

As a matter of law, I thought that I was on very strong grounds to win Andrade's case. Almost a century earlier, the Supreme Court held that the Eighth Amendment prohibits "greatly disproportioned" sentences and stated that "it is a precept of justice that punishment for crime should be graduated and proportioned to the offense." On other occasions, too, the Supreme Court declared sentences unconstitutional for being "grossly disproportionate." In 1983, the Court held that it was grossly disproportionate to sentence a man to life imprisonment with no possibility of parole for passing a bad check for a hundred dollars because of his six prior nonviolent offenses. Justice Lewis Powell, writing for the Court, observed that "the Court has continued to recognize that the Eighth Amendment prohibits grossly disproportionate punishments."

In this and other cases, the Supreme Court said that it would look to three factors in evaluating whether a sentence was grossly excessive: (1) the gravity of the offense and the harshness of the penalty; (2) the sentences imposed on other criminals in the same jurisdiction; and (3) the sentences imposed for commission of the same crime in other jurisdictions.

Under these well-established criteria, I had a very strong argument that Andrade's sentence was grossly disproportionate and thus cruel and unusual punishment. First, Andrade's offense was minor, shoplifting a small amount of merchandise that was recovered before he left the store. But the punishment was extreme: a sentence of fifty years to life in prison.

As for the sentences imposed on others criminals in California, few crimes, even violent crimes, would receive such a sentence. For example, at the time of Andrade's conviction, voluntary manslaughter in California was punishable by up to eleven years in prison; rape was punishable by up to eight years in prison; second-degree murder was punishable by fifteen years to life in prison; and sexual assault on a minor was punishable by up to eight years in prison. As the federal court of appeals noted in ruling in Andrade's favor: "Andrade's indeterminate sentence of 50 years to life is exceeded in California only by first-degree murder and a select few violent crimes."

Finally, in evaluating gross disproportionality, courts are to consider the sentences imposed in other jurisdictions. Justice Stevens noted that California is the "only state in the country in which a misdemeanor could receive such a severe sentence." As Justice Breyer observed in dissent in the companion case, Ewing v. California, prior to California's three-strikes law no one in the history of the United States had ever received a life sentence for shoplifting.

The question might be asked, though, whether the three-strikes law is justified to decrease crime. Careful studies of the effects of the law, however, have shown that it has had no such effect on crime in California. One empirical study concluded that "there is no evidence that Three Strikes played an important role in the drop in the crime rate" in California. The most extensive study of the effects of the three-strikes law, by three prominent professors, also concluded that the "decline in crime observed after the effective date of the Three Strikes law was not the result of the statute." This conclusion is supported by another empirical study that found that "[c]ounties that vigorously and strictly enforce the Three Strikes law did not experience a decline in any crime category relative to the more lenient counties." Analysts at RAND compared crime rates between "three strikes" states and "non-three strikes" states and found that three-strikes laws had no independent effect on the crime rate in states with such statutes.

Moreover, even if the three-strikes law generally has some benefit, there is no evidence that crime has decreased from charging shoplifting or other minor offenses under California's three-strikes law. A state can choose to punish recidivists more harshly, but a life sentence for stealing $153 worth of videotapes makes no sense. The cost of incarcerating a prisoner in California is more than forty thousand dollars a year.

On the morning of November 5, 2002, as I walked from my hotel in Washington, D.C., to the Supreme Court to argue Andrade's case, I was nervous but I felt that I had done everything I could think of to prepare. I had participated in three moot courts, where lawyers peppered me with questions to help me anticipate what the justices were likely to ask. I had spent countless hours rereading the cases and the briefs and planning responses to the expected questions. Although I had argued dozens of cases in the federal court of appeals and had been co-counsel in the Supreme Court a few times, this was my very first time arguing before the justices.

As I walked into the Supreme Court building to the magnificent room where arguments are held, I was aware of what was at stake: if I won, Leandro Andrade was sure to be a free man within weeks of the decision; but if I lost, he would spend the rest of his life in prison for shoplifting. I knew that the odds of his living to age eighty-seven in prison are very small. If I won, others serving life sentences for shoplifting and other minor crimes likely would be released; if I lost, there would be little to give them hope. If Andrade's sentence was not grossly disproportionate, it is hard to imagine the sentence that would violate the Eighth Amendment.

Oral argument in the Supreme Court is an exhilarating though frustrating experience. The courtroom is simultaneously majestic and intimate. The attorney stands at a podium that is only a short distance from the justices. It is easy to see every facial reaction and to observe their body language. The justices are always superbly prepared. Lawyers know to expect that they will be frequently interrupted with questions.

Questions from the justices are welcome because they are the chance to address the justices' concerns. There is no way to know how many cases are won or lost in oral arguments. I have heard justices and judges express widely divergent views on that question. But the lawyer has to assume that the oral argument can make all the difference. Unlike arguments before juries, which are often filled with passion, lawyers before the Supreme Court rarely express emotion. The exchanges with the justices are about legal principles and the meaning of prior Supreme Court decisions.

I was the last of five attorneys to argue that Tuesday morning. The Ewing case was heard first, and in addition to the attorneys for Ewing and the state of California, Assistant Attorney General Michael Chertoff was present on behalf of the Bush administration to argue that Ewing's sentence should be upheld. Chertoff, a law school classmate of mine, later became famous as the head of the Department of Homeland Security. Although the matter before the Court involved California, not federal law, the Bush Justice Department decided to participate in the case and urge the justices to allow states broad latitude to decide the punishment for crimes.

After the justices spent an hour hearing the Ewing case, Chief Justice Rehnquist announced that the Court would hear oral arguments in *Lockyer v. Andrade.* Since I had won in the federal court of appeals, the state of California was the petitioner in front of the Supreme Court and its attorney went first. After he finished speaking, as I rose to the lectern, I realized that the Court had to that point heard more than ninety minutes of oral argument about California's three-strikes law, but no one—not any of the lawyers, not any of the justices—had expressed outrage that a man could spend life in prison for shoplifting.

I decided that I wanted to end my argument with a short, impassioned plea for the justices to remember that Andrade was a human being, a father of three, who was sentenced to spend the rest of his life in prison for stealing videotapes. Chief Justice Rehnquist was legendary for cutting off attorneys, even in midsentence, when time was up. Generally, each lawyer gets thirty minutes before the justices. There are two lights on the top of the podium: a white light that indicates that five minutes remain and a red light, indicating that time is up. As I approached the podium, I decided that if I could, as soon as I saw the white light, I would try to present a conclusion that included some emotion.

I began my argument and I was able to utter only five words before the first question came, predictably from Justice Scalia. My planned first sentence was "For at least a century, this Court has held that grossly disproportionate sentences violate the Eighth Amendment." I got through "For at least a century" when Justice Scalia interrupted. He tried to make a joke by saying that he hadn't realized that he had been on the Court that long. I was startled by the quick interruption and asked him to repeat his question, which stepped on his laugh line.

What makes Supreme Court arguments frustrating is that there is never enough time to answer a justice's question before the next question comes. I recall another case that I argued before the Supreme Court where Justice Stevens asked me a difficult hypothetical. Before I could answer, Justice Kennedy asked me to respond to another fact that he added to Justice Stevens's hypothetical. Just as I started to reply, Chief Justice Rehnquist added yet another wrinkle to the question. I got one sentence out in response to him when Justice Scalia interrupted and asked me a question about something totally different. Throughout the argument, I kept looking for ways to go back and address the unanswered questions from Justices Stevens and Kennedy.

The thirty minutes at the lectern went by incredibly fast, as it always does. I was able to conclude with a short plea for compassion and an expression of outrage at the idea of a man being imprisoned for life for shoplifting. As I sat down, I wished that I had prepared my last few sentences in advance. But overall, I felt good about the argument. There had been no unexpected questions. I have long believed that the key to effective appellate arguments is getting your points across while answering the judge's questions. The last thing I do before going to any appellate argument is make a list of the points I must be sure to make during my presentation. In the Andrade argument, I was able to make all of those points.

I have seen even experienced lawyers make embarrassing mistakes before the justices—calling a justice by the wrong name, misstating a case, getting visibly tripped up by a question. I was relieved that I had not embarrassed myself. Thankfully, there was never that horrible moment that I had feared of wanting the floor to open and swallow me to spare me further shame. After the argument was over, I felt that I would have tremendously enjoyed the experience if not for the weight of how much was at stake.

After argument in the Supreme Court, it usually takes months for the decision to be announced. Over and over again, while driving or taking a shower, I went through the argument in my mind and especially the questions that had been asked by Justices O'Connor and Kennedy, the swing votes on the court. Inferring a vote from questions is always dangerous. But I let myself feel cautiously optimistic that given their questions at the oral argument, at least one of them would rule for Andrade.

The Supreme Court does not inform anyone when a particular decision is going to be announced. However, it is possible to find out the days on which decisions will be released; there's just no way to know which cases will be handed down on those days. A friend, David Pike, who then covered the Supreme Court for the *Daily Journal* (a legal newspaper in California), kindly offered to call me as soon as the Court announced the ruling in *Andrade*. My guess, and it was just a guess based on the Court's calendar, was that the ruling would come down when the Court was in session on February 25, February 26, March 4, or March 5.

On each of the nights before those days, I found it hard to sleep. That's unusual for me; I don't sleep long, but I rarely have insomnia. I slept fine the night before the Supreme Court argument. But the anticipation of the decision and what it would mean was hard to bear. The Court announces its decisions at 10 A.M., eastern time, at the start of its sessions. At 7 A.M. Pacific Time on those days, I anxiously waited for the phone to ring. I figured if I didn't hear anything by 7:15 it meant no decision; it usually takes the Court about fifteen minutes to announce its rulings. On February 25, February 26, and March 4 no phone call came.

March 5 was the Court's last day in session for almost a month. If the decision wasn't announced that day, there would be no ruling for several more weeks. At 7 A.M., as I was getting my younger children ready for school, I listened for the phone. By 7:25, when it was time to leave to take my eight-year-old son to catch the school bus, I was convinced that the decision had not come that day. Just to be sure, I listened carefully to the headlines on the 7:30 news on the radio, and when no mention was made of Supreme Court decisions, I relaxed and walked my son from the car to the bus stop.

Just as my son was boarding the bus, the cell phone in my pocket rang. David Pike immediately said, "Bad news, you lost 5–4. O'Connor wrote the opinion." We spoke for a few more minutes. As I drove to my office, I felt numb. I called my wife to tell her of the decision and then called my oldest son, who was in college in New York, to inform him. Both, along with my other two sons, had been at the Supreme Court in November when I argued the case. My four-year-old daughter was too young to sit still through two hours of legal arguments.

By the time I got to my office, the sense of loss began to hit me.

I immediately went to my computer and downloaded the decision. As I read it, I felt anger that a majority of the Court saw no problem with imposing a life sentence for shoplifting and profound sadness for what the decision meant for Andrade and others in his situation. There were dozens and dozens of media calls. The first came from a friend, Gail Eichenthal, who worked at a local news radio station. I literally was in tears as I tried to do the interview. I tried unsuccessfully to reach Andrade in prison and then to reach his family members and family members of other clients whom I was representing on appeal in three-strikes cases. The mother of Jeff Rico, the man who received a life sentence for stealing a $128 television set, asked what they could do next to overturn their son's draconian sentence. I was at a loss to think of anything. There is no appeal from a Supreme Court decision. I sent copies of the decisions to Andrade, Bray, Brown, and Rico, but I had no hope to offer them.

In *Ewing v. California* and *Lockyer v. Andrade*, the Supreme Court in two 5–4 decisions rejected the defendants' Eighth Amendment arguments and upheld the application of California's three-strikes law to those whose third strike was shoplifting. Both opinions were written by Justice O'Connor and joined by Chief Justice Rehnquist and Justices Scalia, Kennedy, and Thomas. Justice O'Connor expressed the need for great deference to the states in deciding the punishments for crimes. The Court distinguished the earlier cases, which had sentences to be grossly disproportionate. For example, in an earlier decision the Court had said that it was cruel and unusual punishment to send a man to life in prison with no possibility of parole for passing a bad check worth a hundred dollars. But Justice O'Connor said that Andrade's situation was different because he was potentially eligible for parole, albeit not until he was eighty-seven years old.

How did this happen? How could the Supreme Court of the United States conclude that life in prison for shoplifting is not cruel and unusual punishment? Why did the Bush administration choose to defend life sentences for shoplifting when the matter had nothing to do with federal law?

* * *

The answer must begin decades earlier, with Richard Nixon's campaign for the White House, and it is the story of this book. It is a story that affects virtually every area of constitutional law and profoundly touches the lives of people in countless ways. Leandro Andrade's experience is really just an example in a much larger story about what has happened to the Constitution over the last few decades.

Since 1968, conservatives have sought to remake constitutional law and they largely have succeeded. They initially set out to overturn the decisions of the Warren Court, but soon began to aggressively pursue a vision of constitutional law that consistently favors government power over individual rights, especially in the criminal area, and the interests of businesses over individual employees and consumers. Because decisions come one at a time over years and because the Court never overruled the *Roe v. Wade* abortion decision (though it came within one vote of doing so), it is easy to underestimate how successful the conservative assault on the Constitution has been.

In 1968, Richard Nixon repeatedly criticized the Warren Court and said that he would appoint "law and order" justices. The Warren Court is perhaps most famous for ending laws requiring segregation of the races and for banning school prayer. But it also ruled that evidence gained as a result of an illegal police search by state and local police officers cannot be used against a criminal defendant. In one of the most famous Supreme Court decisions ever, *Miranda v. Arizona,* the Court held that before police officers can interrogate a suspect who is in custody, the individual must be warned of his or her right to remain silent, that anything this person says can be used as evidence, and that there is a right to an attorney, including, if needed, one paid for by the government. Any viewer of a police television show in the United States knows these warnings by heart. But this decision was perceived by some, including Nixon, as reflecting a Court that had gone too far in protecting the rights of criminal defendants. Nixon also strongly objected to some of the Court's civil rights decisions, especially those that sought to desegregate schools through busing. Nixon promised the American people that he would appoint "strict constructionists" to the Supreme Court, though that phrase was never defined and was code for justices with a conservative political ideology.

By coincidence, Nixon had four vacancies to fill in his first two years as president. By contrast, President Jimmy Carter had no vacancies on the Supreme Court during his four years in office. Nixon appointed four Republicans: Chief Justice Warren Burger and Justices Harry Blackmun, Lewis Powell, and William Rehnquist. Initially, Burger and Blackmun were both very conservative in their voting on the Court, so much so that they were dubbed "the Minnesota twins" because of their common heritage from that state and their consistently conservative voting. For example, they were two of the three dissenting justices when the Supreme Court held in 1971 that the government could not stop the *New York Times* and the *Washington Post* from publishing the Pentagon Papers, a Defense Department history of America's involvement in the Vietnam War.

Over time, though, Blackmun became progressively more liberal, and by the time he left the Court in 1994, he was likely its most liberal justice. Blackmun is one of the few justices in history whose views shifted significantly while on the bench. In addition to authoring *Roe v. Wade* and being among the most ardent advocates for abortion rights among the justices, in his last year on the Court Blackmun argued that the death penalty is inherently unconstitutional as cruel and unusual punishment. In powerful language, Blackmun declared that he "would no longer tinker with the machinery of death" and would vote to overturn every death sentence that came before him.

Lewis Powell turned out to be fairly moderate: right of center, but not nearly as conservative as Rehnquist or later justices like Scalia and Thomas. But the effect of the four new justices was immediately apparent, especially in cases concerning criminal defendants. In case after case, the four Nixon justices voted together with the more conservative members of the Warren Court, such as Byron White and Potter Stewart. For instance, the new Burger Court quickly recognized situations where confessions could be used even if Miranda warnings were not properly administered. They imposed significant new limits on when convicted defendants could seek a writ of habeas corpus in federal court to raise constitutional challenges to their convictions and sentences. In other areas, the four Nixon justices along with one holdover limited the ability of federal courts to provide remedies for desegregation and unequal schools. Richard Nixon promised to remake the Supreme Court and he did so. Judicial nominations are one of a president's long-lasting legacies. William Rehnquist did not leave the Court until his death in 2005, thirty-one years after Richard Nixon left the White House.

Of the Nixon appointees, only Rehnquist was still on the bench the day that I argued Andrade. But I faced a Court with four other conservatives—O'Connor, Scalia, Kennedy, and Thomas—who had been appointed by Republican presidents, Ronald Reagan and George H. W. Bush.

The Reagan presidency brought the most concerted effort in American history to remake the federal courts in a conservative direction. The Reagan administration was filled with young men and women deeply committed to undoing what they saw as the liberal domination of the judiciary. Some of these young lawyers, such as John Roberts and Samuel Alito, later came to great prominence and are a key part of this story. Nothing was more important to the lawyers in the Reagan administration than appointing hard-core conservative judges and justices.

Some of these conservatives were disappointed in 1981 when Reagan's first pick for the Supreme Court was Sandra Day O'Connor. O'Connor, a judge on an intermediate state appellate court in Arizona, was not well-known in conservative circles at the time of her appointment. No litmus test is more important to conservatives than abortion, and O'Connor had voted for abortion rights while an Arizona legislator. O'Connor, the first woman to serve on the Supreme Court, was easily confirmed and from the outset was a reliable conservative vote in many areas, especially in criminal cases. But she greatly disappointed conservatives in areas such as abortion, affirmative action, and the separation of church and state. Over her almost twenty-five years on the Supreme Court, O'Connor voted with conservatives far more often than liberals, but she was much more moderate than conservatives hoped for a Reagan justice.

Reagan's second chance to appoint a justice occurred in 1986, when Warren Burger stepped down as chief justice. Reagan tremendously pleased his conservative base when he nominated William Rehnquist for chief justice and Antonin Scalia to replace Rehnquist as associate justice. Rehnquist had been the most conservative justice from the time he arrived on the Court in 1972, often writing solitary dissents taking a conservative position. In Scalia, he had an ideological ally. Scalia, a federal court of appeals judge and a former University of Chicago law professor, was well-known within conservative legal circles. He was a frequent speaker at events held by the conservative Federalist Society and had been a top official in the Reagan Justice Department before being named a federal court of appeals judge.

In more than twenty-plus years on the Supreme Court, Scalia has been everything conservatives hoped for and liberals feared. He has forcefully articulated a conservative judicial philosophy, often in colorful language that is quoted in the mainstream press. He is a fierce opponent of abortion rights, all forms of affirmative action, and any attempt to separate church and state.

Civil rights activists debated whether to try to block the confirmation of Rehnquist or Scalia or both. They decided that it was unrealistic to hope to derail both and they concluded that Rehnquist was the more vulnerable target. Rehnquist had more than a decade of conservative decisions as a Supreme Court justice. More importantly, there was strong evidence that he had lied at his confirmation hearings in 1971. While a law clerk for Justice Robert Jackson in the early 1950s, Rehnquist wrote a memo urging the justice to vote to uphold segregation and to reaffirm the infamous decision of *Plessy v. Ferguson,* which in 1896 had decided that separate but equal facilities for blacks and whites were constitutional. This memo surfaced when Rehnquist was nominated for associate justice in 1971, but he successfully convinced the senators that he was playing "devil's advocate" at the request of Justice Jackson. When Rehnquist was nominated for chief justice, civil rights advocates were ready. They had witnesses—including Justice Jackson's secretary and Rehnquist's fellow law clerks—to testify that Jackson had not asked Rehnquist to take this position; Rehnquist was expressing his own views about race. There also were witnesses to Rehnquist impeding the registration of minority voters years earlier when he was a young lawyer in Arizona.

Because the civil rights groups decided to oppose Rehnquist, but not Scalia, Scalia was unanimously confirmed by the Senate. There were thirty-eight votes against Rehnquist's confirmation as chief justice, the largest number in history to vote against a confirmed justice, though that would later be exceeded by the forty-eight votes against Clarence Thomas and the forty-two votes against Samuel Alito.

Reagan's final effort to fill a vacancy on the Supreme Court came a year later and produced a historic battle. When Lewis Powell announced his retirement in 1987, Reagan picked conservative court of appeals judge Robert Bork. Bork had been a Yale law professor before Reagan put him on the federal court of appeals bench. Unlike Scalia, whose writings had mostly been about aspects of administrative law, Bork had extensive writings on constitutional law and they expressed extremely conservative views. For example, Bork opposed any constitutional protection for privacy and contended that the Supreme Court was wrong in protecting a constitutional right of access to contraceptives or to abortion. Bork argued that the Fourteenth Amendment's guarantee of "equal protection of the laws" was limited to protecting racial minorities from discrimination; he did not believe that government discrimination against women should be declared unconstitutional as violating equal protection. He had written that the First Amendment protects only speech related to the political process. Under his view, the government could regulate or ban all other expression.

Bork had long been a hero to conservatives; there is no one whom they wanted more to see on the Supreme Court. He was a villain to liberals. In October 1973, it was Bork, then solicitor general of the United States, who had carried out President Nixon's order to fire Watergate special prosecutor Archibald Cox after the top two officials in the Justice Department refused to do so and resigned.

An intense effort to defeat Bork was immediately mounted and it succeeded. Fifty-eight senators voted against his confirmation, the largest number to vote against any Supreme Court nominee in history. Conservatives later tried to portray this vote as a result of a smear campaign. They coined a verb, to *bork,* to refer to the unfair blocking of a judicial nominee. But Bork was defeated because his views were anathema to most people. I participated in numerous debates and gave countless speeches in the fall of 1987 regarding the Bork nomination. I saw that there was a groundswell of opposition to Bork because most people believe that there is a right to privacy under the Constitution. Every opinion poll shows that a solid majority of people believe that *Roe* was rightly decided. Most people believe that the Constitution prohibits gender discrimination and that the First Amendment's protection of freedom of speech safeguards more just than political expression. When Bork backed away from some of these positions during his confirmation hearings, he was accused of a "confirmation conversion."

After Bork was defeated, Reagan nominated another conservative federal court of appeals judge and former law professor, Douglas Ginsburg. But it was quickly revealed that Ginsburg had smoked marijuana at student parties while a Harvard Law professor. In the era of Nancy Reagan's "Just Say No" campaign, Ginsburg was untenable for the Reagan administration. Reagan then turned to Anthony Kennedy, a federal court of appeals judge in California. Kennedy was known as a conservative, but not an ideologue. He had become a federal court of appeals judge at age thirty-five and was well liked by his colleagues on the bench. A liberal judge on that court told me that "he could work with Anthony Kennedy." Rumor from a good source has it that another of Kennedy's colleagues on the federal court of appeals, a much more conservative judge, assured Attorney General Edwin Meese that Kennedy was a certain vote to overrule *Roe v. Wade*. After the bruising Bork fight, Kennedy was unanimously confirmed by the Senate.

Reagan certainly left his mark on the Court by making Rehnquist the chief justice and by adding Justices O'Connor, Scalia, and Kennedy. But still liberals could occasionally piece together successes when Justices William Brennan, Thurgood Marshall, Blackmun (by then a reliable liberal vote), and Stevens could get Justice Byron White to join them. For example, in 1990, the Supreme Court, with these five justices as the majority, held that the federal government could engage in affirmative action by giving a preference to minority-owned businesses in receiving broadcast licenses from the Federal Communications Commission.

But all of this changed when Marshall resigned from the Court in 1991. The fifth conservative on the bench when I argued Andrade was Clarence Thomas, who was appointed by President George H. W. Bush in 1991 to replace Marshall. Marshall is a legendary figure in American law. As a lawyer for the NAACP Legal Defense Fund, Marshall had argued *Brown v. Board of Education* and played a key role in the litigation that successfully ended segregation. The first African-American to sit on the Supreme Court, Marshall was certainly a liberal, but he also was a unique voice because of his long experience as an advocate for racial equality.

Liberal groups immediately decided to oppose Thomas. He had written several articles arguing that the Court was wrong in protecting privacy, including protecting a right to contraception and abortion. He was an ardent opponent of affirmative action. He was perceived to be at the Scalia end of the ideological spectrum. But Thomas's opponents struggled to get the fifty-one votes needed to defeat him. Civil rights groups, which had been instrumental in persuading southern senators to vote against Robert Bork, were conflicted over whether to oppose an African-American nominee, even one whose views they found abhorrent.

After the Senate completed its hearings on the Thomas nomination, allegations emerged that Thomas had sexually harassed a member of his staff at the Equal Employment Opportunity Commission, Anita Hill. The nation sat mesmerized in October 1991 as Hill testified about the harassment she suffered, and then as Thomas faced the senators and accused Hill of lying. Thomas went on the offensive and called the proceedings "a high-tech lynching for uppity blacks." Thomas was confirmed by a vote of 52–48, the most votes against any justice confirmed for a seat on the Supreme Court. The crucial difference from the Bork confirmation proceedings was that six southern and western Democrats—senators such as Sam Nunn and David Boren—voted against Bork, but in favor of Thomas. As a justice, Thomas has been staunchly conservative, often the sole dissent in 8–1 decisions and frequently going even further than Justice Scalia in urging major changes in constitutional law in a conservative direction.

Two things seemed certain about Thomas as I prepared for the oral argument in the Andrade case. One was that he would ask no questions of me or the other lawyers. Thomas virtually never asks questions, usually going years without speaking a word from the bench. Many theories have been advanced about this: a self-consciousness about speaking in public; a view that lawyers should be permitted to argue their cases without interruption; a sense that he doesn't perceive oral argument to matter much. The other certainty was that I had virtually no chance of getting his vote.

The other four justices on the bench when I argued Andrade—Stevens, Souter, Ginsburg, and Breyer—were widely regarded as being left of center, though none was as liberal as justices of years past, such as William Douglas, Brennan, and Marshall. Stevens and Souter were Republican presidents' appointees who turned out to be very different than expected.

John Paul Stevens had been a successful business lawyer in Chicago before being appointed to the federal court of appeals there. He was well-known to President Gerald Ford's attorney general, Edward Levi, who had been dean of the law school at and then president of the University of Chicago. Stevens had the reputation of being unfailingly polite to lawyers during oral arguments, but also of often asking a series of questions that could devastate a lawyer's position. In his initial years on the Court, Stevens was seen as a justice who often went his own way and was hard to pigeonhole ideologically. Over time, he became one of the most reliably liberal votes on the Court.

The other justice on the bench in November 2002 who had been appointed by a Republican president was David Souter. When Justice Brennan announced his resignation in June 1991, President George H. W. Bush nominated Souter, then a little-known federal court of appeals judge from New Hampshire. Brennan, a Democrat, had been appointed by President Dwight Eisenhower and had been a leader of liberals on the Court for decades. Most credit him with being the architect of the Warren Court's constitutional vision. After a long tenure on the New Hampshire Supreme Court, Souter had been on the federal bench only a very short time before being chosen for the U.S. Supreme Court. Law professors and Senate staffers pored over Souter's opinions looking for any information that would give a sense of his views on issues like abortion. There was nothing to be found. After having read hundreds of New Hampshire Supreme Court decisions, New York University law professor Burt Neuborne said that the only conclusion he could draw was that New Hampshire's supreme court had a really boring docket.

It turns out that the Bush administration knew no more about Souter's ideology than his critics did. White House Chief of Staff John Sununu and Senator Warren Rudman, both from New Hampshire, had enthusiastically praised Souter to the Bush administration, but soon after arriving on the Court, Souter demonstrated that he was independent and more likely to vote with the liberals than with the conservatives on a wide range of issues. At oral arguments, he asked very precise, straightforward, and incisive questions.

The final two justices on the bench when I argued *Andrade* were both picks of President Bill Clinton. When Byron White stepped down in 1993, he was replaced by federal court of appeals judge Ruth Bader Ginsburg. White, though appointed by

President John F. Kennedy, was no liberal. He and Rehnquist were the only dissenters in *Roe v. Wade*. White wrote a forceful dissent in *Miranda v. Arizona* and usually voted with the conservative justices in criminal cases. He often was the fifth vote for conservative results.

Ginsburg replacing White is the only instance since 1968 where a justice has been replaced by someone more liberal. Ginsburg was a law professor and an American Civil Liberties Union lawyer before being nominated for the federal court of appeals by President Carter. Ginsburg created the ACLU women's rights project and had argued the leading Supreme Court cases concerning gender equality.

A year later, in 1994, Harry Blackmun stepped down and President Clinton nominated federal court of appeals judge Stephen Breyer to replace him. Breyer, a Harvard law professor, before going on the federal appellate court, was not as liberal as Blackmun. For example, Breyer cast the decisive fifth vote in 5–4 decisions to allow random drug testing of high school students participating in extracurricular activities, to permit the government to detain an American citizen as an enemy combatant, and to allow a large Ten Commandments monument to remain at the corner between the Texas Capitol and the Texas Supreme Court. Still, in the vast majority of instances in which the Court is ideologically divided, Breyer is in agreement with the more liberal justices.

This was the Court that I stood before in November 2002. It was composed of three very conservative justices—Rehnquist, Scalia, and Thomas; two moderate conservative justices—O'Connor and Kennedy; and four moderate liberal justices—Stevens, Souter, Ginsburg, and Breyer. It is, of course, the Court that will be best remembered for its momentous decision on December 12, 2000, in *Bush v. Gore*, which was the first time in American history that the Supreme Court decided a presidential election. In a 5–4 decision, with the five most conservative justices—Rehnquist, O'Connor, Scalia, Kennedy, and Thomas—in the majority, the Court halted the counting of uncounted votes in Florida and effectively made George W. Bush the forty-third president of the United States.

Since then, the Supreme Court has become substantially more conservative. In 2005, John G. Roberts, Jr., was nominated and confirmed to replace Rehnquist as chief justice. Roberts, after being a law clerk to Rehnquist, worked in the Reagan Justice Department and later was deputy solicitor general under Kenneth Starr during the first Bush administration. Before becoming a federal court of appeals judge, Roberts worked at a law firm and specialized in representing business interests before the Supreme Court. Conservatives were delighted with the choice of Roberts. Everything Roberts had ever written or done indicated that he would be a consistent, conservative vote on the Court. In his first four years, there is not a single instance in which he has disappointed conservatives. His replacing Rehnquist did not change the ideology of the Court; Roberts is ideologically indistinguishable from his predecessor. But a fifty-year-old conservative justice did replace an eighty-year-old one.

President George W. Bush nominated Harriet Miers to replace Sandra Day O'Connor, but conservatives quickly derailed that nomination. Liberal senators and activists stayed remarkably quiet as conservatives opposed her as lacking sufficient qualifications and as being too unpredictable in her judicial ideology. After the Miers nomination was withdrawn, President Bush nominated federal court of appeals judge Samuel Alito for the O'Connor seat. Conservatives were thrilled. In fifteen years as a federal court of appeals judge, Alito virtually always voted in a conservative direction. Years earlier he had been dubbed "Scalito" because his views so closely matched Antonin Scalia's.

I was asked to testify at the Alito confirmation hearings and read more than two hundred of his published opinions. On every significant issue—abortion, death penalty, civil rights, separation of church and state—Alito was on the far right of the ideological judicial spectrum. Despite intense opposition, Alito was confirmed, though with forty-two senators voting against him. So far, he too has been everything conservatives hoped for and liberals feared.

Thus the Court is even more conservative than it was in 2002 when I argued *Andrade*. There are four very conservative justices—Roberts, Scalia, Thomas, and Alito—who virtually always vote together on matters defined by ideology, such as issues of abortion, gun control, civil liberties, and the war on terror.

As in 2002, in the most recent Court term, there were four moderate liberal justices. Justices Stevens, Ginsburg, and Breyer remain on the Court, but David Souter resigned in 2009, at the relatively young age for a departing justice of sixty-nine years old. Sonia Sotomayor was nominated and confirmed to replace Souter, but she does not change the overall ideology of the Court. After reading hundreds of Sotomayor's opinions from her time as a federal court of appeals judge, I concluded that she will be a moderate liberal on the Court. In 5–4 cases where the Court is split along ideological lines, she is very likely to vote in the same way that Souter would have done. One area where she may be more conservative than Souter is criminal justice. Perhaps owing to the many years she spent as a state court prosecutor early in her career, her rulings on the federal court of appeals were more pro–law enforcement than might be expected for a relatively liberal judge.

With Roberts, Scalia, Thomas, and Alito consistently on one side, and Stevens, Ginsburg, Breyer, and Souter (and now Sotomayor) on the other, that leaves Kennedy as the swing justice who usually casts the deciding vote in 5–4 cases. In the 2006–2007 Supreme Court term (properly referred to as October Term 2006 because of the month and year it began), there were twenty-four 5–4 decisions out of sixty-eight cases resolved by the Court that year. Justice Kennedy was in the majority in every one them. In its most recent term, October Term 2008, there were seventy-five decisions and twenty-three were decided by a 5–4 margin. Justice Kennedy was in the majority 92 percent of the time, including in eighteen of twenty-three 5–4 cases, more than any other justice.

Today's Supreme Court is the Anthony Kennedy Court. Kennedy sometimes disappoints conservatives, such as in his refusal to overturn *Roe v. Wade*, his opinions protecting rights for gays and lesbians, and his opinions concluding that the death penalty is unconstitutional when used for crimes committed by juveniles or for the crime of child rape. But he is a predictable vote against affirmative action programs, in favor of laws regulating abortion, for permitting government support for religion, and for striking down campaign finance laws. Of the twenty-three 5–4 decisions in October Term 2008, for example, the justices lined up along expected ideological lines in sixteen of them, with Roberts, Scalia, Thomas, and Alito on one side, and Stevens, Souter, Ginsburg, and Breyer on the other. In eleven of these sixteen cases, Anthony Kennedy sided with the conservatives.

The Barack Obama presidency is unlikely to change the ideological composition of the Court, at least in the short term. The vacancies between January 20, 2009, and January 19, 2013, are likely to come from one side of the ideological aisle. So far President Obama has had two appointments to the Supreme Court. Both could be labeled as moderate liberals; both left of center, but neither as liberal as a Douglas, a Brennan, or a Marshall.

The nomination and confirmation of Sotomayor is likely to provide a blueprint for future Obama picks for the high court. President Obama was able to please his political base while investing almost no political capital in securing Sotomayor's confirmation. A more liberal justice in the mold of a Douglas, a Brennan, or a Marshall would face a far more difficult confirmation process and require more effort on the part of the president.

In fact, President Obama followed this script in selecting Elena Kagan to replace Justice Stevens. In April 2010, shortly before his ninetieth birthday, Stevens announced his resignation after thirty-five years on the Supreme Court. Kagan offered President Obama a seemingly easy confirmation process. She has little paper trail; she was never a judge and has no judicial opinions to scrutinize and has written relatively few law review articles. On the other hand, the lack of a paper trail also means that no one, including the president, can be sure of her ideology and likely votes once confirmed. All expect that she will be left of center, but whether she will be similar to Stevens, or more toward the middle or perhaps even more liberal, is impossible to know.

It is expected that President Obama is likely to have another vacancy to fill in the next couple of years. There are always rumors that Justice Ginsburg, who is seventy-seven and has had health problems, might retire.

These could be the only vacancies for Obama, even if he is elected to a second term.

John Roberts turned fifty-five years old in January 2010. If he remains on the Court until he is ninety, he will be chief justice until 2045. Samuel Alito turned sixty; Clarence Thomas has been on the Court for eighteen years, but will be only sixty-two in 2010. Both Scalia and Kennedy will be seventy-four in 2010. The best predictor of a long life expectancy seems to be confirmation for a seat on the U.S. Supreme Court.

Thus, absent unforeseen events, the five conservative justices are likely to remain another decade. The election of 2008 was very different from the election of 2004 with regard to the composition of the Supreme Court. If Al Gore or John Kerry had replaced Rehnquist and O'Connor, they would have done so with individuals vastly different from Roberts and Alito. There would be six liberal, or at least moderate liberal, justices on the high court. The story of constitutional law, now and for decades to come, would be vastly different.

This, then, is how we got the Court that I faced in *Andrade* and that we have today. This book is about what the composition of that Court means. I want to show what the conservative assault on the Constitution has already accomplished and what is likely to happen in the years ahead. I seek to show that the changes are not just about legal rules or abstract principles. They affect people in the most intimate and important aspects of their lives.

But to understand what conservatives have accomplished it is necessary to look beyond the Supreme Court and beyond the judiciary. The assault on the Constitution is the result of a concerted effort by conservatives to alter foundational constitutional principles. The focus needs to be not just on the courts, but also on policies developed during the presidencies of Nixon, Ford, Reagan, Bush, and Bush.

As described in the pages of this book, conservatives—in the executive branch and on the courts—have sought to create unprecedented, unchecked executive power, including the power to torture and detain individuals indefinitely without a trial or even due process. They have sought to obliterate the long-standing wall separating church and state, allowing the government almost unlimited authority to support religion and to make religion a part of government activities. They have sought to abolish any constitutional protection for privacy and, most of all, to eliminate constitutional protections for abortions. They have sought to greatly reduce constitutional protections for criminal defendants, including their ability to ask a federal court for protection from unconstitutional state procedures or results. They have worked to eliminate all affirmative action and to institute a vision of the Constitution that will perpetuate deep racial inequalities in American society. Most successfully, they have closed the courthouse doors, especially to people bringing civil rights claims.

In some areas, the story starts with the Republican platform of 1964. Ideas that then seemed radical and unthinkable were later adopted and became the official orthodoxy of Republican presidents. In most areas, the policies trace back to Richard Nixon or at least to Ronald Reagan. Some of the key players—such as Dick Cheney and Donald Rumsfeld—unite this story as they were integral parts of several Republican administrations. Young lawyers who served in the Reagan administration and were deeply committed to its conservative agenda, such as John Roberts and Samuel Alito, came to be Supreme Court justices. It is a mistake to see the policies of the Bush administration or the Roberts Court in isolation from a larger conservative movement that has sought to alter, and in many areas succeeded in altering, basic precepts of constitutional law.

I start with American public education because of the importance of education and also because it is a place where the conservatives have been markedly successful. In a series of 5–4 decisions in the 1970s, the 1990s, and the 2000s, justices appointed by Republican presidents have prevented effective desegregation of schools or equalization of spending. The result, by every measure, is schools that are increasingly separate and unequal.

In Chapter 2 I examine the tremendous growth of presidential power and what it has meant for the loss of individual liberties. During the Nixon presidency, there was talk of the "imperial presidency" with assertions of great presidential powers. The Reagan and first Bush presidencies built on this principle and then the George W. Bush administration relied on these predecessors' theories to take claims of uncheckable presidential power to unprecedented heights. Chapter 2 focuses less on what the Supreme Court has done and more on how Nixon, Reagan, and Bush have tried to greatly expand the scope of presidential power.

A major concern of the right wing is the separation of church and state. For decades, it was understood that the First Amendment's prohibition on the establishment of religion meant that there was a wall separating church and state, a wall that kept American governments secular. But conservatives, especially starting with the Reagan presidency, have sought to eliminate any such notion. They argue that the government should have broad latitude to aid religion and to include religion in government activities. With the arrival of Chief Justice Roberts and Justice Alito, there now appear to be five votes for radically changing the law in this area in a manner that conservatives have advocated for decades.

Chapter 4 covers the rights of criminal defendants and of prisoners. No group in American society is more politically vulnerable. Yet none has fared worse in the Supreme Court over the last few decades. Starting with the Nixon presidency, there has been a successful effort to limit the rights of criminal defendants in both federal and state court. This effort has resulted in legislation and court decisions that have tremendously favored the government in criminal cases and greatly increased the likelihood that innocent people will be convicted of crimes.

Conservatives have devised a jurisprudence that above all was designed to overrule *Roe v. Wade*. There are likely four votes on the current Court to do so—Roberts, Scalia, Thomas, and Alito. But the Obama presidency makes a fifth vote to overrule *Roe* unlikely for the foreseeable future. However, while Justice Kennedy has shown that he won't vote to overturn *Roe*, he is a consistent fifth vote to allow almost any government regulation of abortion up to a total ban.

Individual liberties, of course, include more than abortion rights. The conservative assault on individual rights has dramatically lessened constitutional protection from harm by the government, for freedom of speech, and for other aspects of privacy.

Chapter 6 considers access to the courts. American lawyers like to say that our country guarantees anyone who suffers an injury the chance to have his or her day in court. The reality is far different. Increasingly, those with injuries cannot sue in court, no matter how meritorious their claims. Once more, a series of 5–4 decisions, with the most conservative justices in the majority, has significantly changed the law and made it much harder to hold the government, its officers, and businesses accountable.

The concluding chapter pulls all of these strands together to show that the whole is greater than the sum of the parts. A conservative approach to the Constitution that began with the Republican platform of 1964 gained momentum with Richard Nixon and came to fruition with Ronald Reagan and two Bush presidencies. It has changed virtually every area of constitutional law in a profoundly conservative direction.

Looking at many different areas helps to show that the conservative assault on the Constitution is not a product of a neutral method of constitutional interpretation or a commitment to judicial restraint. Quite the contrary: conservative justices are very willing to be activist in striking down laws and overturning precedents with regard to affirmative action programs, or invalidating gun control laws, or imposing new limits on punitive-damage awards to injured individuals. Conservatives who espouse a need to be true to the framers' intent are willing to abandon it when it does not support the results they want.

The conservative assault on the Constitution is driven not by methodology or interpretive philosophy but by ideology. Antonin

Scalia, one of the prime architects of the Court's conservatism, finds in the Constitution no limits on government aid to parochial schools. He believes that the Constitution allows prayers in public schools. He rejects a constitutional right to abortion, but finds a right of individuals to have handguns. He wants to strictly limit the ability of federal courts to order desegregation of elementary and secondary schools, but refuses to allow colleges and universities to engage in affirmative action to remedy the great disparities in the American educational system. Justice Scalia professes that he follows the original meaning of the Constitution, but his are the views of the 2008 Republican platform, not of the Constitution's framers.

There are two very different constitutional visions. Justices like Brennan and Ginsburg on the one side, as compared with Scalia and Thomas on the other, disagree on virtually every major matter of constitutional law. All are interpreting the same constitutional text. Their divergence is a result of their markedly different political ideologies and worldviews. Liberals and conservatives in the late twentieth and early twenty-first centuries sharply disagree about matters such as school desegregation, affirmative action, presidential power, separation of church and state, individual liberties such as abortion rights and gay rights, protections for criminal defendants, and civil rights.

This book describes how to a large extent the conservative vision has triumphed on these issues in constitutional law and what it means for people's lives and for society. For those who do not share this conservative vision, it is a book which describes significant setbacks. Indeed, throughout the book, I describe the setbacks that I have suffered as a lawyer fighting for a very different vision of equality and individual freedom.

But I do not believe that these setbacks are permanent. I conclude in the final chapter by suggesting that things can change; the Constitution can be reclaimed from the conservative assault that has triumphed for the last quarter of a century. Congress can pass laws restoring rights that the Court has taken away. The Obama administration can restore a commitment to checks and balances. Over time, the Supreme Court can undo the damage it has done to civil liberties and civil rights.

But it is important to understand what has happened over the last few decades and why. Ultimately, it is the explanation for why the Supreme Court decided that Leandro Andrade can spend fifty years in prison for shoplifting.

1.

Separate and Unequal Schools

The case attracted no national media attention and is little remembered. But the brief that I was asked to write tells a great deal about what has happened to American public education over the last half century. The litigation involved tremendous inequities in funding the Alabama public schools. As is true in almost every state, there was a vast disparity between the amount spent per pupil in wealthier school districts as compared with poorer ones. For example, the Mountain Brook city school system, which ranked highest in state and local revenues of Alabama's 129 school systems in the 1989–90 school year, had $4,820 available to spend per pupil. This amount was more than double the resources available to the Roanoke, Alabama, city schools, the lowest revenue system, which had only $2,371 per pupil. On May 3, 1990, the American Civil Liberties Union brought a lawsuit on behalf of the Alabama Coalition for Equity challenging the disparities in school funding as violating the Alabama constitution.

The problem for their lawsuit was that in 1973, in *San Antonio Independent School District v. Rodriguez*, the U.S. Supreme Court ruled 5–4 that such disparities in school funding do not violate the U.S. Constitution. The Court held that there is no constitutional right to education and thus that differentials in spending between wealthy and poor school districts within a metropolitan area are constitutionally permissible. If I were to list the most important, and the worst, Supreme Court decisions during my lifetime, *Rodriguez* would be high on this list.

Since *Rodriguez*, any challenges to disparities in school funding must be brought under state constitutions. States are allowed to provide more rights under their state constitutions than the U.S. Constitution offers, but not fewer. A number of states, including Arizona, California, Texas, and New Jersey, have found that disparities in school funding violate their state constitutions even though *Rodriguez* concluded that this situation did not offend the U.S. Constitution.

Alabama was not one of these states. Alabama had amended its state constitution by voter initiative in 1956 to declare that there was no right to public education in the state. Amendment 111 stated that "nothing in this Constitution should be construed as creating or recognizing" that education is a right. This was done to allow Alabama public schools to close rather than desegregate. Alabama was so determined to resist the end of Jim Crow education, as decreed by *Brown v. Board of Education*, that its voters amended their constitution to allow school districts to close *all* schools to avoid having to desegregate them.

The ACLU's lawsuit faced a major obstacle: Alabama argued that it did not need to provide public education at all under its state constitution, so it could not be said that inequities in funding were impermissible.

The litigation was being handled for the ACLU by Helen Hershkoff, a law school classmate of mine (and now a law professor at New York University). Helen asked if I would write a friend of the court brief to the Alabama trial court arguing that the provision in the Alabama constitution violated the U.S. Constitution. But I was stumped as to how to do this because of the Supreme Court decision that there is no right to education under the U.S. Constitution. The Alabama provision declaring that there was no right to education in the state never mentioned race and over several decades the Supreme Court had ruled that such laws that do not mention race can be successfully challenged as violating equal protection only if there is proof that they had both a racially discriminatory impact and a racially discriminatory purpose. There was no doubt as to the latter for the Alabama law, but there was no evidence that the disparities in school funding in the state had a racially discriminatory effect.

After some initial successes for the lawsuit in the Alabama courts, in 1997 the Alabama Supreme Court concluded that there were disparities in school funding, but refused to provide any remedy. In 2002, the same court then dismissed the case. Tremendous disparities in funding in Alabama and across the country remain. At the same time schools across the country are becoming increasingly racially segregated.

Of course, no longer are there laws mandating segregation of the races, but as a result of a series of U.S. Supreme Court decisions, the ability of judges and legislatures to remedy racial separation is very limited. The result is that American public schools are increasingly separate and unequal. The statistics are stark and startling.

Harvard professor Gary Orfield's study *Schools More Separate: Consequences of a Decade of Resegregation* carefully documents how during the 1990s America's public schools became substantially more racially separate. In the South, for example, he shows that "[f]rom 1988 to 1998, most of the progress of the previous two decades in increasing integration in the region was lost. The South is still more integrated than it was before the civil rights revolution, but it is moving backward at an accelerating rate."

The percentage of African-American students attending majority-white schools has steadily decreased since 1986. In 1954, at the time of *Brown v. Board of Education,* only 0.001 percent of African-American students in the South attended majority-white schools. In 1964, a decade after *Brown,* that percentage was just 2.3. From 1964 to 1988, there was significant progress: the percentage rose to 43.5 in 1988. But since then the percentage of African-American students attending majority-white schools has gone in the opposite direction. By 1991, the percentage in the South had decreased to 39.2 and over the course of the 1990s it went down to 32.7 in 1998.

Orfield shows that nationally the percentage of African-American students attending majority-black schools and schools where over 90 percent of the students are black also has increased. In 1986, 62.9 percent of black students attended schools that were 50–100 percent made up of minority students; by 1998–99, this percentage had increased to 70.2.

Orfield's research, most recently in a report released in January 2009, shows that during the last decade the problem of racially segregated schools has continued to get worse. By 2006–2007, 73 percent of African-American students attended schools that were 50–100 percent minority students; 38.5 percent attended schools that were 90–100 percent minority students. Orfield's research also shows that the nation's teaching force, too, is largely segregated; students rarely encounter teachers of races different from their own.

Quite significantly, Orfield shows that the same is true for Latino students. The historic focus for desegregation efforts has been to integrate African-American and white students. The burgeoning Latino population requires that desegregation focus on this minority as well. The percentage of Latino students attending schools where the majority of students are of minority races, or almost exclusively of minority races, increased steadily over the last two decades. In the 2006–2007 school year, 78 percent of Latino students attended schools that were 50–100 percent minority students, and 40 percent attended schools that were 90–100 percent minority students. Orfield notes that "[Latinos] have been more segregated than blacks for a number of years, not only by race and ethnicity but also by poverty."

The overall statistics for major-city public schools could not be more discouraging for those who believe in desegregation. In Chicago, by the academic year 2002–2003, 87 percent of public school enrollment was black or Hispanic; less than 10 percent of children in the schools were white. In Washington, D.C., 94 percent of children were black or Hispanic; less than 5 percent were white. In St. Louis, 82 percent of the student population was black or Hispanic; in Philadelphia and Cleveland, 79 percent; in Los Angeles, 84 percent; in Detroit, 96 percent; in Baltimore, 89 percent. In New York City, nearly three-fourths of the public school students were black or Hispanic.

The tragic reality is that American schools are separate and unequal. To a very large degree, education in the United States is racially segregated. By any measure, predominantly minority schools are not equal in their resources or their quality. Wealthy suburban school districts are almost exclusively white; poor inner-city schools are often composed exclusively of African-American and Hispanic students. Studies have shown that across the United States significantly more is spent on the average white child's education compared with the average black child's schooling. Moreover, disproportionately more white children than minority children attend private schools, with their greater resources and better student-faculty ratios. According to the most recent national statistics, private elementary schools are 86 percent white and private high schools are 87 percent white.

Some question whether desegregation and equal expenditures really matter. They argue that children can learn just as well no matter what the racial composition of the classes and that there is no proof that expenditures make a difference in terms of educational achievement. I believe that both of these arguments are attempts to rationalize what should be a national embarrassment, what Jonathan Kozol expressed in the titles of two books about the American educational system, *Savage Inequalities* and *The Shame of the Nation: The Restoration of Apartheid Schooling in America.*

More than a half century ago, in *Brown v. Board of Education,* the Supreme Court explained why segregation of schools is so harmful. Chief Justice Earl Warren, writing for the Court, said: "Such considerations apply with added force to children in grade and high schools. To separate them from others of similar age and qualifications solely because of their race generates a feeling of inferiority as to their status in the community that may affect their hearts and minds in a way unlikely ever to be undone."

Although Chief Justice Warren was speaking of government-mandated segregation, there is significant evidence that racial integration matters in educational achievement. Justice Breyer, in a recent opinion, summarized it this way: "One commentator, reviewing dozens of studies of the educational benefits of desegregated schooling, found that the studies have provided 'remarkably consistent' results, showing that: (1) black students' educational achievement is improved in integrated schools as compared to racially isolated schools, (2) black students' educational achievement is improved in integrated classes, and (3) the earlier that black students are removed from racial isolation, the better their educational outcomes."

Even if it cannot be proven that children achieve more in integrated classrooms, the benefits of diversity are enormous. Students learn from each other's lives and experiences. Students have the chance for interracial associations that can change attitudes and break down stereotypes. Again, Justice Breyer, in his recent opinion, summarized the research:

> [O]ne study documented that "black and white students in desegregated schools are less racially prejudiced than those in segregated schools," and that "interracial contact in desegregated schools leads to an increase in interracial sociability and friendship." Other studies have found that both black and white students who attend integrated schools are more likely to work in desegregated companies after graduation than students who attended racially isolated schools. Further research has shown that the desegregation of schools can help bring adult communities together by reducing segregated housing. Cities that have implemented successful school desegregation plans have witnessed increased interracial contact and neighborhoods that tend to become less racially segregated.

Former federal court of appeals judge Nathaniel Jones was correct when he coined the phrase "green follows white." What he meant by this comment was that there will always be more money and more resources for predominantly white schools than for schools made up mostly of minority students. The only way to ensure equal educational opportunity, or even adequate resources for students of color, is to have them educated in the same school system as whites. The Supreme Court in *Brown* got it exactly right when it said that separate can never be equal.

Admittedly, there is an endless debate over the relationship of expenditures to educational achievement. After having read so many of these articles and studies, I am left to shrug and ask whether poorer students shouldn't have the same chance to be disappointed by expenditures of money for schools as wealthier students. Money matters in terms of class size, student-faculty ratios, classes like art and music, Advanced Placement classes, libraries, facilities, guidance counselors, and so much else. In selecting schools for their children, these are the factors all parents look to if they can make choices. No one was surprised that Barack and Michelle Obama sent their daughters to private schools in Chicago and the District of Columbia rather than to local public schools. They made the same choice so many parents with the means to do so make: selecting the schools with more resources, smaller classes, better student-faculty ratios, higher graduation rates.

Separate and unequal schools have a dramatic effect on society. In 2006, 28.4 percent of white Americans reported having graduated from college, compared with 18.5 percent of blacks and 12.5 percent of Latinos. Unemployment rates for African-Americans and Latinos are far greater than for whites. Every study shows that average income levels rise and chances of unemployment fall as education increases. Education always has been the vehicle for social mobility, and educational opportunities in this country depend enormously on the race and wealth of the student.

There are undoubtedly many causes for the failure to achieve equal educational opportunity in the United States. None of the recent presidents—not Reagan, nor either Bush, nor Clinton, nor even Obama so far—has done anything to advance desegregation. None has used the powerful resources of the federal government, including the dependence of every school district on federal funds, to further desegregation or equality in education. "Benign neglect" would be a charitable way of describing the attitude of recent presidents to the problem of segregated and unequal education; there has been neglect, but there has been nothing benign about it. The only major education initiative in recent de-cades, President Bush's "No Child Left Behind," sought neither to advance desegregation nor to equalize funding among schools in the same metropolitan area. The Bush plan sought to improve ed-ucation but made no effort to deal with the two crucial underlying problems in American education: the racial separation of students and the great inequities in educational expenditures.

Nor has the federal government, or for that matter state or local governments, acted to deal with housing segregation. In a country deeply committed to the ideal of the neighborhood school, resi-dential segregation often produces school segregation. But it has been decades since the last law was enacted to address housing discrimination, and efforts to enhance residential integration seem to have vanished.

The fact that American public schools are increasingly separate and unequal is in large part a product of the conservative assault on the Constitution. Like so much in this book, it is a story that begins with Richard Nixon, specifically with his campaign for the White House and with the four justices that he appointed to the Supreme Court. A series of decisions from the Supreme Court, with the Nixon, Reagan, and Bush appointees in the majority, has gone a long way to ensuring racial segregation of students and inequity in American public education.

Barry Goldwater carried only six states in 1964 and five were in the Deep South. Southern states that had voted consistently Democratic since the Civil War and the Republican presidency of Abraham Lincoln. Kevin Phillips devised a "southern strategy" for Richard Nixon to win the presidency in 1968. Key to this strategy was an appeal to white voters on the issue of race.

Nixon's opposition to school desegregation was a central as-pect of the strategy. No area of desegregation had proven more controversial or more difficult than education. There had been massive resistance throughout the South to efforts to eliminate segregated schools. During the 1968 campaign, Nixon strongly opposed forced busing of white children to minority neighbor-hoods and children of color to predominantly white schools to achieve racial balance. Since public schools in the United States are largely based on neighborhoods, residential segregation meant that there often would be little chance for desegregating most public schools without some busing. Opposing busing thus both symbolized and epitomized Nixon's opposition to desegregation.

Once elected, President Nixon continued to oppose busing. In August 1971, he declared: "I am against busing as that term is commonly used in school desegregation cases. I have consistently opposed the busing of our Nation's schoolchildren to achieve a racial balance, and I am opposed to the busing of children simply for the sake of busing." Of course, no one was proposing busing "simply for the sake of busing." It was all about achieving desegregation. Never did President Nixon confirm the importance of achieving the mandate of *Brown v. Board of Education* and desegregating America's public schools. His message was a negative one: efforts at desegregation, especially through busing, had gone too far.

In the spring of 1971, the United States Supreme Court, in *Swann v. Charlotte-Mecklenburg Board of Education*, expressly approved busing as a tool for desegregation. President Nixon voiced strong disagreement with the decision. In March 1972, he proposed legislation to effectively overrule the decision by barring federal courts from ordering busing. Historians have suggested that, in part, this was an effort to appeal to white voters to help defeat a third-party challenge from the right by George Wallace.

President Nixon explained his proposal: "My first proposal to the Congress is a moratorium on all new and additional busing of schoolchildren. That would stop any further busing now." There is little doubt that this action would have been unconstitutional. Congress cannot overrule a Supreme Court case interpreting the Constitution and Congress cannot tell federal courts what remedies they are allowed to impose. In addition to proposing this legislation, which was never enacted, Nixon ordered his Justice Department not to pursue busing as a remedy and he fired a liberal official in the Department of Health, Education, and Welfare who espoused a different view.

A decade later, the Reagan administration was widely perceived as hostile to civil rights and school desegregation. William Bradford Reynolds, the assistant attorney general for the Civil Rights Division in the United States Department of Justice, was regarded by civil rights groups as a strong adversary to desegregation and especially affirmative action. These groups mobilized and blocked his appointment to be associate attorney general.

The Reagan administration and its Justice Department opposed judicial remedies in school desegregation cases, especially those that involved busing. It reversed the position that the Carter administration had taken and unsuccessfully urged the Supreme Court to uphold the constitutionality of a Washington state initiative that banned school busing. It proposed to "shift control over education policy away from the Federal Government and back to State and local authorities." In other words, it sought to end efforts by the federal government and the federal courts to desegregate the schools. One aspect of this effort was the Reagan administration's dramatically cutting funds for school desegregation programs.

The greatest effects of these two presidencies on school equality, though, came from the justices that they appointed to the Supreme Court. The importance of the federal judiciary to achieving desegregation and equal educational opportunity cannot be overstated. African-Americans and Latinos lack adequate political power to achieve desegregation or equal educational opportunity through the political process. Only the judiciary can achieve these aims. This was true when *Brown* was decided and it is true today.

The courts are indispensable to effective desegregation, but over the last thirty years, the courts, and especially the Supreme Court, have failed. There have been three sets of Supreme Court decisions—in the 1970s, in the early 1990s, and in 2007—that have contributed significantly to separate and unequal schools. Had the Supreme Court decided these key cases otherwise, the nature of public education today would be very different. The explanation for the Court's rulings is simple: justices appointed by Presidents Nixon, Reagan, Bush, and Bush have undermined de-segregation and efforts to equalize educational opportunities. Four justices appointed by President Nixon are largely to blame for the decisions of the 1970s; the cases were 5–4 decisions with those four justices in the majority. Five justices appointed by Presidents Reagan and Bush are responsible for the decisions of the 1990s and the last decade that have contributed substantially to resegregation and inequalities of schools.

The 1970s

The 1970s were a particularly critical time in the battle to desegregate American schools. From *Plessy v. Ferguson*, which upheld the constitutionality of "separate but equal" in 1896, until *Brown* in 1954, government-mandated segregation of schools existed in every southern state and many northern states. As mentioned above, when *Brown* was decided only 0.001 percent of African-American students in the South attended majority white schools. After *Brown*, southern states used every imaginable technique to obstruct desegregation. Some school systems attempted to close public schools rather than desegregate. The Alabama constitutional provision that I was asked to help challenge, which denied any right to public education, is an example. Some school boards adopted so-called "freedom of choice" plans that allowed students to choose the school where they would enroll and the result was continued segregation. In some places, there was outright disobedience of desegregation orders. The phrase "massive resistance" appropriately describes what occurred during the decade after *Brown*.

The result was that during that decade, little desegregation occurred. In the South, just 1.2 percent of black schoolchildren were attending schools with whites. In South Carolina, Alabama, and Mississippi, not one black child attended a public school with a white child in the 1962–63 school year. In North Carolina, only one-quarter of one percent—or .26 percent—of the black students attended desegregated schools in 1961; the figure did not rise above 1 percent until 1965. Similarly, in Virginia in 1964 only 1.63 percent of blacks were attending desegregated schools.

But the persistent efforts at desegregation had an impact. One by one, the obstructionist techniques were defeated. Finally, by the mid-1960s, desegregation began to proceed. By 1968, the integration rate rose to 32 percent and by 1972–73, 91.3 percent of southern schools were desegregated.

Many factors explain the delay between *Brown* and any results in desegregation. Efforts to thwart *Brown* had to be defeated. The 1964 Civil Rights Act, which in Title VI tied federal funds to eliminating desegregation, was crucial. Virtually every public school system depends on federal money. Title VI, and its enforcement by the Johnson administration, gave schools a tremendous financial incentive to change their ways.

But also important was renewed attention by the Supreme Court to segregated schools. In *Brown*, in 1954, the Court found that separate but equal is unconstitutional in the realm of public education, but it did not order a remedy. The Court asked for new briefs and arguments for the following year on the question of the appropriate solution. A year later, in *Brown II*, the Court considered the issue of remedy, but did virtually nothing: the Court sent the case back to the lower courts to achieve desegregation "with all deliberate speed." The phrase is an oxymoron, and it certainly gave no instructions to the lower courts responsible for implementing *Brown* as to what they were supposed to do. The Court provided no deadlines or timetables; it prescribed no techniques or approaches to desegregating schools to comply with the Constitution.

In 1958, the Supreme Court ruled that the governor of Arkansas could not disregard the U.S. Constitution and obstruct the desegregation of the Little Rock public schools. But that was the only Supreme Court decision about school segregation in the years after *Brown* until 1964. That year the Court lamented that "[t]here has been entirely too much deliberation and not enough speed" in achieving desegregation.

It was not until 1971, in *Swann v. Charlotte-Mecklenburg Board of Education,* that the Supreme Court attempted to provide guidance to lower courts in structuring remedies to desegregate schools. The Court approved such techniques as redrawing attendance zones and busing of students. This is the case that caused President Nixon to propose a federal statute to prevent school busing.

One must ask whether it would have made a difference had the Supreme Court in *Brown II,* or a case soon thereafter, mandated timetables for desegregation and detailed the remedies to be imposed. There is no way to know whether such efforts would have hastened desegregation. But it is too easy to assume that timetables and prescribed remedies would have made little difference in the face of massive resistance. Had the Court dictated timetables, outlined remedies, and been more actively involved from 1954 to 1964, results might well have been different, at least in some places.

By the 1970s, there finally had been substantial progress toward desegregation. But two crucial problems emerged: white flight to suburbs threatened school integration efforts, and perhaps more importantly, there were pervasive inequalities in funding, especially between urban and suburban schools. The Court's handling of these issues was critical to the future of American public education. In each instance, the Supreme Court, with four Nixon appointees in the majority, ruled against the civil rights plaintiffs and dramatically limited the efforts at desegregation and equal educational opportunity. The segregation and inequities in public education today are very much a consequence of these decisions.

White flight to suburban areas—in part to avoid school desegregation, and in part as a result of a larger demographic phenomenon—endangered successful desegregation. In virtually every urban area, the inner city was increasingly composed of racial minorities. By contrast, the surrounding suburbs were almost exclusively white, and what little minority population resided in suburbs was concentrated in towns that were almost exclusively black. School district lines parallel town borders, meaning that racial separation of cities and suburbs results in segregated school systems. For example, by 1980, whites constituted less than one-third of the students enrolled in the public schools in Baltimore, Dallas, Detroit, Houston, Los Angeles, Miami, Memphis, New York, and Philadelphia.

By the 1970s it was clear that effective school desegregation required interdistrict remedies. There were simply not enough white students in many major cities to achieve desegregation. Likewise, suburban school districts could not be desegregated without interdistrict remedies because of the scarcity of minority students in the suburbs.

As mentioned above, in the landmark case of *Swann v. Charlotte-Mecklenburg Board of Education*, the Supreme Court addressed the issue of the federal courts' power to issue remedies in school desegregation cases. The Supreme Court said that federal courts have broad authority in formulating remedies in desegregation cases. But *Swann* focused exclusively on remedies *within* a school district. It did not address interdistrict remedies.

The Court considered this situation three years later, in *Milliken v. Bradley*, and imposed a substantial limit on the judiciary's remedial powers in desegregation cases. The case involved the segregation of the Detroit public schools. Following the pattern that is common throughout the United States, Detroit had a student population that was almost entirely minority, but the city was surrounded by suburbs that were almost entirely white. For example, of the fourteen schools that opened in Detroit in 1970–71, eleven opened with more than 90 percent of their students being African-American and one opened with less than 10 percent African-American students. Many of the school systems in the surrounding suburbs were composed almost entirely of white students. The federal district court found that without including the suburbs in the desegregation plan, many schools in Detroit would inevitably remain between 75 and 100 percent black.

A federal district court devised a remedy for the racial separation in the Detroit-area schools that included both the city and 53 of 87 suburbs. No one in the litigation disputed that the area-wide remedy could have been successful in achieving desegregation.

Nonetheless, the Supreme Court in a 5–4 decision ruled this plan impermissible and held that "[b]efore the boundaries of separate and autonomous school districts may be set aside by consolidating the separate units for remedial purposes or by imposing a cross-district remedy, it must first be shown that there has been a constitutional violation within one district that produces a significant segregative effect in another district." In other words, courts can include suburbs in desegregation efforts only if it can be shown that the suburban districts had violated the U.S. Constitution. This is usually an insurmountable burden. So many factors contributed to the pattern of predominantly minority city schools surrounded by a ring of white suburban schools that it is difficult to prove that this situation resulted from identifiable constitutional violations. Since *Milliken*, there have been only a few successful efforts at court-imposed interdistrict remedies for school segregation.

Milliken has had a devastating effect on the ability to achieve desegregation in many areas. Duke professor Charles Clotfelter, in a careful study of American schools, concluded that 60 percent of segregation is a result of *Milliken v. Bradley;* or put another way, American schools would be 60 percent less segregated if interdistrict remedies were possible.

Common sense and experience explain why this is so. I grew up in Chicago, an urban area in which the city is predominantly minority, but there are surrounding suburbs that are virtually all white. For example, on the west side of the city, the Austin neighborhood is almost entirely composed of African-Americans and Latinos. But just across the border, Oak Park and especially River Forest are overwhelmingly white. An interdistrict remedy could help to desegregate both the Chicago public schools and the nearby suburban schools. Little would be required except redrawing attendance zones. But *Milliken* ensured that this would not happen. Chicago public schools are now more than 87 percent African-American and Latino. Without an interdistrict remedy that includes suburban schools there is relatively little that can be done to desegregate Chicago public schools in a meaningful way; there are just not enough white students to desegregate the city of Chicago's public schools. At the same time, there remain overwhelmingly white suburban districts, like New Trier and Glenbrook.

Likewise in the Los Angeles area, my home for much of the last thirty years, there are predominantly white school systems, such as Beverly Hills, surrounded by overwhelmingly minority schools. Transferring students across these district boundaries could lessen racial separation. But *Milliken* means that it can't and won't happen.

The segregated pattern in major metropolitan areas—blacks in the city and whites in the suburbs—did not occur by accident, but rather was the product of many government policies and social norms. Moreover, *Milliken* has had the effect of encouraging white flight. Whites who wish to avoid school desegregation can do so by moving to the suburbs. If *Milliken* had been decided differently, one of the incentives for such moves would have been eliminated.

Milliken was a 5–4 decision, with the four recent Nixon appointees—Burger, Blackmun, Powell, and Rehnquist—joining with Potter Stewart, an Eisenhower appointee, to create the majority. Nixon's pick for chief justice, Warren Burger, wrote the opinion for the Court. *Milliken* remains the law to this day and continues to prevent courts from devising desegregation remedies.

The second significant problem confronting the Supreme Court in the early 1970s was the growing disparity in school funding among districts within the same metropolitan area. In 1972 sociologist and education expert Christopher Jencks estimated that on average, 15 to 20 percent more money was being spent on each white student's education than on each black child's schooling. This was true throughout the country. For example, in the early 1970s, the Chicago public schools spent $5,265 for each student's education; but in the Niles school system, just north of the city,

$9,371 was spent on each student's schooling. In Camden, New Jersey, $3,538 was spent on each pupil; but in Princeton, New Jersey, the figure was $7,725. These disparities also corresponded to race: in Chicago, the majority of the students were African-American; in Niles Township, the schools were 91.6 percent white and 0.4 percent black.

There is an easy explanation for these funding disparities. In most states, education is substantially funded by local property taxes. Wealthier suburbs have significantly larger tax bases than poorer cities, so suburbs can tax at a low rate and still spend a great deal on education. Cities must tax at a higher rate and nonetheless often have much less to spend on schools per pupil.

The Court had the opportunity to remedy this inequality in education in *San Antonio Independent School District v. Rodriguez* in 1973. *Rodriguez* challenged the Texas system of funding public schools largely through local property taxes. There were seven public school districts in the San Antonio, Texas, area. The Edgewood Independent School District, with approximately 22,000 students enrolled in its twenty-five elementary and secondary schools, was one of the poorer ones. It was in a residential neighborhood that had little commercial or industrial property. The residents were predominantly of Mexican-American descent: approximately 90 percent of the student population was Mexican-American and more than 6 percent was African-American. Edgewood had the lowest average property value ($5,960) and the lowest median annual family income ($4,686) in the metropolitan area, but it taxed its property at the highest rate: an equalized tax rate of $1.05 per $100 of assessed property. The result, when combined with state and federal funds, was an expenditure of $356 per pupil annually.

By contrast, Alamo Heights was the most affluent school district in San Antonio. Its six schools, educating approximately 5,000 students, were overwhelmingly white, 18 percent Mexican-American and less than 1 percent African-American. Its local tax rate was $0.85 per $100, significantly lower than that in Edgewood. But that tax rate yielded more revenue than in Edgewood, allowing the district to spend significantly more on each child's education, $594 per pupil.

The plaintiffs challenged this system on two grounds: it violated equal protection as impermissible wealth discrimination and it denied the fundamental right to education. The Court rejected the former argument by holding that discrimination based on wealth does not violate the Constitution. Unlike discrimination based on race or gender, which are subjected to careful judicial scrutiny, the Court said that courts should defer to legislative judgments when it comes to matters of wealth discrimination. No Supreme Court decision since *Rodriguez* has found any discrimination based on wealth to be unconstitutional.

Moreover, the Court rejected the claim that education is a fundamental right. The Court said: "It is not the province of this Court to create substantive constitutional rights in the name of guaranteeing equal protection of the laws." Nixon appointee Justice Lewis Powell, writing for the majority, then concluded: "Education, of course, is not among the rights afforded explicit protection under our Federal Constitution. Nor do we find any basis for saying it is implicitly so protected." Although education obviously is inextricably linked to the exercise of constitutional rights such as freedom of speech and voting, the Court nonetheless decided that education itself is not a fundamental right. Thus the Court concluded that the significant disparities in school funding did not offend the U.S. Constitution.

Rodriguez was a 5–4 decision. As in *Milliken*, the four Nixon appointees—Burger, Blackmun, Powell, and Rehnquist—joined with Stewart to create the majority. It is easy to imagine that this case would have been decided differently if it had come to the Supreme Court a few years earlier, during the Warren era, or if Hubert Humphrey had defeated Richard Nixon in 1968 and had made those four appointments to the high court.

Subsequently, the Court reaffirmed that there is no right to education under the U.S. Constitution. *Kadrmas v. Dickinson Public Schools* in 1988 involved a challenge brought by a poor family to a state law authorizing local school systems to charge a fee for use of school buses. The family lived sixteen miles from the school, too far for the children to walk, and they could not afford the fee for the school bus. The parents had no way to get their children to school, so the family sued for the right to have its children bused there. The Court ruled against the family and reiterated its holdings from *Rodriguez*: there is no constitutional right to education, and discrimination against the poor, even as to something as basic as education, does not offend equal protection. Once more it was a 5–4 decision, split exactly along ideological lines, with the five most conservative justices composing the majority. The Reagan administration participated in the litigation and urged the Court to rule as it did.

These decisions are tragically wrong in holding that there is no fundamental right to education. Education is essential for the exercise of constitutional rights, for economic opportunity, and ultimately for achieving equality. Chief Justice Warren eloquently expressed this view in *Brown v. Board of Education:* "Today, education is perhaps the most important function of state and local governments. Compulsory school attendance laws and the great expenditures for education both demonstrate our recognition of the importance of education to our democratic society. It is required in the performance of our most basic public responsibilities, even service in the armed forces. It is the very foundation of good citizenship. Today it is a principal instrument in awakening the child to cultural values, in preparing him for later professional training, and in helping him to adjust normally to his environment. In these days, it is doubtful that any child may reasonably be expected to succeed in life if he is denied the opportunity of an education."

The combined effects of *Milliken* and *Rodriguez* cannot be overstated. *Milliken* helped to ensure racially separate schools and *Rodriguez* meant that they would be unequal. American public education today is characterized by wealthy white suburban schools spending a great deal on education surrounding much poorer black and Latino city schools that spend much less on education. In virtually every major city, twice as much is spent on education in wealthy predominantly white suburbs as in city schools that are overwhelmingly composed of children of color. In the Chicago area, $17,291 is spent per pupil in the Highland Park and Deerfield schools, which are only 10 percent black and Latino, compared with $8,482 on each child's education in the Chicago public schools, which are 87 percent black and Latino. In the Philadelphia area, $17,261 is spent per pupil in the Lower Merion schools, which are 9 percent black and Latino, compared with the Philadelphia public schools, where $9,299 is spent per pupil in a school system that is 79 percent black and Latino. In the New York area, $22,311 is spent per pupil in a system that is 9 percent black and Latino, compared with $11,627 in the New York City schools, which are 72 percent black and Latino.

The 1990s

Despite the obstacles created by these Supreme Court decisions, courts in many metropolitan areas were still able to fashion effective desegregation orders. In some areas, *Milliken* made this impossible; but in other places desegregation was achieved, even though *Rodriguez* precluded federal courts from equalizing educational expenditures among districts.

However, in a series of three decisions in the 1990s, the Supreme Court ordered an end to most of the desegregation orders across the country. The Court made it clear that even successful desegregation decrees were to be ended, even when that would mean the substantial resegregation of the public schools. Once more, it was the conservative justices, appointed by Republican presidents, who were in the majority in these cases.

In *Board of Education of Oklahoma City v. Dowell*, in 1991, the issue was whether a desegregation order should continue when its end would mean a resegregation of the public schools. Oklahoma schools had been segregated under a state law mandating separation of the races in education. It was not until 1971—seventeen years after *Brown*—that desegregation was ordered. A federal court order was successful in desegregating the Oklahoma City public schools; almost no children were attending schools that were composed of students of more than 90 percent of one race.

Evidence proved that ending the desegregation order would result in dramatic resegregation of these schools. Ending the federal court's remedy would mean that over one-half of Oklahoma City's elementary schools would have student bodies that would be either 90 percent African-American or 90 percent non-African-American.

Nonetheless, the Supreme Court held that the school desegregation order should be lifted. In an opinion written by Chief Justice William Rehnquist, with the four most conservative justices then on the Court joining to form the majority, the Court said that once a "unitary" school system had been achieved, a federal court's desegregation order should end *even if it will mean resegregation of the schools.*

The Court did not define "unitary system" with any specificity. The Court simply said that the desegregation decree should be ended if the board "has complied in good faith" and "the vestiges of past discrimination have been eliminated to the extent practicable." The phrase "unitary system" refers to school systems not split in two according to race. The Court was thus saying that once a federal court order ending the dual system had been in effect for several years, the order should be ended, even when this would mean the rapid resegregation of the public schools. In fact, this has been exactly the experience in Oklahoma City as the schools quickly resegregated.

The Court reaffirmed and expanded on this opinion a year later in *Freeman v. Pitts*, which involved the DeKalb County, Georgia, public schools. Like Oklahoma City, this was a school system that had once been segregated by law. The Supreme Court held that a federal court desegregation order should end when it is complied with, even if other desegregation orders for the same school system remain in place.

A federal district court ordered desegregation of various aspects of the Georgia school system. Part of the desegregation plan had been met; the school system had achieved desegregation in pupil assignment and in facilities. Another aspect of the desegregation order, concerning assignment of teachers, had not yet been fulfilled. The school system planned to construct a facility that likely would benefit whites far more than blacks given its location. Nonetheless, the Supreme Court held that the federal court could not review the discriminatory effects of the new construction because the part of the desegregation order concerning facilities had already been met. The Court said that once a portion of a desegregation order is met, the federal court should cease its efforts as to that part of the order and remain involved in only those aspects of the plan that have not been achieved.

Finally, in *Missouri v. Jenkins*, in 1995, the Court ordered an end to a school desegregation order for the Kansas City, Missouri, schools. Missouri law had once required the racial segregation of all public schools. It was not until 1977 that a federal district court ordered the desegregation of the Kansas City public schools. The federal court's desegregation effort made a difference. In 1983, twenty-four schools in the district had an African-American enrollment of 90 percent or more. By 1993, no elementary-level student attended a school with an enrollment that was 90 percent or more African-American. At the middle school and high school levels, the percentage of students attending schools with an African-American enrollment of 90 percent or more declined from about 45 to 22 percent.

In an opinion written by Chief Justice Rehnquist and with Republican appointees O'Connor, Scalia, Kennedy, and Thomas making up the majority, the Court ordered an end to the desegregation efforts. The Court ruled that the district court's order that attempted to attract nonminority students from outside the district was impermissible because there was no proof of an interdistrict violation. Chief Justice Rehnquist applied *Milliken v. Bradley* to conclude that the interdistrict remedy—incentives to attract students from outside the district into the Kansas City schools— was not allowed because there was proof only of an intradistrict violation.

Additionally, the Court ruled that the continued disparity in student test scores did not justify continuance of the federal court's desegregation order. It concluded that the U.S. Constitution requires equal opportunity and not any result, and that therefore disparities between African-American and white students on standardized tests was not a sufficient basis for concluding that desegregation had not been achieved. The majority held that once a desegregation order is complied with, the federal court effort should be ended. Disparity in test scores is not a basis for continued federal court involvement.

The three cases together sent a clear signal to lower courts: the time has come to end desegregation orders, even when the effect will be resegregation. Lower courts have followed this lead. For example, the United States Court of Appeals for the Fourth Circuit ended the desegregation remedy for the Charlotte-Mecklenburg schools ordered by the Supreme Court in *Swann*. Harvard professor Gary Orfield has documented the substantial resegregation of the Charlotte-area public schools. Between 1993 and 2000, there was a doubling in the number of black students attending schools with minority enrollments of 80 percent of more. Similarly, the United States Court of Appeals for the Eleventh Circuit ended the desegregation order for the Tampa, Florida, schools despite strong evidence of continued segregation and likely significant increases in racial separation with the lifting of the decree. These are just a few of the many examples across the country where federal courts have ended previously successful desegregation orders and caused substantial increases in racial separation in public schools. Orfield documents how these decisions have contributed significantly to the resegregation of American public education.

During the Vietnam War, Senator George Aiken said that the United States should declare victory and withdraw from Vietnam. In these decisions of the 1990s the Supreme Court declared victory over the problem of school segregation and withdrew the judiciary from solving the problem.

2007

The effect of the Supreme Court's decisions in the 1970s and the 1990s was to greatly limit the power of the federal courts to achieve desegregation or equalize educational opportunity. Even the judicial remedies that survived the 1970s decisions were rapidly ended after the 1990s rulings. But there was still the possibility of school districts implementing desegregation plans on their own. The Supreme Court's decision in 2007 in *Parents Involved in Community Schools v. Seattle School Dist., No. 1* ended many of these efforts. Once more it was a 5–4 decision, with the five most conservative justices appointed by Presidents Reagan, Bush, and Bush—Roberts, Scalia, Kennedy, Thomas, and Alito—composing the majority.

The case involved two school systems, in Seattle and Louisville, that had adopted desegregation plans. The Seattle plan applied at the high school level. The district operates ten regular public high schools. Under the plan adopted in 1998, students could pick the school they wished to attend. If too many students listed the same school as their first choice, the district used a series of "tiebreakers" to determine who would gain admission to the oversubscribed school. The first factor considered gave preference for students who had a sibling currently enrolled in the school. The second factor looked to race if the school was not racially balanced. In other words, race was one factor considered in assigning students if the schools were oversubscribed.

Unlike Seattle, where the schools had never been segregated by law, the Jefferson County schools in Louisville had been racially segregated until this segregation was declared unconstitutional in 1973. A desegregation order was imposed by the federal court in 1975. In 2000, as a result of the Supreme Court's decisions from the 1990s, the federal court lifted its desegregation order. The school board then adopted its own desegregation plan. Approximately 34 percent of the district's 97,000 students were black; most of the remaining 66 percent were white. The desegregation plan adopted by the school board required all nonmagnet schools to maintain a minimum black enrollment of 15 percent, and a maximum black enrollment of 50 percent. In both the elementary schools and high schools, race was one factor used to assign students to schools to achieve desegregation.

The Supreme Court struck down both programs and created a

significant obstacle to school boards implementing their own desegregation programs in the future. Chief Justice Roberts's opinion was joined in its entirety by Justices Scalia, Thomas, and Alito, and in part by Justice Kennedy, the fifth justice in the majority.

All five justices in the majority agreed that the government may use race as a factor to achieve desegregation only if it can show that its actions are necessary to achieve a compelling purpose. The use of race to achieve desegregation is thus treated exactly the same way by the courts as the use of race to discriminate against minorities. Chief Justice Roberts, writing for a plurality of four, found that Seattle and Louisville lacked a compelling interest for their desegregation efforts. He stressed that the school systems were not seeking to remedy constitutional violations and he rejected the argument that diversity in classrooms was a sufficient government interest to allow the desegregation efforts. Roberts was emphatic: "The principle that racial balancing is not permitted is one of substance, not semantics. Racial balancing is not transformed from 'patently unconstitutional' to a compelling state interest simply by relabeling it 'racial diversity.'"

By contrast, Justice Kennedy and the four dissenters said that desegregating schools *is* a compelling government interest. But Justice Kennedy joined with the other four conservative justices in holding that the school districts failed to show that race-neutral means could not achieve desegregation. Justice Kennedy, like the four Justices in the plurality, said that race can be used in assigning students only if there is no other way of achieving desegregation. Proving that every possible alternative will fail is usually a difficult, if not insurmountable, task.

The decision is troubling on many levels. First, it will create a huge obstacle to school systems adopting desegregation plans. For obvious reasons, desegregating schools often requires taking into account the race of the students. Assigning students randomly, without regard to their race, cannot achieve the goal. Justice Breyer, in his dissenting opinion, attached an appendix listing dozens of voluntary desegregation plans that would be in jeopardy after the Court's holding. Many have since been ended. The earlier Supreme Court decisions greatly limited what courts could do to desegregate schools and equalize educational opportunity. *Parents Involved in Community Schools* is important because the ruling restricts the ability of school districts to create effective voluntary desegregation plans.

Second, Chief Justice Roberts's opinion forcefully argued that the Constitution requires that the government be color-blind— that the constitutional guarantee of equal protection means that the government cannot use race as a factor, even to achieve desegregation, except in the most compelling circumstances. Writing for four justices, he contended that any use of race by the government inherently violates equal protection. Chief justice Roberts concluded his majority opinion by quoting from the briefs of the plaintiffs who were challenging school segregation in *Brown v. Board of Education:* "[T]he Fourteenth Amendment prevents states from according differential treatment to American children on the basis of their color or race." Roberts then asked: "What do the racial classifications at issue here do, if not accord differential treatment on the basis of race?"

He ended his opinion by declaring: "For schools that never segregated on the basis of race, such as Seattle, or that have removed the vestiges of past segregation, such as Jefferson County, the way 'to achieve a system of determining admission to the public schools on a nonracial basis,' is to stop assigning students on a racial basis. The way to stop discrimination on the basis of race is to stop discriminating on the basis of race."

Roberts disregards the distinction between the government using race to subordinate racial minorities, as was the case with laws requiring segregation, and the use of race to benefit minorities and to achieve diversity. They are not the same. The Seattle and Louisville plans that used race as one factor in pupil assignments to achieve desegregation share no similarity to state laws that mandated that white and black children be educated separately because of an assumption of white superiority and black inferiority. The former is motivated by the desire to remedy past discrimination and to foster diversity; the latter was based on racism. "Color blindness" sounds noble, but there is every difference in the world between using race to discriminate and using race to desegregate. The Jim Crow laws struck down in *Brown* were based on a belief in the superiority of one race and the inferiority of another; the Louisville and Seattle plans were based on a desire to advance equal educational opportunity.

Although the Court's conservative justices often profess to follow the original meaning of the Constitution, here they ignored it. The Congress that ratified the Fourteenth Amendment did not believe in color blindness as a constitutional principle. It created numerous programs, such as the Freedmen's Bureau, to provide benefits based on race and it voted to segregate the District of Columbia public schools.

The hypocrisy of the decision in *Parents Involved in Community Schools* is that it is activism by the very conservative justices who preach against judicial activism. The Court struck down desegregation plans adopted by popularly elected school boards. Nowhere was there the deference to the government, and specifically to school boards, that the conservatives proclaim in other areas when it serves their political agenda. Of course, my objection is not to the court being antimajoritarian; it is that in *Brown* v. *Board of Education.* The problem is that the Court sees no difference between invalidating laws requiring segregation and invalidating laws to end segregation.

In the decisions of the 1990s, the Supreme Court ordered an end to federal court desegregation orders to return control of schools to elected local leaders. But when cities and school boards attempted on their own to achieve desegregation, the Court declared these efforts unconstitutional.

As Justice Breyer noted in his dissent, the immediate effect of the Court's decision in *Parents Involved* will be to make it far harder for the government to achieve successful desegregation efforts. Equally troubling, Chief Justice Roberts's proclamation of a requirement that the government be color-blind raises the real possibility that in the near future conservatives will be able to achieve their long-professed goal of finding virtually all government affirmative action plans to be unconstitutional.

In *Grutter v. Bollinger*, in 2003, the Supreme Court held that colleges and universities have a compelling interest in diversity in their classrooms and may use race as one factor among many in admissions decisions to benefit minorities and to enhance diversity. Specifically, the Court ruled that the University of Michigan Law School could consider race in its admissions decisions to increase diversity among its students. The decision was 5–4, with Justice O'Connor writing for a majority joined by Justices Stevens, Souter, Ginsburg, and Breyer. With Justice O'Connor now replaced by Justice Alito, and with Alito joining the opinion espousing the view that the government must be color-blind, this decision seems in great jeopardy. Moreover, Justice O'Connor's majority opinion in *Grutter* expressly said that the government did not have to prove that there was no way to achieve diversity without considering race, whereas all five justices in the majority in *Parents Involved in Community Schools* said that this is the government's burden.

There thus seem five votes—Roberts, Scalia, Kennedy, Thomas, and Alito—to overrule *Grutter* and hold that affirmative action programs are unconstitutional. No one doubts that Roberts, Scalia, Thomas, and Alito will vote this way, but I have heard some people express hope that Justice Kennedy will join with the more liberal justices to preserve *Grutter's* holding. It must be remembered, though, that Justice Kennedy dissented in *Grutter*, along with Rehnquist, Scalia, and Thomas. In fact, in his more than twenty years on the Supreme Court, Justice Kennedy never has voted to uphold any affirmative action program.

If the conservatives on the Court achieve this long-sought goal, there will be a devastating effect on the composition of classrooms in colleges and universities. Because of the long history of race discrimination, and the continuing inequities in elementary and high schools, there will be relatively few African-American and Latino students at the elite colleges and universities if affirmative action is outlawed.

To take law schools, the area I know best, as an example, in 2009, in the entire United States, there were only twelve African-American students with LSATs above 170 and grade point averages above 3.5. In the entire country, there were only 118 African-Americans with LSATs above 165. To put this in perspective, the University of California, Irvine, School of Law, where I am dean, had a median LSAT of 167 and a median GPA of 3.61 in its first year of existence. Schools like Duke and Berkeley are at about 169 for their median LSAT; Harvard, Yale, and Stanford have median LSATs over 170.

The effect of ending affirmative action was evident in 1996 when California voters adopted Proposition 209, which prohibited state and local governments from discriminating or giving preference based on race or gender in education, employment, or contracting. In the five years following the adoption of Proposition 209, there was a sharp difference in racial composition between the public and private law schools in California. The University of Southern California and Stanford law schools, both at private universities, had student bodies that were respectively more than 11 percent and more than 9 percent African-American. The University of California, Berkeley, and the University of California, Los Angeles, law schools were respectively more than 3 percent and more than 2 percent African-American.

In his vehement dissent in *Grutter,* Justice Clarence Thomas said that the desire for diversity in the classroom is simply an aesthetic preference for students with different colors of skin. He is wrong. Colleges and universities have long recognized that diversity in the classroom matters. It always has been easier for an outstanding student from Montana to get into Harvard or Yale than an outstanding student from Boston or New York City. Those with unusual talents, for example, in athletics or music, also have long been given preference in admissions. Never have colleges and universities admitted students solely on the basis of grades and test scores. Children and grandchildren of those who attended the school, so-called "legacies," always have been given preferential treatment in admissions.

I have been a law professor for thirty years now and have taught constitutional law in classes that are almost all white and in those that are racially diverse. The conversations are vastly different and the education of all is enhanced when the classroom is racially mixed. It is different to talk about racial profiling by the police when there are African-American and Latino men in the room who can talk powerfully about their experience of being stopped for no reason other than driving while black or brown. Preparing students for the racially diverse world they will experience requires that they learn in racially diverse classrooms. This is exactly why the Court found diversity to be a compelling interest in *Grutter v. Bollinger.*

But the likely conservative ending of affirmative action programs must be understood in the context of the overall effect on the American educational system. Because of decisions by conservatives on the Supreme Court in the 1970s and 1990s and in 2007, American public elementary and high schools are increasingly segregated and terribly unequal in the resources available for education. Not surprisingly, white students who are the beneficiaries of unequal resources tend to do far better in the statistical measures used for college, professional school, and graduate school admissions. If as I expect the Supreme Court ends affirmative action programs meant to compensate for this inequality, the result will be a further institutionalization of inequalities between the races.

As I mentioned at the start of this chapter, the ACLU's lawsuit challenging the inequities in the Alabama schools was initially successful. The evidence presented to the trial court was compelling. A heavily minority elementary school in Wilcox County did not have a single working piece of playground equipment. Science labs were more than twice as likely to be available in the more affluent schools. More than half the wealthier school districts had audiovisual production facilities, but only 17 percent of the poorer schools had them. In 1993, a state trial court judge, Eugene Reese, found that the funding of the Alabama public schools was inequitable.

Four years later, the Alabama Supreme Court agreed with this conclusion but overruled the proposed remedy of equalizing funding in the state's school system. The litigation languished with no remedy imposed until 2002, when the Alabama Supreme Court dismissed the case. Thus neither the federal nor the state constitution provides any remedy for the inequalities in funding the Alabama public schools.

Thirty years ago, in a prophetic dissent in *Milliken v. Bradley*, Justice Thurgood Marshall reminded us of what is at stake in the fight for equal educational opportunity:

> [W]e deal here with the right of all children, whatever their race, to an equal start in life and an equal opportunity to reach their full potential as citizens. Those children who have been denied that right in the past deserve better than to see fences thrown up to deny them that right in the future. Our nation, I fear, will be ill served by the Court's refusal to remedy separate and unequal education, for unless our children begin to learn together, there is little hope that our people will ever learn to live together.

Nowhere has the conservative assault on the Constitution and the effect of the conservative justices on the Supreme Court been more apparent or more important than in its re-creation of separate and unequal schools.

2.

The Imperious Presidency

Salim Gherebi is about fifty years old and has been a prisoner at the American military base at Guantanamo Bay, Cuba, since the spring of 2002. He has been my client since July 2002. He is about my height, five feet seven, and slim in build with a long, graying beard. He has an intense gaze and his fingers are deformed, some fused together and misshaped. When we spoke through an interpreter at Guantanamo, he answered in a quiet voice. He is the father of three children; his wife was pregnant with the youngest when he was apprehended in Afghanistan. He is of Libyan descent and is a devout Muslim.

Although I have represented him for almost eight years, I can honestly say, without fear of disclosing any classified information or violating any confidence, that I do not know why he is being held prisoner. He may be a very dangerous man or, like many others, he may have been taken to Guantanamo by mistake. Since he has never had a trial or even a meaningful factual hearing, it is impossible to know.

The story of my representing Gherebi began over the Martin Luther King holiday weekend in January 2002. At that time the news media first reported that the United States was bringing prisoners—shackled, blindfolded, and drugged—to Guantanamo, where they were to be housed in cages measuring eight feet by eight feet.

A Los Angeles civil rights lawyer, Stephen Yagman, called me at home and was very upset about these media reports. He felt that someone should sue on behalf of these detainees to make sure they were treated in accord with the requirements of the law. A federal statute allows a habeas corpus petition to be brought on behalf of a person being held in custody. A habeas corpus petition is a legal proceeding dating back to English law that allows a court to order the release of a prisoner who is held in violation of the law. Yagman's concern was that the treatment of these prisoners violated the United States Constitution and international law and that there was no one to sue on their behalf. He asked if I would join him as a lawyer in handling the matter. I did some quick legal research and confirmed that federal law allowed individuals to bring habeas petitions on behalf of others without their knowledge or consent. I also read every media report and was concerned that what the United States was doing seemed in clear violation of the Constitution and the Geneva Conventions, the treaty signed by the United States that governs the detention and treatment of prisoners.

Yagman put together a coalition of clergy members, professors, and journalists to be the plaintiffs in the suit; it was titled *Coalition of Clergy v. Bush*. The case was filed on an emergency basis on Monday, January 21, in the federal district court in Los Angeles. Although Washington, D.C., seemed a more logical place to sue, we both lived in Los Angeles and thought that we could argue that the president and the secretary of defense should be able to be sued in any federal court. We were acting pro bono, that is, without compensation, so minimizing costs was important.

The news media immediately picked up the story of the suit. I was flying to New York that day for a speech on Tuesday. When I landed late in the evening my cell phone message box was filled to capacity. Every call was from a journalist, including requests to appear on every national morning news show the next day. My speaking obligation made this very difficult; besides, I did not want it to seem that I was doing this for publicity. I thought that the complaint filed in federal court spoke for itself and decided not to do media appearances. In hindsight, I regret not taking this initial opportunity to explain why what the United States was doing was wrong and illegal.

During the Vietnam War, even though the Viet Cong violated conventional rules of warfare, the United States gave those whom they captured the protections assured by the Geneva Conventions. The United States created a formal system of hearings to separate the combatants from the civilians. These hearings became an ongoing part of American military procedures. During the Gulf War, the United States continued this practice and conducted almost 1,200 hearings, finding 310 detainees were prisoners of war and that the rest were refugees. These hearings were a mechanism prescribed by international law to ensure that individuals were not held prisoner by mistake.

The Bush administration, though, did not follow this procedure for those brought to Guantanamo; it did not provide them any hearings and for years steadfastly maintained that it did not need to do so. The detention and treatment of these prisoners has been inconsistent with the Constitution and treaties ratified by the United States such as the Geneva Accords and the International Covenant of Political and Civil Rights.

On Tuesday morning, I discovered that I had more than two hundred new e-mail messages. Virtually every one of them was hateful, and many quite ugly. Some wished that my family would die in a Bin Laden bombing. Only a couple expressed support for the lawsuit. Later that day, when I called my office, I learned that it had been deluged with hate phone calls. Some had been so offensive and threatening that campus security had been called by one of the faculty secretaries who had been answering the calls.

The case was assigned to a federal district judge in Los Angeles, Howard Matz. He set oral arguments for mid-February. I was to argue for the plaintiffs and Paul Clement, the deputy solicitor general of the United States, flew out from Washington to represent the government. Clement's presence was a clear signal of the seriousness with which this lawsuit was taken by the government. At the time, Clement was only thirty-five years old and was a rising star in conservative legal circles. After graduating from Harvard Law School, he had clerked for conservative federal court of appeals judge Laurence Silberman and then for Supreme Court justice Antonin Scalia. In the second Bush term, Clement would become the solicitor general of the United States, the prestigious official who represents the United States government before the Supreme Court.

At the beginning of the hearing, Judge Matz handed Clement and me copies of his twenty-five-page draft opinion. He said that we could have fifteen minutes to read it, but we could not show anyone. He said that he would then return to the bench for oral argument. The draft opinion dismissed our lawsuit, primarily because the judge said that we did not have standing to sue on behalf of the Guantanamo detainees. The oral argument then commenced. I had the strange experience of trying to convince a judge to change his mind when he had made his decision and already written an opinion. The low point for me came when after I cited several cases to support my point, Judge Matz said, "Professor, you know the cases better than I do, but you're not convincing me." I failed. The next day, Judge Matz released his opinion saying that our standing was a "close question," but that we could not sue for the Guantanamo detainees.

Yagman and I appealed Judge Matz's dismissal to the United States Court of Appeals for the Ninth Circuit. The oral argument was held in July in Pasadena. Only two of the judges were on the bench; the third, John Noonan, was participating by telephone and other than an occasional cough there was no way to know that he was there. Once more, Paul Clement flew in to represent the United States. My argument was a simple one: the federal statute allowed habeas petitions to be brought on behalf of another person and that was especially important in situations where a person cannot sue for himself or herself and there is no one else to sue. This, I argued, was exactly that situation.

The two judges on the bench that day, Kim Wardlaw and Marsha Berzon, both Clinton appointees, were skeptical of my position. Repeatedly they asked me to show that the detainees in Guantanamo could not sue on their own or have others connected to them sue. I am not prone to sarcasm and strongly advise my students never to use it in court, but finally my frustration grew. In my rebuttal I said: "Those in Guantanamo have not sued and very few suits had been filed on their behalf. There are two explanations: One is that they like being incarcerated and held in cages. The other is that they do not have the knowledge or where-withal to go to federal court and their families don't know where they are or have the resources to help them. The latter seems far more plausible."

In November 2002, the court of appeals unanimously affirmed the dismissal of our lawsuit. The court of appeals said that in order to have standing we would need the permission of the detainees or at least must have tried to form a relationship with them and we would need to show that no one else could represent them. As to the latter, Judge Berzon in her opinion said, "Here, however, Coalition has not proven except by assertion that the remaining detainees have no relationship with anyone who could appropriately serve to litigate the legality of the detention." I am not sure what we or anyone could have done to meet either of these requirements since the government at that point would not let us visit the detainees in Guantanamo.

However, the problem solved itself when the brother of a detainee, Belaid Gherebi, contacted Stephen Yagman after reading the account of the oral argument in the newspaper. Gherebi said that he had a brother, Salim, being held in Guantanamo and asked if we would represent him. Over time, others detained in Guantanamo obtained lawyers, often through the requests of family members living in other countries. Many of the nation's most prestigious law firms began representing detainees.

Yagman and I filed a new complaint and asked Judge Matz to allow us to submit our earlier briefs on behalf of Gherebi in arguing that the detention violated the Constitution and international law. Matz agreed that no new briefing was needed and that we now had standing to sue since we had been retained by a family member to represent a detainee, but then ruled against us and dismissed the suit on behalf of Gherebi. He said that federal courts lack the authority to review the detention of those in Guantanamo. We appealed to the Ninth Circuit, which heard the case in August 2003. In December, it held in our favor, overruling the strong objections of the Bush administration and holding that the federal court had the authority to hear the petition for habeas corpus filed on behalf of Gherebi. This was an enormous victory at the time; it was the first court to rule in favor of a Guantanamo detainee. The United States Court of Appeals for the District of Columbia Circuit had come to the opposite conclusion.

In June 2004, the Supreme Court reversed the D.C. Circuit in *Rasul v. Bush* and came to the same conclusion as the Ninth Circuit had, holding that federal courts can grant habeas corpus to the Guantanamo detainees. Justice Stevens wrote for the Court and Justices Rehnquist, Scalia, and Thomas dissented. The Bush administration then successfully pushed the Republican-controlled Congress to adopt a law, the Detainee Treatment Act, providing that no federal court could grant habeas corpus to anyone held at Guantanamo. The Supreme Court never ruled on the constitutionality of this law, but in 2006 it said that this law would be deemed to apply only prospectively to those apprehended in the future and not to those already held. In response, in the fall of 2006, at the strong urging of the Bush administration, Congress adopted the Military Commissions Act. It provided that noncitizens held as enemy combatants shall not have access to the federal courts via a writ of habeas corpus. The law said that any decisions rendered by a military tribunal could be reviewed in the United States Court of Appeals for the District of Columbia Circuit. But the law did not require military tribunals, and if none were held, a person could be held without judicial review indefinitely. Also, review in the federal court of appeals was limited to issues applicable under the U.S. Constitution and federal statutes; no claims under international law could be brought. Since the earliest days of the nation, the Supreme Court had held that treaties and other international law are enforceable in the United States. In fact, the 2006 decision invalidated the Bush system of military commissions for violating the Geneva Conventions.

On June 12, 2008, six and a half years after the first detainees were brought to Guantanamo, the Supreme Court held in

Boumediene v. Bush that the Military Commissions Act was unconstitutional. It was a 5–4 decision, with Justice Anthony Kennedy writing for the Court, joined by the four most liberal justices, Stevens, Souter, Ginsburg, and Breyer. Justice Scalia wrote an impassioned dissent in which he declared that innocent Americans would die because of the Court's ruling. He said that federal courts would release dangerous terrorists and they would come back and commit acts of violence in the United States. He urged the Court to leave the matter entirely to the president and Congress.

The Supreme Court's decision did not release a single detainee, but it did mean that the federal courts could hear their claims and could order their release if the law required this. In fact, on remand from the Supreme Court in the case of detainee Zakhdar Boumediene, in November 2008, federal district court judge Richard Leon found that there was no evidence justifying holding the detainees in the case before him. This was telling because Judge Leon, an appointee of President George W. Bush, had ruled in favor of the Bush administration at every step of the proceedings. In a strongly worded ruling he said that he had reviewed the entire record, including that portion filed in secret, and there was no basis for the continued detention of all but one of the detainees before him. He ordered their release and he urged the United States not to appeal; he said that innocent people had been held long enough. The government did not appeal and this group of detainees was released from custody.

We know now that many who were held in Guantanamo were brought there by mistake. The United States paid warlords to name those with ties to the Al Qaeda terrorist network, responsible for the attacks of September 11, 2001. Not surprisingly some named rivals to get them out of the way and some gave names just to collect the bounties. Some prisoners held at Guantanamo, of course, might be very dangerous. But the position of the Bush administration was that the government could hold anyone it chose, citizen or noncitizen, indefinitely as an enemy combatant without any need for a hearing or due process. In fact, the government argued repeatedly in the lower federal courts, in the Supreme Court, and in the press that it had the authority to detain even American citizens as enemy combatants and hold them until the end of the war on terror, which President Bush said will continue long beyond any of our lifetimes.

The abuses of power and violations of rights during the Bush administration were enormous. The claim of the authority to detain individuals indefinitely without a hearing or due process is one example, but others include massive illegal electronic eavesdropping, torture unlike anything ever done before by the American government, and an enormous degree of secrecy about all of these activities. For all of these actions, the Bush administration claimed inherent executive power to act and argued that any federal law limiting its conduct was an unconstitutional infringement of presidential prerogatives. It repeatedly contended that no court had the power to review its actions. Each of these actions warrants close examination, but first it is important to situate them in historical context and especially in the context of efforts by Republican presidents since Richard Nixon to greatly expand presidential powers. The conservative assault on the Constitution described in this chapter has come through the executive branch, not the courts. In fact, for the most part, the Bush administration lost its arguments in the Supreme Court, though many of its actions never were reviewed there.

In one sense, what occurred during the Bush administration was simply one of the worst aspects of American history repeating itself. Throughout our history, threats, especially foreign-based threats, have brought a repressive response. In hindsight we have realized that no security was gained from the violation of basic civil rights.

This experience began early in American history, in the nation's first decade. There were concerns about the country's ability to survive during its early years. In 1798, Congress enacted the Alien and Sedition Act, which made it a federal crime to falsely criticize the government or government officials. Numerous individuals were sentenced to prison for speech that was mild and ineffectual, tamer than what Jay Leno or David Letterman or Jon Stewart say today on a nightly basis. In the election of 1800, Thomas Jefferson campaigned against the law and when elected pardoned those who had been convicted under it. In 1964, the Supreme Court said that the law had been declared unconstitutional in "the court of history." The act violated the most basic principles of the First Amendment for no apparent gain to the nation's security.

During the Civil War, President Abraham Lincoln suspended the writ of habeas corpus. Called the "Great Writ" in England, habeas corpus provides a procedure where those held in violation of the Constitution can seek court relief. Even in times of war, the government should not be holding people in violation of the Constitution. The suspension of the writ of habeas corpus meant that innocent people were wrongly held with no remedy. Hundreds and perhaps thousands were detained for their speech criticizing how the Civil War was being fought. There is no indication that these detentions helped the war effort in any meaningful way; they just silenced dissenters. After the Civil War, Lincoln's action suspending habeas corpus was declared unconstitutional. Suspending habeas corpus is not a power granted to the president by the Constitution.

During World War I, in 1917 and 1918, Congress enacted two laws that made criticizing the war effort and particularly the draft a federal crime. People received long prison sentences for mild disagreement with the government. In one famous case, an individual was sentenced to ten years in prison for circulating a leaflet arguing that the draft was involuntary servitude in violation of the Thirteenth Amendment. In another case, the famous socialist Eugene Debs was sentenced to ten years in prison for saying to his audience, "You are good for more than cannon fodder; there's more that I'd like to say but I can't for fear of going to prison." The Supreme Court upheld both of these convictions and sentences, even though there was not the slightest evidence that the speech had any effect on military recruitment or the war effort.

During World War II, 110,000 Japanese-Americans, some aliens and others citizens—70,000 were citizens—were uprooted from their homes and placed in what President Franklin Roosevelt called "concentration camps." Not one Japanese-American ever was indicted for espionage or any crime against the security of the United States. The invasion of basic human rights was enormous. This was the first time in American history that race alone determined who would be incarcerated behind barbed wire. Tragically, in 1944, the Supreme Court upheld the evacuation of Japanese-Americans, a decision widely regarded by constitutional scholars and historians as one of the worst mistakes in Supreme Court history.

During the late 1940s and early '50s, the McCarthy era, Congress enacted laws such as the Smith Act, which punished speech and associational activity. It was the age of suspicion where merely being suspected of being a communist could cause people to lose their jobs or even their freedom. In the leading case decided by the Supreme Court, individuals were sentenced to twenty years in prison simply for studying and teaching works by Marx and Lenin. They were convicted of the crime of conspiracy to advocate the overthrow of the United States government. They were not charged with plotting or conspiring to overthrow the government, or even for advocating it, but for conspiracy to advocate. Their activities had no identifiable effect whatsoever. But the Supreme Court upheld their convictions, saying that the harm of a revolution is so great that there is no need for the government to show that the speech increases the likelihood of this harm in order to justify punishment.

University of Chicago law professor Geoffrey Stone, in a magnificent book, Perilous Times, shows how throughout American history the response to crises has been repression and how in hindsight we realize we were not made any safer from the loss of rights. I believe that is the story of what has occurred since 9/11: there have been significant violations of basic constitutional principles without any proof that they have made the country safer. But in some ways what the Bush administration did was different because no other administration in American history has gone so far in its assertions that no law applied to its actions and in its claims of unreviewable, uncheckable executive power.

The expansive claims of executive power, and the conduct that resulted from them, like so much in this book, trace their origins to the presidencies of Richard Nixon and Ronald Reagan. In fact, the architects of much of the Bush administration's approach to executive power, men such as Dick Cheney and Donald Rumsfeld, developed their views during the Nixon, Ford, and Reagan years. Rumsfeld was the head of the Office of Economic Opportunity during the Nixon presidency and hired Cheney as his assistant. Rumsfeld served as Gerald Ford's White House chief of staff and chose Cheney to be his deputy. Rumsfeld and Cheney asserted broad executive powers and received legal opinions supporting their views from the young lawyer heading the Office of Legal Counsel in the Justice Department: Antonin Scalia.

Over thirty years ago, during the Nixon presidency, noted historian Harvard professor Arthur Schlesinger wrote *The Imperial Presidency*. He documented the great growth in executive power during the Nixon years. One important and representative example was the Nixon administration's assertion of the power to impound federal funds allocated and appropriated by Congress. Nixon claimed that the president had the authority to block the spending of money that had been authorized and appropriated in a spending bill passed by Congress and signed by the president. The president certainly can veto any appropriations bill. But Nixon argued that even if a presidential veto had been overridden by Congress or even if he had signed the bill, he still had presidential authority to impound funds and prevent them from being spent.

This was a tremendous expansion of presidential control over spending and it was declared unconstitutional by several lower federal courts. Nothing in the Constitution remotely suggests such authority. Article I of the Constitution gives Congress the power to tax and spend and this always has been regarded as a quintessential legislative power. Nixon's efforts to impound funds led Congress to adopt the Impoundment Control Act of 1974, which effectively forbids the practice. The Nixon administration then argued that this act was an unconstitutional limit on executive power, claiming uncheckable authority to stop Congress from spending money. Dick Cheney, for example, has taken this position and argued that the Impoundment Control Act unconstitutionally restricts executive power. This position is impossible to reconcile with the long-established view that Congress has the power of the purse.

Another example of the assertion of broad powers during the Nixon years, and one that resurfaced on a much broader scale during the recent Bush presidency, was its assertion of authority to engage in warrantless wiretapping for the sake of domestic security. The Nixon administration apparently engaged in significant electronic eavesdropping without warrants, contending that this action was part of the inherent power of the presidency to protect domestic security. In 1972, the United States Supreme Court unanimously ruled against the Nixon administration and held that the president may not authorize such warrantless electronic surveillance. There is no authority for it in the Constitution and it violates the Fourth Amendment's requirement that searches—and wiretapping is a form of a search—be based on a warrant issued by a judge. The warrant requirement is a key check on police and executive power intended by the framers of the Constitution.

The Supreme Court's emphatic disapproval of warrantless wiretapping in 1972 may have had a little-noted but profound consequence: it may have been the explanation for the break-in at the Democratic National Headquarters in the Watergate building. The late Rutgers law professor Arthur Kinoy argued that the Nixon White House was tipped off that the Supreme Court was about to disapprove of warrantless wiretapping and the purpose of the break-in was to retrieve bugs that had been placed in the DNC headquarters.

The Supreme Court's decision invalidating warrantless wiretapping for domestic security led Congress to pass the Foreign Intelligence Surveillance Act, which allows the government to go before a special, secret court to obtain a warrant when the government is gathering information about foreign intelligence activities. The act is explicit that *all* electronic eavesdropping in the United States must be approved either by a federal judge under a federal law adopted earlier (Title III of the Omnibus Crime Control Act of 1968) or under the Foreign Intelligence Surveillance Act.

The claim of broad, uncheckable presidential power grew during the Reagan presidency. This was particularly evident during the major scandal of the Reagan administration: Iran-Contra. The Boland Amendment, amendments to federal appropriation bills, barred any "agency or entity of the United States involved in intelligence activities" from spending funds "to support military or paramilitary operations in Nicaragua." The Boland Amendment was passed by Congress and signed into law by President Reagan.

High-level members of the Reagan administration intentionally violated the Boland Amendment by raising funds from third parties to fund the Contras—the opposition to the government of Nicaragua—by secretly selling arms to Iran to fund the Contras. The congressional Iran-Contra committee documented this activity, which led to the successful prosecution of White House aide Oliver North, whose conviction was later overturned because testimony gained under immunity was used against him. Interestingly, when the House committee issued a report detailing the illegal actions that occurred within the Reagan administration in channeling money to the Contras, a congressman from Wyoming, Dick Cheney, dissented and argued that the Boland Amendment was an impermissible restriction on the president's power to conduct foreign policy. The Republican minority report to the House committee declared: "[The] Constitution gives the President some power to act on his own in foreign affairs.... Congress may not use its control over appropriations, including salaries, to prevent the executive or judiciary from fulfilling Constitutionally mandated obligations."

This is an astounding assertion that the president has inherent power to spend money in foreign policy that Congress cannot limit or control. It is inconsistent with the grant of the spending power to Congress in Article I of the Constitution. It also is inconsistent with the most basic historical interpretations of checks and balances.

Many years later, while vice president, Cheney said that his philosophy of executive power was reflected in that minority report. "If you want reference to an obscure text, go look at the minority views that were filed with the Iran-Contra Committee.... [T]hey were actually authored by a guy working for me....I do believe that especially in the day and age we live in, the nature of the threats we face ... the president of the United States needs to have his constitutional powers unimpaired, if you will, in terms of the conduct of national security policy."

Cheney has repeatedly taken the position that limits on executive power, like the Impoundment Control Act and the Boland Amendment and the War Powers Resolution, which requires congressional approval for long-term American involvement in foreign hostilities, are unconstitutional infringements of executive power. It is a view of uncheckable executive power that has little precedent in American history. Other presidents certainly had expanded executive power; what made the Bush-Cheney position different is the claim that the courts could not review the president's actions and that Congress could not limit them. It is a view of executive power that led to serious abuses of the law during the presidency of George W. Bush.

What's wrong, though, with the Nixon, Reagan, Bush approach to executive power, especially in areas of foreign policy and fighting terrorism? Since leaving office, Dick Cheney has been vociferous in defending his view that they are needed to protect the nation.

At the risk of saying the obvious, checking executive power was a central goal of the American Constitution. For the framers of the Constitution, executive power was the authority most to be feared. Having endured the tyranny of the king of England, the framers viewed the principle of separation of powers as the central guarantee of a just government.

James Madison wrote in *The Federalist Papers* that the strict separation of powers was essential to preserve democracy in a republic: "No political truth is certainly of greater intrinsic value or is stamped with the authority of more enlightened patrons of liberty than that ... [t]he accumulation of all powers legislative, executive and judiciary in the same hands, whether of one, a few or many, and whether hereditary, self appointed, or elective, may justly be pronounced the very definition of tyranny."

In the past, the Supreme Court has served an essential role in the system of separation of powers by checking executive power and rejecting presidential actions that usurp the powers of other branches of government or prevent them from carrying out their constitutional duties. In cases like *Youngstown Sheet & Tube Co. v. Sawyer*, which rejected President Truman's effort to seize the steel mills during the Korean War, and *United States v. Nixon*, which rejected President Nixon's effort to invoke executive privilege to keep the Watergate tapes from being used as evidence in court, the Court imposed essential limits on executive power.

The key flaw in the Bush administration's approach was that it ignored the basic framework of the Constitution that two branches of government should be involved in all major government actions. Arrests and especially detentions are initiated by the executive and are required by the Fourth, Fifth, and Sixth Amendments to be approved by the judiciary. Searches, including electronic eavesdropping, are requested by law enforcement and must be approved by the courts under the Fourth Amendment. Government treatment of individuals, such as how they can be questioned, is regulated by the Constitution, statutes, and treaties; it is not simply a matter of executive prerogative. More generally, a key elegance of the Constitution is that generally two branches of government must be involved for any major action; making a law requires involvement of Congress and the president; enforcing a law requires involvement of the executive and the judiciary. Appointing a judge or an ambassador or a cabinet member requires appointment by the president and approval by the Senate. Making a treaty or going to war involves the president and Congress. The Bush administration claim of inherent, uncheckable executive power cannot and should not be reconciled with this framework.

A central flaw in the reasoning of the Bush administration was in not realizing how its unchecked powers could be abused. Top officials—including the president, the vice president, and the attorney general—saw the ends as justifying the means particularly when the means were being used against very dangerous individuals. But, of course, once a power exists, without checks there is always the great danger that it will be used against others. And there are some means, like torture, that are not acceptable at all.

The framers of the Constitution were deeply concerned that an unchecked executive would lead to abuses of power. The experience during the Bush administration is modern confirmation that their fears were justified.

Warrantless Electronic Eavesdropping

In December 2005, the *New York Times* revealed that the National Security Agency was intercepting electronic communications by telephone and e-mail between people in the United States and others in foreign countries without a warrant or probable cause. The National Security Agency traditionally never intercepted calls in the United States; its doing so was a major change in policy. *New York Times* reporter Eric Lichtblau, who broke the story with his colleague James Risen, explained that "the idea that the NSA was running the operation was a seismic shift in how domestic surveillance was carried out." He quoted a former government official that it "is almost a mainstay of this country that the NSA only does foreign searches."

The *New York Times* had the story of the NSA surveillance for a year before it published it. Top Bush administration officials, including the president himself, implored the *New York Times* not to reveal the story. The president told the publisher and editors that "blood would be on their hands" if they disclosed the secret spying.

It is now known that the NSA spying on people in the United States was very controversial even within the Bush administration. Attorney General John Ashcroft had serious doubts about its legality, as did top Justice Department officials such as Jack Goldsmith. It has been revealed that at one point Alberto Gonzales, when still White House counsel, went to Ashcroft's hospital room, where Ashcroft was recovering from a gallbladder attack and was under sedation, to try to get his signed authorization for the spying program.

After the *New York Times* revealed the program, the Bush administration acknowledged and vehemently defended the warrantless wiretapping. On several occasions, Attorney General Gonzales said that there might be other warrantless eavesdropping beyond what has been disclosed and reported in the media.

The Fourth Amendment says that searches, including government wiretapping and electronic surveillance, require a judicially approved warrant. The Foreign Intelligence Surveillance Act (FISA) says explicitly that the government may engage in electronic eavesdropping only by getting a warrant either from a federal district court or from the Foreign Intelligence Surveillance Court. The Bush surveillance program violated this law.

The president and his administration claimed two sources of power for engaging in warrantless surveillance: his power as commander in chief and his authority under the joint resolution Authorization for Use of Military Force, passed a week after the September 11 attacks. Neither provides for such authority.

The president, as commander in chief of the military, has no power to violate the Bill of Rights. If presidential power can trump the Fourth Amendment's requirement for a warrant for electronic eavesdropping, there is no reason why it cannot be used to override any other constitutional provision. The same reasoning would allow warrantless searches of people's homes in violation of the Fourth Amendment. In fact, under this reasoning, the president could suspend freedom of speech or the press as commander in chief.

Nor does the resolution authorizing military force provide a basis for such presidential power. After September 11, Congress authorized the use of troops and arms to respond to the terrorists; the resolution says nothing about eavesdropping. Authorizing "military force" does not include every other action that the government wants to take in the name of the war on terrorism.

The Supreme Court made this distinction clear in its decision in 2006 in *Hamdan v. Rumsfeld*. The issue was the legality of the military commissions created by President Bush in an executive order to try those being detained in Guantanamo. The Supreme Court held that there was not adequate statutory authority for the military commissions created by presidential executive order and that they violated the Uniform Code of Military Justice and the Geneva Conventions. In an important footnote, the Court said: "Whether or not the President has independent power, absent congressional authorization, to convene military commissions, *he may not disregard limitations that Congress has, in proper exercise of its own war powers, placed on his powers.*" The Court concluded that the Authorization for Use of Military Force (AUMF) adopted after September 11 did not authorize military tribunals.

This decision is important because the Bush administration repeatedly pointed to the AUMF as authorizing its actions in the war on terrorism, including providing it authority for warrantless electronic eavesdropping. Justice Stevens's majority opinion in *Hamdan* shows that the Supreme Court is unwilling to read the AUMF as a blank check for presidential actions, especially when they contradict statutory provisions.

The warrantless electronic eavesdropping is particularly unnecessary because the government could have gone to the Foreign Intelligence·Surveillance Court and obtained warrants. Between 1978 and 1999, that court granted more than 11,883 warrants and denied none. More recent statistics indicate that the government receives a FISA warrant more than 99 percent of the time when one is requested. The only argument that the administration gave for not doing so is that these warrants require a great deal of paperwork. But if time is of the essence, the act even allows the government to apply for a warrant after the eavesdropping occurred.

The American Civil Liberties Union brought suit to have the warrantless wiretapping declared illegal and unconstitutional. A federal district court in Michigan agreed. But the United States Court of Appeals for the Sixth Circuit reversed in a 2–1 decision, with two Republican appointees composing the majority and one Democratic appointee dissenting. The majority said that the plaintiffs lacked standing to bring the lawsuit because they could not show that their own conversations had been illegally intercepted.

The plaintiffs were a group of individuals who regularly communicate with people in foreign countries that were the targets for the eavesdropping. The plaintiffs said that their communications were chilled by the knowledge that they were likely being intercepted. The Sixth Circuit ruled, though, that this was not enough; to have standing the plaintiffs had to demonstrate that their phone conversations or e-mail messages had been monitored by the government. Since the NSA does not disclose who it is eavesdropping on, there would be no way for anyone to meet this requirement. The Sixth Circuit approach would mean that no one could challenge the NSA program, no matter how unconstitutional and illegal. The U.S. Supreme Court denied review.

Torture

In 2002, the Office of Legal Counsel (OLC) in the United States Department of Justice issued a memorandum that said that the president could authorize torture of human beings in violation of treaties ratified by the United States and federal statutes that prohibit such conduct. The so-called "torture memo" argued that the antitorture treaty and statute could not prohibit the president from ordering the use of torture in interrogations of enemy combatants, because it claimed that such a prohibition would violate the president's constitutional powers. The commander in chief, according to the memo, had the power to authorize any interrogation techniques; restrictions imposed by laws or treaties were an unconstitutional infringement of executive powers. This was the same position Congressman Dick Cheney took twenty years earlier in the minority report in arguing that the Boland Amendment was unconstitutional.

In a memo dated August 1, 2002, OLC redefined torture to be only suffering "equivalent in intensity to the pain accompanying serious physical injury, such as organ failure, impairment of bodily function, or even death." Mental suffering, according to the memo, had to "result in significant psychological harm" and "be of significant duration, e.g., lasting for months or years." By this definition, methods long deemed torture—bamboo shoots under fingernails, threats to one's family, waterboarding—were not torture.

The torture memos were written by two law professors working in the Justice Department: Jay Bybee (now a federal court of appeals judge) and John Yoo (now at the University of California, Berkeley, School of Law). The Department of Justice ultimately withdrew the torture memos. But as Professor Neil Kinkopf notes, "[t]he withdrawing memo, however, does not repudiate or even question the substance of the Torture Memos reasoning on the issue of presidential power."

The significance of the torture memo in terms of the Bush administration's views of executive power cannot be overstated. Top officials of the U.S. government were claiming no less than that the government could torture human beings, notwithstanding laws and treaties specifically forbidding this. It is an assertion of executive power that recognizes no limits and acknowledges no checks and balances.

It had a real effect. Jane Mayer, in her deeply disturbing book *The Dark Side*, describes how government agents explicitly relied on the Bybee/Yoo memos to justify engaging in torture. She explains that from the time of George Washington's command of the revolutionary army, this country always prided itself on humane treatment of prisoners. The United States was instrumental in drafting and ensuring the ratification of the Geneva Conventions, which govern how those captured in battle are to be treated. In part, it is a sense that our own humanity is degraded when we engage in such practices. In part, too, it is the knowledge that there is little evidence that torture produces useful information; those being tortured will say anything that they think will end the pain. But also quite importantly, it is a way of protecting

Americans who may be caught on foreign battlefields. I have
given countless speeches since 9/11 on civil liberties and national
security and I have discovered that those who often agree with
me the most are those who have served in the military or have
loved ones serving in the military. They repeatedly ask: How can
this country expect foreign countries to follow the law in the
treatment of American prisoners if our government doesn't follow international law in the treatment of foreign prisoners? After
the revelation of torture by American soldiers and agents, former
secretary of state Colin Powell lamented that "[t]he world is beginning to doubt the moral basis of our fight against terrorism."

In the popular press, there developed an academic debate over
whether torture might be justified to stop the ticking time bomb;
if authorities had a suspect who knew of a hidden bomb, would
torture be justified to gain the information? This is the stuff of the
television program *24*, but it gives a false impression of what the
Bush administration did. Jane Mayer describes how government
officials systematically implemented a policy that included torture. These were not individuals being tortured to reveal a ticking
time bomb; she describes individuals being routinely tortured,
including some who were apprehended by mistake. She tells of
someone dying as a result of torture administered in questioning.
The Red Cross issued a report corroborating much of what is in
Mayer's book and again documenting torture inflicted by Americans at the direction of Americans.

Government memos that were disclosed authorize techniques
including waterboarding, which makes a person feel as if he or
she is drowning. It has been regarded as torture throughout the
world since the early twentieth century. Two suspected Al Qaeda
leaders, Khalid Sheikh Mohammed and Abu Zubaydah, were subjected to waterboarding a combined total of 266 times. Prisoners
were shaved and stripped naked and required to stay that way
through long periods of time wearing only a diaper. One detainee
was kept naked for a month, during which he was questioned
by many female interrogators. Prisoners were subjected to sleep
deprivation of up to ninety-six hours. They were forced to stand

in uncomfortable positions for long periods of time and often suffered excruciating pain.

Mayer tells the story of Khaled el-Masri, a car salesman from Ulm in Germany who was stopped at a border crossing between Serbia and Macedonia. He was confused with someone with a similar name and taken into custody. According to Mayer, a CIA official in Langley, Virginia, believed that el-Masri had ties to Al Qaeda and on this hunch el-Masri was held for 149 days without word to his family or anyone else. He was stripped, fed putrid food, and lost sixty pounds; he was "roughed up" during the interrogations. Ultimately, CIA officials realized that they had the wrong man and decided to release him. Mayer describes his release: "The CIA meanwhile, had flown Masri to Tirana, Albania, driven him blindfolded down a long, winding, potholed road, handed him back his possessions, and dropped him near the border with Serbia and Macedonia, where he was told to start walking and not look back."

Masri sued for his capture and treatment, which violated countless requirements of international law. The United States, though, moved to dismiss the case on the grounds that for a court to consider it could reveal "state secrets" about the United States' rendition program. The federal courts agreed and Masri's case was dismissed without ever being heard.

The memos from the Department of Justice reveal that torture was authorized at the highest levels of American government. The techniques described are "cruel, inhumane, and degrading treatment," which is forbidden by international and American law. Nothing has yet come to light to indicate that useful information was gained from torture. In fact, Mayer suggests that some who provided useful information stopped cooperating after being tortured.

Detentions

One of the most disturbing acts of the Bush administration was its claim of authority to suspend the Bill of Rights by detaining an

American citizen apprehended in the United States as an enemy combatant without complying with the Constitution's requirements. The phrase "enemy combatant" is not part of international or American law. It is difficult to find it used before the last decade. Since this creates a new category of prisoners not covered by existing law, the Bush administration argued that the protections of international and American law did not apply.

Jose Padilla is an American citizen who was apprehended at Chicago's O'Hare Airport in May 2002. He allegedly was planning to build and detonate a "dirty bomb," a crude radioactivity dispersal device, in the United States. He was imprisoned for almost four years before he was indicted. Instead the government held him as an enemy combatant and claimed that no court had jurisdiction to review Padilla's detention.

After his arrest, Padilla was taken to New York. An attorney filed a petition in the Southern District of New York to meet with him. Shortly thereafter, Padilla was transferred to a military prison in South Carolina. But the litigation over his detention and rights remained in New York and ultimately in the United States Court of Appeals for the Second Circuit. The Second Circuit ruled in Padilla's favor and held that the government did not have the authority to hold an American citizen apprehended in the United States as an enemy combatant.

At the oral argument in the Supreme Court, the United States argued that Padilla had no right to any hearing or due process; his only right, the government asserted, was to answer the questions from his interrogators. The Supreme Court, in a 5–4 decision, concluded that the New York court lacked jurisdiction to hear Padilla's habeas corpus petition. The Court said that a person must bring a habeas petition where he or she is being detained against the person immediately responsible for the detention. Padilla needed to file his habeas petition in South Carolina against the head of the military prison there.

Justice Stevens wrote for the four dissenters and lamented that Padilla, who already had been held for more than two years, had to begin all over again. But there seems no doubt that Padilla had five votes on the Supreme Court that it is illegal to hold him as an enemy combatant. In a footnote near the end of his dissenting opinion, Justice Stevens expressly stated that he agreed with the Second Circuit that there was no legal authority to detain Padilla as an enemy combatant. Justice Scalia, who was in the majority in the Padilla case, was emphatic in his dissent in a companion case that an American citizen cannot be held without trial as an enemy combatant unless Congress suspends the writ of habeas corpus.

Nonetheless, the United States Court of Appeals for the Fourth Circuit, in an opinion by conservative judge Michael Luttig, then ruled that Padilla could be held as an enemy combatant. As the case was heading back to the Supreme Court, the government indicted Padilla and ended his status as an enemy combatant. As Judge Luttig noted, surely this was because the government knew based on the earlier ruling that it likely would lose in the high court. The Supreme Court then denied review because the controversy over whether Padilla could be held as an enemy combatant was over; he had been charged with a crime. The result is that the government's authority to detain an American citizen as an enemy combatant was never decided by the Supreme Court.

But Padilla is not the only instance of the Bush administration claiming the power to detain people without judicial review. Yaser Hamdi is an American citizen who was apprehended in Afghanistan and brought to the base at Guantanamo Bay. There it was discovered that he was an American citizen and he was taken to a military prison in South Carolina. He was held as an enemy combatant and was never charged with any crime. His situation was identical to that of John Walker Lindh, the "American Taliban," except that Walker was indicted and pled guilty to crimes. The Bush administration took the position in the lower federal courts and the Supreme Court that Hamdi could be held indefinitely as an enemy combatant without any due process.

Although the Court, in a 5–4 vote with Justice Scalia dissenting, held that Hamdi could be detained as an enemy combatant, it ruled against the Bush administration and held by an 8–1 margin that Hamdi had to be given due process. The five justices in the majority were O'Connor Rehnquist, Kennedy, Breyer, and Thomas. Although the Court did not specify the procedures that must be followed in Hamdi's case, the justices were explicit that Hamdi had to be given a meaningful factual hearing. At a minimum, this must include notice of the charges against him, the right to respond, and the right to be represented by an attorney. Only Justice Thomas rejected this conclusion and accepted the government's argument that the president could detain enemy combatants without any form of due process.

Almost immediately after the Supreme Court's decision in Hamdi's case in 2004, the United States reached an agreement with him that led to his release. Hamdi agreed to renounce his citizenship, leave the country, and never take up arms against the United States. In exchange, he was allowed to go free.

No president other than perhaps Abraham Lincoln during the Civil War ever has claimed the power to detain American citizens without any form of due process or judicial review. The Bush administration's assertion of executive power was unnecessary. There was no reason why these individuals could not be charged and tried. Padilla, for instance, ultimately was tried in a federal district court and convicted of aiding terrorist activity and given a long prison sentence.

Similarly, Ali Al-Marri was held by the Bush administration for almost seven years as an enemy combatant before the Obama administration ordered him tried. Al-Marri was not a citizen, but a lawful long-term resident alien and a graduate student at Bradley University in Peoria, Illinois. Beginning in 2002, he was held as an enemy combatant without trial. The Supreme Court granted review in his case in 2008, but before it could be heard the Obama administration acted. Al-Marri was convicted and sentenced to six years in prison. Again, this procedure could have occurred many years earlier.

What was so frightening about the Bush administration's assertion of the power to detain citizens was that it had no stopping point. If the government can detain individuals as enemy combatants without judicial review or trial, what is to stop it from designating anyone an enemy combatant and holding the person for the rest of his or her life? Why couldn't Timothy McVeigh or Terry Nichols, the individuals responsible for the Oklahoma City bombing, have been held as enemy combatants? In fact, why would this approach be limited to the war on terror? Why couldn't the government designate drug dealers as enemy combatants in the war on drugs and hold them indefinitely? The Bush administration's claim of authority to detain citizens and lawful resident aliens as enemy combatants without judicial review was no less than an assertion of uncheckable power to suspend the Constitution.

Another example of the Bush administration's claim of authority to detain was its abuse of the power to hold material witnesses. Federal law allows the government to detain an individual as a material witness under very limited circumstances: it must be shown that the person's testimony is needed in a criminal case and that there is no way to obtain it except by detaining the individual. The statute, 18 U.S.C. §3144, is explicit that "[n]o material witness may be detained because of inability to comply with any condition of release if the testimony of such witness can adequately be secured by deposition, and if further detention is not necessary to prevent a failure of justice."

The Bush administration, however, used this statute to detain individuals whom it wanted to investigate but whom it did not have probable cause to arrest or hold. The federal court of appeals in a recent decision tells the story of Abdullah Al-Kidd, a United States citizen and a married man with two children. He

> was arrested at a Dulles International Airport ticket counter. He was handcuffed, taken to the airport's police substation, and interrogated. Over the next sixteen days, he was confined in high security cells lit twenty-four hours a day in Virginia, Oklahoma, and then Idaho, during which he was strip searched on multiple occasions. Each time he was transferred to a different facility, al-Kidd was handcuffed and shackled about his wrists, legs, and waist. He was eventually released from custody by court order, on the

conditions that he live with his wife and in-laws in Nevada, limit his travel to Nevada and three other states, surrender his travel documents, regularly report to a probation officer, and consent to home visits throughout the period of supervision. By the time al-Kidd's confinement and supervision ended, fifteen months after his arrest, al-Kidd had been fired from his job as an employee of a government contractor because he was denied a security clearance due to his arrest, and had separated from his wife. He has been unable to obtain steady employment since his arrest.

As the federal court of appeals says, "Al-Kidd was not arrested and detained because he had allegedly committed a crime." Rather, he was held under the federal material witness statute. But the government was not holding him because it wanted to secure his testimony, as the statute requires. His detention had absolutely nothing to do with obtaining testimony from him. Rather, Al-Kidd was detained so that the government could investigate him. The material witness statute was used because the government did not have enough evidence to arrest him.

The United States Court of Appeals ruled that Al-Kidd could sue then attorney general John Ashcroft and other top Bush administration officials who authorized this conduct. The court said that the law was "clearly established" that this is illegal and unconstitutional. In an opinion written by Judge Milan Smith, appointed to the federal bench by President George W. Bush, the court declared: "All seizures of criminal suspects require probable cause of criminal activity. To use a material witness statute pretextually, in order to investigate or preemptively detain suspects without probable cause, is to violate the Fourth Amendment."

There is no way to know how many others, like Al-Kidd, were illegally held. A 2002 article in the *Washington Post* said that half of those being detained in the war on terror were detained as material witnesses. Al-Kidd's situation almost surely was not unique.

In terms of numbers, the most significant claim of authority to detain without judicial review concerns the detainees in Guantanamo Bay, Cuba. Since January 2002, the U.S. government has held more than six hundred individuals as prisoners at the naval facility there.

The Bush administration repeatedly argued that there could be no judicial review of its actions in holding prisoners in Guantanamo. It argued that federal courts lacked jurisdiction to hear a writ of habeas corpus brought on behalf of the Guantanamo prisoners. As explained above, the Supreme Court consistently has ruled against the Bush administration on this matter.

The case that came to the Supreme Court in 2004 involved two habeas corpus petitions that had been filed on behalf of the Guantanamo detainees. *Rasul v. Bush* was a suit brought by the father of an Australian detainee, the father of a British detainee, and the mother of another British detainee. *Al-Odah v. United States* was brought by fathers and brothers of twelve individuals being held at Camp X-Ray in Guantanamo.

In both cases, the government moved to dismiss, contending that the federal courts lacked authority to hear habeas corpus petitions by those being held in Guantanamo. In March 2003, the United States Court of Appeals for the District of Columbia Circuit affirmed the dismissal of the case for lack of jurisdiction and ruled that no court in the country could hear the petitions brought by the Guantanamo detainees.

The Supreme Court reversed the D.C. Circuit and held, 6–3, that those held in Guantanamo do have access to the federal courts via a writ of habeas corpus. After *Rasul*, many habeas petitions were heard in the lower federal courts. While they were pending, Congress, at the urging of the Bush administration, enacted the Detainee Treatment Act and the Military Commissions Act of 2006. These laws provided that noncitizens held as enemy combatants cannot challenge their detention in a writ of habeas corpus. On June 12, 2008, the Supreme Court in a 5–4 decision in *Boumediene v. Bush* declared this an unconstitutional suspension of the writ of habeas corpus. The four most conservative justices—Roberts, Scalia, Thomas, and Alito—vehemently dissented and would have sided with the Bush administration's claim that the Guantanamo detainees could be held indefinitely without judicial review.

Subsequently, some detainees have been released. Some have their habeas petitions now pending in federal court. President Obama pledged to close Guantanamo within a year of taking office, but that pledge was not kept primarily because of congressional opposition to placing the remaining detainees anywhere in the United States.

Salim Gherebi remains in Guantanamo, where he has been since late spring of 2002. He and others have been imprisoned for eight years without a trial or a meaningful hearing. One of the most frustrating aspects of the Guantanamo detentions is that none of the courts has felt it necessary to expedite the proceedings. The detainees have lost years of their lives as the proceedings have dragged on and on.

Secrecy

The discussion of the abuses of executive power as a result of the war on terrorism is made difficult by the tremendous secrecy surrounding the actions of the Bush administration. To take the example of detentions, how many individuals have been detained by the federal government as part of the war on terror since September 11? How many have been held as material witnesses?

How many have been sent to rendition camps? After initially denying it, the Bush administration acknowledged that terror suspects were taken to "black hole sites" in places like Egypt, Saudi Arabia, Jordan, and Pakistan, where torture was known to be practiced. Jane Mayer noted that the "number of renditions grew and hundreds of suspects were deposited indefinitely not just in foreign prisons but also in U.S.-run facilities in Afghanistan, Cuba, and the C.I.A.'s top-secret black site prisons." No one knows how many individuals were subject to such "extraordinary renditions." Estimates range anywhere from 100–150 to several thousand terror suspects.

A few years ago, I debated Michael Chertoff, the director of the Department of Homeland Security. I asked him how many people have been held as part of the war on terror. He said that he could not disclose the information because of national security. I asked how knowing the number of people being held, whether dozens or hundreds or thousands, could reveal anything that remotely could harm national security. There was no answer.

Unprecedented secrecy pervaded much of the Bush administration's approach. Soon after September 11, the Bush administration announced that it would hold many immigration proceedings in total secrecy, with no one allowed to be present except the government's lawyer, the person to be deported, and his or her lawyer (if there was one). All present would be subject to an order preventing disclosure of what occurred. Certainly there might be some cases where such secrecy might be necessary for national security. But what was striking about the Bush administration's approach was its claim that it could order closure of proceedings without any need to show in a particular case the need for secrecy.

A federal court of appeals declared this conduct unconstitutional. It emphasized that deportation proceedings have been traditionally open to the public, but can be closed if the government demonstrates a need for secrecy. Judge Damon Keith eloquently wrote for the court:

> Today, the Executive Branch seeks to take this safeguard away from the public by placing its actions beyond public scrutiny. Against non-citizens, it seeks the power to secretly deport a class if it unilaterally calls them "special interest" cases. The Executive Branch seeks to uproot people's lives, outside the public eye, and behind a closed door. Democracies die behind closed doors. The First Amendment, through a free press, protects the people's right to know that their government acts fairly, lawfully, and accurately in deportation proceedings. When government begins closing doors, it selectively controls information rightfully belonging to the people. Selective information is misinformation. The Framers of the First Amendment "did not trust any government to separate the true from the false for us." They protected the people against secret government.

Another federal court of appeals came to an opposite conclusion and the Bush administration changed its policy before the

Supreme Court could hear the matter. But I have heard stories from lawyers of secret trials and secret appeals in federal court. In one case, an appeal of such a secret proceeding made news when the convicted individual filed a public petition for Supreme Court review objecting to the constitutionality of such a secret proceeding that apparently existed on no docket of any court. The government filed its opposition to review in secret and the Supreme Court denied review. Secret trials and appeals are reminiscent of star-chamber proceedings from the Middle Ages, not legal proceedings in a democracy.

Of course, I recognize that there are times when secrecy is essential for national security and other essential government needs. But there is no need for keeping secret things like the numbers of individuals who have been detained or routine deportation proceedings.

To a large extent, the claims of unreviewable, uncheckable executive power during the Bush years have been repudiated. In some instances, the Bush administration itself backed away from its policies in the face of substantial media and public criticism. The Bush Justice Department, for example, expressly rescinded the torture memos written by John Yoo and Jay Bybee. Attorney General Alberto Gonzales ended the policy of warrantless wiretapping by the National Security Agency and announced that the government would comply with the requirements of the Fourth Amendment and of federal law in seeking warrants for electronic surveillance.

In some instances, the courts have curtailed abuses. The Supreme Court declared illegal the military tribunals that President Bush had authorized by executive order to try noncitizens accused of terrorist acts. As mentioned earlier, the Supreme Court declared it unconstitutional for Congress to suspend the writ of habeas corpus for those held in Guantanamo as enemy combatants. Other executive abuses were stopped by lower federal courts. A federal district court judge in New York declared unconstitutional the practice of the government obtaining personal information about individuals through "national security let-ters" where there was no judicial review and where the entity disclosing the information could not tell the subject that the information had been turned over to the government. A national security letter allows the FBI to obtain information, even personal information, by a letter requesting it. The person disclosing the information cannot tell the target that it has been requested. Ann L. Aiken, a federal judge in Oregon, put it well when she ruled against the government and declared: "For over 200 years, this na-tion has adhered to the rule of law—with unparalleled success. A shift to a nation based on extraconstitutional authority is prohib-ited, as well as ill-advised."

Upon taking office, President Obama renounced some of the worst aspects of the Bush administration's assault on the law. For example, he prohibited torture and extreme interrogation by government officials or those contracting with the government. As mentioned, President Obama announced that the prisons at Guantanamo would be closed within a year, although he has failed to accomplish this. Supporters of the Bush administration's Guantanamo policy take the failure of the Obama administration to close the facility as vindication. But many factors account for the failure to move detainees: strong congressional opposition to moving detainees to the United States; lack of political will to deal with the situation; and the reality that once executive power grows, it is difficult for even administrations of a different political party to relinquish it.

Attorney General Eric Holder announced that alleged 9/11 mastermind Khalid Sheikh Mohammed would be tried in federal court, not in a military tribunal, where any conviction would lack legitimacy. Unfortunately, pressure, including from New York of-ficials, may cause the Obama administration to back down on this. But federal courts have shown over many years that they can handle the security and demands of terrorism trials. Perhaps most importantly, unlike his predecessor, President Obama pledged that his administration would comply with international and domestic law in all of its practices.

In other areas, though, the approach of the Obama administration raises concerns. The Obama Justice Department continues to aggressively assert the state secrets doctrine to keep courts from hearing cases of those who claim to have had their rights violated. It proposes to use military tribunals, not federal courts, to try some terror suspects. Nor has Obama completely renounced the practice of rendition.

Still, there is no doubt that there is a tremendous difference between the Bush and the Obama administrations in their approach to presidential power and the war on terror. The architects of the Bush policies are unrepentant. Former vice president Dick Cheney at every opportunity criticizes the Obama presidency for abandoning the Bush administration's approach. John Yoo continues to defend what he did during his years in the Bush Justice Department.

Those who defend their actions are fond of quoting Justice Robert Jackson's statement that "the Constitution is not a suicide pact." Of course this is true. But what is missing from the defense of the Bush administration's actions is any evidence that these actions were needed to protect the nation. Never has it been demonstrated that complying with the Constitution, which has served the country so well for so long, poses any threat to the nation.

Justice Louis Brandeis wrote, "Experience should teach us to be most on our guard to protect liberty when the government's purposes are beneficent. Men born to freedom are naturally alert to repel invasion of their liberty by evil-minded rulers. The greatest dangers to liberty lurk in insidious encroachment by men of zeal, well-meaning but without understanding." Louis Brandeis, of course, never knew Dick Cheney or John Yoo or Donald Rumsfeld, but if he had, he could not have described them more accurately.

3.

Dismantling the Wall Separating Church and State

I was sitting in my office when I received a collect phone call from Thomas Van Orden. Although the name was unfamiliar to me, I accepted the call. He explained to me that he had just lost a case in the federal court of appeals in which he had challenged the presence of a large Ten Commandments monument that sits directly at the corner between the Texas Capitol and the Texas Supreme Court in Austin. Van Orden wanted to know if I would take his case to the United States Supreme Court. He explained that he used to be a lawyer, that he was a graduate of the law school at Southern Methodist University, but that he was no longer a member of the bar and thus was ineligible to appear in the Supreme Court.

I explained that I had not yet seen the federal court of appeals decision, but that I would review it and call him back. He matter-of-factly explained that he was homeless and that he would have to call me back. I was obviously surprised to hear this, but we agreed that he would call me at a designated time at the end of the week.

I read the decision by the United States Court of Appeals for the Fifth Circuit, written by one of the more conservative judges on that court, and it was exactly as Van Orden had described. The monument is six feet high and three feet wide and takes the shape of the tablets that some religions believe that God gave to Moses. It contains the following words written in large letters:

The Ten Commandments

I AM the LORD thy God.
Thou shalt have no other gods before me.
Thou shalt not make to thyself any graven images.
Thou shalt not take the Name of the Lord thy God in vain.
Remember the Sabbath day, to keep it holy.
Honor thy father and thy mother that thy days may be long
*   upon the land which the Lord thy God giveth thee.*
Thou shall not kill.
Thou shall not commit adultery.
Thou shall not steal.
Thou shalt not bear false witness against thy neighbor.
Thou shalt not covet thy neighbor's house.
Thou shalt not covet thy neighbor's wife nor his manservant
*   nor his maidservant, nor his cattle nor anything that is his*
*   neighbor's.*

On the monument, above the text of the Ten Commandments, there are two small tablets with what appears to be ancient script. Also above the Ten Commandments is a large American eagle grasping the American flag and an eye inside a pyramid, which is similar to the symbol on the back of the one-dollar bill. At the bottom of the monument, below the Ten Commandments, there are two small Stars of David and also two Greek letters, chi and rho, superimposed over each other to represent the name Christ. These other symbols are much smaller than the text of the Ten Commandments, which occupies most of the space on the monument. Under the Ten Commandments are the words "Presented to the people and youth of Texas by the Fraternal Order of Eagles of Texas, 1961."

Although there are several other monuments on the grounds of the Texas Capitol, the Ten Commandments monument is the closest to the capitol of any of them. No other monument on the capitol's grounds expresses a religious message. The Ten Commandments monument is on government property and is owned by the state of Texas. Under Texas law, any monument on the capitol grounds must be approved by the state legislature; erecting a monument without legislative approval is a criminal offense punishable by imprisonment and an impeachable offense if done by a government official.

The gift of the monument was accepted by a joint resolution of the Texas House and the Texas Senate in early 1961. Around this time, the Fraternal Order of Eagles donated hundreds, and perhaps thousands, of Ten Commandments monuments to governments all over the country. These monuments were paid for by movie producer Cecil B. DeMille, who did so to help promote his movie *The Ten Commandments,* starring Charlton Heston.

Thomas Van Orden said that he spent many of his days on the grounds of the Texas Capitol, often using the library in the supreme court building. He told me that he was upset seeing a Ten Commandments monument at the seat of the state government. He said that although he was raised and remained a Christian, he thought that the government should be secular. He litigated the case on his own in the federal district court, but lost. Sometime later, I saw the district court judge who ruled against Van Orden and he told me how very impressed he was with Van Orden's handling of the litigation. Van Orden then briefed and argued the case on his own in the federal court of appeals, where he also lost.

I never learned how Van Orden came to be homeless or to lose his law license. After the U.S. Supreme Court granted review, I flew to Texas to meet with him. He is a tall man whose appearance gave no clue as to his homelessness. He was cleanly shaven and clothed in a dress shirt and jeans. I discovered that he is intensely private and proud. He forbade me to give his e-mail address to reporters. At the time the case was being heard by the U.S. Supreme Court, I received requests for interviews with him from every major network, from media outlets including the *Today* show, *People* magazine, and several network news shows. I relayed all of these to him, but I believe he did few interviews.

I offered to pay his way to Washington to hear the Supreme Court argument. He said that he could not take my money for this purpose. I thought for a moment and offered to bring him to Duke Law School, where I was teaching, to meet with the students and talk about his case. I said that it is customary to pay speakers an honorarium and his would be sufficient to cover his costs to come to Washington to watch his case being argued. I explained that my students would benefit enormously from hearing the story of his bringing and litigating the case. He thought about it for a time, but declined.

This should have been an easy case. The First Amendment prohibits Congress from making any law "respecting the estab-lishment of religion." In 1947 the Supreme Court held that, like the rest of the First Amendment, this provision applies to state and local governments as well. In fact, in that case, all nine of the justices agreed that the Establishment Clause—as the provi-sion is known—was meant, in the words, of Thomas Jefferson, to "erect a wall between church and state. That wall must be kept high and impregnable." The 1947 case *Everson v. Board of Educa-tion* involved whether a school district could provide bus service to take children to and from parochial school when it provided the same service for students in the public schools. The Court, 5–4, allowed this aid to religious schools, but with all nine of the justices agreeing that Thomas Jefferson's metaphor was the guid-ing principle for understanding the Establishment Clause.

Separating church and state simply means that the government should be secular; the place for religion is in people's homes, churches, synagogues, and mosques. Separating church and state is not an expression of hostility to religion, but instead affirms the lessons that history teaches about the importance of government being strictly secular. James Madison, another of the founders, said: "The purpose of the separation of church and state is to keep forever from these shores the ceaseless strife that has soaked the soil of Europe in blood for centuries." There are many reasons why separating church and state is so vital.

First, the Establishment Clause protects freedom of conscience by ensuring that the government is not aligned with a particular religion, or even religion generally. A government identified with a specific faith inevitably causes people to feel pressure, sometimes subtle and sometimes overt, to conform their religious beliefs and practices.

Separating church and state means that people will not be not be taxed to support religions other than their own. Jefferson's famous statement concerning the need for a wall separating church and state, and Madison's "Memorial and Remonstrance Against Religious Assessments," were made in opposition to a state tax to aid the church.

Jefferson spoke of the unconscionability of taxing people to support religions that they do not believe in. The Supreme Court has described Jefferson's belief that "compelling a man to furnish contributions of money for the propagation of opinions which he disbelieves is sinful and tyrannical." Madison said: "[T]he same authority which can force a citizen to contribute three pence only of his property for the support of any one establishment, may force him to conform to any other establishment."

It is wrong to make me support a church that teaches that my religion or my beliefs are wrong or even evil. It violates my freedom of conscience to force me to support religions that I do not accept. Justice Souter explained that "compelling an individual to support religion violates the fundamental principle of freedom of conscience. Madison's and Jefferson's now familiar words establish clearly that liberty of personal conviction requires freedom from coercion to support religion, and this means that the government can compel no aid to fund it."

Second, the Establishment Clause serves a fundamental purpose of inclusion in that it allows all in society, those of every religion and those of no religion, to feel that the government is theirs. When the government supports religion, inescapably those of different religions feel excluded. I have been at banquets or events that include sectarian Christian prayer. I immediately feel that as a Jew I am in the wrong place. When the government is overtly aligned with religion, those of different faiths or who do not have religious beliefs inevitably feel that they are in the wrong place, that they are outsiders with regard to their government.

Treating all religions equally does not solve this problem. In a society that is overwhelmingly Christian, those of minority faiths feel marginalized and unwelcome when religion is overtly a part of the government. If treating all religions equally were the only constraint imposed by the Establishment Clause, a school could begin each day with a prayer so long as every religion got its due. If a school reflected America's religious diversity, the vast majority of days would begin with Christian prayers. Those with no religion would be made to feel that it was not their school, as would those of minority religions who routinely were subjected to prayers of Christian faiths.

This goal of inclusion is central, not incidental, to the Establishment Clause. Justice O'Connor has explained: "Direct government action endorsing religion or a particular religion is invalid because it sends a message to nonadherents that they are outsiders, not full members of the political community, and an accompanying message to adherents that they are insiders, favored members of the political community."

Consider the most blatant violation of the Establishment Clause: a city or state declares a particular religion, say Catholicism, to be the official religion. Assuming that the government took no actions to limit free exercise by those of other faiths, why is such a declaration unacceptable?

It is worth noting that under Justice Clarence Thomas's view this situation would be entirely acceptable. He repeatedly has argued that the Establishment Clause does not apply to state and local governments. His view, expressed in many opinions, is that the Establishment Clause was meant to prevent the federal government from establishing churches that would have competed with state churches that existed at the time the First Amendment was adopted. This view, of course, would mean a dramatic change in the law since state and local governments would be unconstrained by the Establishment Clause. Utah could declare itself to be a Mormon state; Georgia could officially be a Baptist state; Connecticut could deem itself to be a Catholic state. State and local governments never could be found to violate the Establishment Clause no matter what they did. Thankfully, though, Justice Thomas is the only member of the Supreme Court to take this radical position.

The pronouncement that there is an official religion makes all of a different faith feel unwelcome. They are made to feel that they are tolerated guests, not equal members of the community. Just as bad, those of the favored religion are made to feel that they are special members of the community. In Justice O'Connor's words, nonadherents are made to feel outsiders and adherents are made to feel insiders.

The very core of the Establishment Clause prevents the government from taking actions that divide people in this way. The clause is meant to prevent the majority, through government power, from making those of other religions feel unwelcome. If the majority of an audience wants to hear prayers, of course it may do so, but not at an official government function, especially one where the audience is compelled to be present.

The problem is much greater today than when the First Amendment was adopted, because the country is far more religiously diverse now. Justice William Brennan observed that "our religious composition makes us a vastly more diverse people than were our forefathers. They knew differences chiefly among Protestant sects. Today the nation is far more heterogeneous religiously, including as it does substantial minorities not only of Catholics and Jews but as well of those who worship according to no version of the Bible and those who worship no God at all."

This explains why religious symbols do not belong on government property. A city hall with a large cross on its roof makes those of different religions feel unwelcome, that it is not their government. At the oral argument in *Van Orden v. Perry*, Justice Kennedy asked me why those who don't like the Ten Commandments monument at the seat of the Texas state government can't simply avert their eyes. My response was that this has no stopping point—a city could put a large Latin cross atop its roof, or many crosses, and simply proclaim that those who don't like it should look away. Not looking doesn't make the constitutional problem go away. A cross atop city hall violates the Establishment Clause even if people remember to avert their eyes.

That was the core of my argument to the Court in *Van Orden v. Perry*. The Ten Commandments is a sacred text in many religions, including mine, and it conveys a message that is thoroughly and essentially religious: there is a God and that God has decreed rules for behavior. These include rules for religious observance, such as "Thou shalt have no other gods before me," "Thou shalt not make to thyself any graven images," "Thou shalt not take the name of the Lord thy God in vain," and "Remember the Sabbath day." There also are rules governing behavior that are not inherently religious, such as "Thou shalt not kill," "Thou shalt not commit adultery," and "Thou shalt not steal." But in the Ten Commandments these prescriptions, too, convey and define God's command and rule. They are not secular; they express a religious faith and vision.

Also, very importantly, there is not one version of the Ten Commandments. Each faith that considers the Decalogue, as it is sometimes called, to be sacred has its own version and the differences are often enormously important. For example, in Jewish versions of the Ten Commandments, the First Commandment is "I the Lord am your God who brought you out of the land of Egypt, the house of bondage." This relationship between God and the Jews is a central part of the faith and is celebrated by a prayer recited in virtually every Jewish service. In the Protestant version, the First Commandment is "Thou shalt have no other gods before me"; in the Catholic version, it is "I am the Lord thy God. Thou shalt not have strange gods before me." The monument between the Texas Capitol and the Texas Supreme Court adopts the Protestant version of the First Commandment.

The Second Commandment also varies among these religions. For Jews, the second commandment states: "You shall have no other gods besides me. You shall not make for yourself a sculptured image." In contrast, the Catholic version of the Second Commandment is "Thou shalt not take the name of the Lord thy God in vain." The prohibition against graven images, included in the

Jewish Second Commandment, is not included in the Catholic version of the Ten Commandments. This, of course, is not surprising given the role of statues and other religious images in Catholicism. The Texas monument adopts the Lutheran version, which places "Thou shalt not make to thyself any graven images" as part of the First Commandment. These differences in the first two commandments among religions are reflected throughout the texts of the varying versions of the Ten Commandments. The fact that Jews, Catholics, Lutherans, and other Protestants all have different First and Second Commandments leads to a different numbering system throughout the rest of their versions of the commandments. For example, the Seventh Commandment for Catholics is a prohibition on stealing, while this is the Sixth Commandment for Protestants and Jews.

Differences in the content among the religions and their versions of the Ten Commandments often matter enormously. For instance, the Jewish version of the Ten Commandments says, "You shall not murder." But the King James Version of the Bible, which is the basis for the Texas monument, says, "Thou shalt not kill." Some religions place great weight on this difference, seeing the prohibition on all "killing" as broader than the outlawing of murder.

The differences in the wording of the Second Commandment among religions also are extremely important to matters of religious faith and practice. The Catholic Church's version, which does not prohibit graven images, has been a source of great tension, and even violence, among religions since at least the Reformation.

Thus Texas, in placing this monument on government property, is making an inherently sectarian choice by adopting one religion's—the Protestant faith's—version of the Ten Commandments. For the state of Texas to declare a prohibition on graven images offends the religious precepts of Catholics. The monument's prohibition of killing, as opposed to murder, is inconsistent with the Jewish Bible. And the entire monument is an affront to adherents of other religions that do not include the Ten Commandments in their scripture and, in fact, reject some of what it expresses.

Third, the separation of church and state is important because it protects religion from the government. If the government provides assistance, inescapably there are and should be conditions attached. For example, when the government gives money, it must make sure that the funds are used for their intended purpose. This necessarily involves the government placing restrictions on the funds and monitoring how they are spent. Such government entanglement is a threat to religion.

This concern is not new. Roger Williams, the founder of Rhode Island, for example, worried that "worldly corruptions ... might consume the churches if sturdy fences against the wilderness were not maintained." Justice Souter also expressed this concern as a fundamental basis for the Establishment Clause: "[G]overnment aid corrupts religion. . . . In a variant of Madison's concern, we have repeatedly noted that a government's favor to a particular religion or sect threatens to taint it with 'corrosive secularism.' "

Fourth, coercion is inherent without a separation of church and state. If supervisors in a government office hold prayer breakfasts, even if they are voluntary, employees feel the pressure to be there. If schools have prayers, students feel pressure to participate.

The more the government is aligned with religion, the greater the likelihood of coercion. Government support for faith-based organizations has exactly this effect. There has been a significant trend in recent years toward allowing churches, synagogues, and mosques to directly receive government money for providing social services. One of President George W. Bush's first acts was to create an office of faith-based programs in the White House. No longer would religious institutions need to create a secular arm in order to take government money. President Barack Obama, unfortunately in my view, has expressed his support for such direct government aid to churches, synagogues, and mosques.

For example, across the country criminal defendants are increasingly being placed in drug and alcohol rehabilitation programs that are operated by religious institutions and that are pervasively religious. In recent years, the federal government has significantly increased the availability of funds for drug and alcohol rehabilitation programs and has expressly authorized faith-based organizations to receive government money to provide these services. At the same time, courts are increasingly placing those accused of some crimes, such as crimes involving drugs and alcohol, in treatment programs rather than prison. Although this makes great sense, the result of these two trends has been that individuals are forced to participate in religious indoctrination in order to avoid prison. Often the criminal defendant must participate in programs such as Alcoholics Anonymous and Narcotics Anonymous, programs in which the Christian faith and God play a central role in treatment. Recently, I was talking with a judge on the Los Angeles Superior Court who regularly hears domestic abuse cases. He said that in a significant percentage of these matters the underlying problem is alcohol. He explained that it was his practice to often include in the sentence a requirement that the defendant participate in Alcoholics Anonymous. He said that he did this for a long time until realizing that this was an overtly Christian program and he was deeply troubled by the Establishment Clause ramifications of what he was doing. He looked for a secular equivalent and could not find one. Alcoholics Anonymous, of course, does wonderful work, but ordering a person to participate or face jail raises serious constitutional problems because its treatment program and its message are pervasively religious.

Sometimes within prison, inmates are placed in programs that are completely sectarian and they must participate or face longer sentences. In one recent case, a federal district court and a federal court of appeals found a violation of the Establishment Clause when a program in an Iowa prison based on evangelical Christianity facilitated the earlier release of inmates who participated.

Another case that I was involved in provides a powerful illustration of this conflict. In February 2001, Joseph Hanas was charged in Michigan with possession of marijuana with intent to deliver. He was placed on probation. In January 2003, Hanas violated the conditions of his Drug Court program when he was ticketed for being a minor in possession of alcohol. The court decided that in order for Hanas to remain in the Drug Court program, rather than being sentenced to prison, he had to successfully complete a residential program called the Inner City Christian Outreach Residential Program. Hanas was given no other option if he wanted to avoid incarceration than to participate in this specific program.

Hanas complied with the terms of the sentence and took residence in the Inner City Christian Outreach Residential Program. Once there, he discovered that the program, run by a pastor of the Pentecostal faith, was pervasively religious. While in the residential program, Hanas was proselytized to accept the Pentecostal faith and was not allowed to practice his own Roman Catholic religion. For example, the pastor confiscated Hanas's rosary and Catholic Bible because, according to the pastor, they were items of "witchcraft." When Hanas asked to see his Catholic priest, the pastor forbade him from doing so. The pastor further told Hanas that to be certified as having successfully completed the program, he would need to participate in a Pentecostal service and declare that he had been "saved."

Hanas then returned to the Drug Court and objected to his placement on the grounds that it interfered with his religious freedom. Hanas asked to be transferred to a secular treatment program. Hanas and his lawyer, along with an attorney for the ACLU participating as a friend of the court, objected that the Inner City Christian Outreach Residential Program was a Pentecostal program designed to convert him to the Pentecostal faith, that it demeaned his Roman Catholic faith, and that there were no drug or alcohol counselors on staff. They also objected that Hanas was prohibited from practicing his religion and from attending Alcoholics Anonymous meetings.

The Drug Court acknowledged that the Inner City Christian Outreach Residential Program was a "religious based program," but denied Hanas's request for reassignment to a different residential treatment program. The judge was angry at him for objecting and removed him from the Drug Court program and sentenced him as a regular criminal defendant to six months in jail and probation for a term of four years. Hanas objected, to no avail, that he was being punished by being jailed solely for asserting his rights of religious freedom. The only basis for Hanas being removed from the Drug Court program and being placed in jail and on probation was his objecting to being in the Pentecostal program. In fact, Pastor Rottier, the director of the Inner City Christian Outreach Program, testified on the record that Hanas had "done good" while he was in their program.

I represented Hanas in seeking review in the Supreme Court. As faith-based programs are becoming all the more common, stories like that of Joseph Hanas are also becoming more common. Unfortunately, the Supreme Court denied review.

A separation of church and state prevents coercion. The Supreme Court long has held that coercing a person into participating in religious activities violates both the Free Exercise and the Establishment clauses of the First Amendment. Yet, without a separation of church and state, coercion—whether in schools or in prisons or elsewhere—is inevitable.

All of this explains why the Supreme Court for decades espoused the view that the Establishment Clause was meant to separate church and state. Yet, when I stood before the justices in March 2005 to argue Thomas Van Orden's challenge to the Texas Ten Commandments monument, there were only three justices—Stevens, Souter, and Ginsburg—who espoused the view of Thomas Jefferson that there should be a wall that separates church and state.

Four justices—Rehnquist, Scalia, Kennedy, and Thomas—repeatedly had said that they rejected the notion of a separation of church and state. Their view was that this idea was unduly hostile to religion and impermissibly limited the ability of the majority to govern as it wished. They took the position in numerous cases that the government violated the Establishment Clause only if it literally established a church or coerced religious participation. By this view, religious symbols on government property never infringe the First Amendment. In light of their prior opinions, I knew that there was no chance to get them to vote that the Texas Ten Commandments monument violated the Establishment Clause.

The remaining two justices on the bench at the time—O'Connor and Breyer—rejected both of these views as too extreme. In a series of opinions over twenty years, Justice O'Connor said that the government violates the Establishment Clause if it symbolically endorses a religion or a particular religion. For example, she had said that a nativity scene by itself on government property is not allowed because it is a symbolic endorsement of Christianity, but a nativity scene becomes permissible if it is accompanied by symbols of other religions and by secular symbols. Justice Breyer also had taken this view that the Establishment Clause is violated if the reasonable observer would see the government as endorsing religion.

I knew that to win in *Van Orden,* I needed to persuade Justice O'Connor and Justice Breyer. But how did it come to be that the Court had gone from having nine justices who believed in the strict separation of church and state to just three? The answer reflects a major change in the political landscape.

As recently as the 1940s, religions such as Southern Baptists and Orthodox Jews strongly favored the separation of church and state. Perhaps because they were fearful of government regulation of religion and perhaps because they could not imagine the government helping their faiths, they espoused the view that the Establishment Clause prevented government aid to religion and religion's involvement with government.

This attitude began to change, though, with the 1964 election. The Barry Goldwater campaign for president engaged southern Christian evangelicals who opposed desegregation. Some who had been part of the Goldwater campaign became architects of a new Republican Party, one founded less on anticommunist appeals. They called themselves "the New Right."

Paul Weyrich, who had been a volunteer for Goldwater in 1964, founded the Heritage Foundation in 1973—a think tank to promote the ideas of the New Right. Weyrich also founded ALEC, the American Legislative Exchange Council, in 1973 to coordinate the work of "religious right" state legislators. It was funded primarily by large corporations, industry groups, and conservative foundations—including R. J. Reynolds Tobacco, Koch Industries, and the American Petroleum Institute. In 1979 Weyrich coined the term "Moral Majority." The goal was to politicize members of fundamentalist, Pentecostal, and charismatic churches, a constituency that had been basically apolitical. Speaking in Dallas in 1980, Weyrich captured the spirit of this new movement. He said, "We are talking about Christianizing America. We are talking about simply spreading the gospel in a political context." Jerry Falwell, who became the leader of the Moral Majority, said, "[G]et them saved, get them Baptized, and get them registered."

The 1980 presidential election saw the emergence of the religious right as a major political force. Thousands of fundamentalist preachers participated in political training seminars that year, and by June more than two million voters had been registered Republican. Their goal was to register five million new voters by November. In the 1980 elections, the newly politicized religious right succeeded in unseating five of the most liberal Democratic incumbents in the U.S. Senate and provided the margin that helped Ronald Reagan defeat Jimmy Carter. Many other conservative organizations formed in the 1980s to harness religion as a political force.

The Reverend Timothy LaHaye founded the American Coalition for Traditional Values—a network of 110,000 churches—committed to getting Christian candidates elected to office. In 1979, LaHaye and his wife, Beverly, founded Concerned Women for America (CWA), claiming a membership of six hundred thousand. With prayer and action meetings, the women were, and still are, a formidable lobbying force.

The result of this has been to link conservative Republican politics to the religious right. Nixon was the first president to institute weekly White House chapel services. According to historian Gary Wills, the institution of prayer breakfasts was an attempt by the Nixon White House to woo the rising evangelical community. Nixon proposed substantial increases in government funding for parochial schools, including tax credits for parents who were paying tuition for religious education for their children.

Nixon, though, was mild in his opposition to the separation of church and state compared with Ronald Reagan. President Reagan was a frequent critic of the idea of such a wall. He said that in drafting the First Amendment our founding fathers "sought to protect churches from government interference" but "never intended to construct a wall of hostility between government and the concept of religious belief itself." Reagan urged the "reawaken[ing] of America's religious and moral heart, recognizing that a deep and abiding faith in God is the rock upon which this great nation is founded."

Reagan repeatedly criticized the Supreme Court's decisions banning prayer in public schools and he said that "well meaning Americans in the name of freedom have taken freedom away. For the sake of religious tolerance they've forbidden religious practice in our classrooms." On May 17, 1982, President Reagan proposed an amendment to the Constitution to allow prayer in public schools. It read: "Nothing in this Constitution shall be construed to prohibit individual or group prayer in public schools or other public institutions. No person shall be required by the United States or any state to participate in prayer." In presenting the amendment to Congress, he described school prayer as a "simple freedom" and a "fundamental part of our American heritage." In his 1983 State of the Union Address, Reagan declared that "God should never have been expelled from America's classrooms in the first place."

In 2004, when George W. Bush won a close reelection bid over challenger John Kerry, one out of four Republican voters self-identified as an evangelical Christian. Religions such as Southern Baptists, which as recently as the 1940s urged a separation of church and state, shifted to opposing any such notions. The religious right forcefully argued that the insistence on a secular government was impermissible hostility to religion.

This attitude became powerfully apparent on the U.S. Supreme Court as conservative justices joined the bench and urged a change in the interpretation of the Establishment Clause. In 1989, the Court heard a case that involved religious symbols on government property at two government buildings in Pittsburgh, Pennsylvania. One involved a county courthouse where there was a large stairway display case. In it, in December, was placed a nativity scene. The other case involved a Pittsburgh city building. In front of it in December was placed a menorah, a Christmas tree, and a proclamation about tolerance in the holiday season.

The Supreme Court found that the nativity scene was unconstitutional, but that the menorah and tree display was constitutional. The decision was the result of a Court deeply divided over how to approach the Establishment Clause. Three justices—Brennan, Marshall, and Stevens—took the position that both the nativity scene and the menorah and tree were unconstitutional. Their view was that religious symbols do not belong on government property. This is the view about separation of church and state that the Supreme Court had followed for decades.

Four justices—Rehnquist, White, Scalia, and Kennedy—took the view that both religious symbols are constitutional. Justice Kennedy wrote for them and argued that the Establishment Clause should be interpreted to accommodate religion into government and government into religion. He urged that the government should be found to violate the Establishment Clause only if it literally establishes a church or coerces religious participation. Under this view, religious symbols on government property never violate the Establishment Clause. This is a view that rejects any notion of a wall separating church and state. It was exactly the view of the president who appointed Anthony Kennedy to the Supreme Court, Ronald Reagan.

Justices O'Connor and Blackmun cast the swing votes. They said that the nativity scene was unconstitutional because it was a symbolic endorsement of Christianity. For them the key question was whether the government is symbolically endorsing religion or a particular religion. Earlier the Supreme Court had ruled that nativity scenes on government property are permissible so long as they are accompanied by symbols of other religions and by secular symbols as well. The nativity scene by itself in the staircase of the county courthouse was for Justices O'Connor and Blackmun an impermissible symbolic endorsement for Christianity. A nativity scene is obviously a religious depiction; religious Christians would be appalled to hear such a sacred event declared to be secular. By contrast, they said that the menorah, a Jewish religious symbol, was allowed because it was part of an overall holiday display and was accompanied by other symbols, a Christmas tree and a proclamation of tolerance.

The case remains important in defining when religious symbols, such as nativity scenes, are allowed on government property. Even more significant, though, was the explicit attack on the notion of separation of church and state launched by the four most conservative justices. Under their view, urged by conservative organizations and the religious right, government would have tremendous latitude to advance religion.

For a brief time in the early 1990s, it appeared that there were five justices to take this position. But they never found the occasion for a decision where they could join in a majority opinion adopting this view. The closest they came was in 1992 in *Lee v. Weisman*. The Weisman family had a daughter, Deborah, about to graduate from the local public middle school in Providence, Rhode Island. Their older children had previously graduated from the same school and the Weismans had been upset by clergy members delivering religious invocations and benedictions at the graduations.

Deborah's father, Daniel, went to see the principal, Robert E. Lee, and objected to the clergy-delivered prayer at the public school graduation. Lee said that he would solve the problem by inviting the Weismans' rabbi to deliver the invocation and benediction. This, of course, did not address Daniel Weisman's concern; his objection was to a prayer at the public school event. It wasn't more acceptable just because the prayer came from his religion. The Weismans sued arguing that the clergy-delivered prayer violated the Establishment Clause.

The administration of President George H. W. Bush participated in the case and urged the Court to rule in favor of the principal and the school. In a brief submitted by Solicitor General Kenneth

Starr and Deputy Solicitor General John G. Roberts, Jr., the Bush administration argued that the Court should abandon the view of the Establishment Clause that had been followed for decades and instead find that the government violates the First Amendment only if it coerces religious participation or literally establishes a church.

This was the position that the four most conservative justices took in the *Allegheny County* case and it had become the conservative approach to the Establishment Clause. It sought to replace any notion of a separation of church and state with government accommodation of religion.

A deeply divided Court, in a 5–4 decision, found that clergy-delivered prayers at public school graduations violate the Establishment Clause. Interestingly, five justices adopted the test urged by the Bush administration, but only four of them agreed with its conclusion that this made the prayer constitutional. Justice Kennedy wrote for the majority and said that clergy-delivered prayers are inherently coercive. He explained that graduation is an important event in the lives of children and their families. There thus was great pressure to be present and it was not realistic for children to leave the stage during the time of the prayer. Justice Kennedy declared, "True, Deborah could elect not to attend commencement without renouncing her diploma; but we shall not allow the case to turn on this point. Everyone knows that in our society and in our culture high school graduation is one of life's most significant occasions. A school rule which excuses attendance is besides the point."

The other four justices in the majority—Stevens, Blackmun, O'Connor, and Souter—wrote separately to say that they believed that coercion was not necessary to find a violation of the Establishment Clause. A long line of cases had held that prayer in schools, even voluntary, nondenominational prayer, is unconstitutional. In 1962, in the famous "school prayer" case, *Engel v. Vitale,* the Court had declared unconstitutional a requirement that students in New York begin each school day by reciting a prayer composed by the New York Board of Regents. A year later, in

Abbington School District v. Schempp, the Court invalidated a Texas law requiring that a verse of the Bible be read at the beginning of each school day, accompanied by a recitation of the Lord's Prayer. These were the decisions that President Reagan sought to overturn with his proposed constitutional amendment to allow prayer in public schools.

Although these cases were tremendously controversial, they reflected the notion that religious observations, including prayer, do not belong in public school classrooms. This idea is not hostility to religion, but rather a view that government should be secular and the place for prayer is in people's hearts, homes, and places of worship, but not in schools.

Justice Scalia wrote a vehement dissent in *Lee v. Weisman,* joined by Justices Rehnquist, White, and Thomas. In it he called on the Court to repudiate these earlier decisions and to make clear that the government violates the Establishment Clause only if it coerces religious participation or creates a church. He ridiculed the notion of psychological coercion, which Justice Kennedy had relied upon. At the end of his dissent, Justice Scalia said that the Court was far too concerned with the few students who did not want prayer at graduation and wrongly ignored the majority that wanted it. He wrote, "The reader has been told much in this case about the personal interest of Mr. Weisman and his daughter, and very little about the personal interests on the other side. They are not inconsequential. Church and state would not be such a difficult subject if religion were, as the Court apparently thinks it to be, some purely personal avocation that can be indulged entirely in secret, like pornography, in the privacy of one's room." For Justice Scalia and the other three dissenters, it was the desire by most parents and children for prayer that should be controlling.

The difference between the majority and the dissent is over whether the Bill of Rights, including the Establishment Clause, is designed to protect the majority or the minority. If the Establishment Clause has any effect, it always will be applied to restrict the government's ability to advance religion. The majority's preferences are typically reflected in the government's actions; the Bill of Rights protects the minority. Justice Scalia's deference to the majority's desire for religion in government would not only obliterate any notion of a wall separating church and state, it would leave very little of the Establishment Clause. The Establishment Clause always limits the ability of government to advance religion.

Over the years that followed, leading up to when I argued *Van Orden v. Perry*, in March 2005, there were four justices, but never the crucial five, who took Justice Scalia's position. Justice Byron White retired in 1993 and was replaced by Justice Ruth Bader Ginsburg; Justice Harry Blackmun retired in 1994 and was replaced by Justice Stephen Breyer. Both of these new justices rejected the Scalia position and adhered to the view that the Establishment Clause separates church and state.

To be sure, there were differences between Justices Ginsburg and Breyer. Justice Ginsburg was more the strict separationist. This was initially evident in a decision in 2000, *Mitchell v. Helms*. The issue was whether Louisiana could give instructional equipment, such as computers and audiovisual equipment, to parochial schools. The program provided this equipment to all schools in the state, public and private, secular and religious.

Four of the justices—Rehnquist, Scalia, Kennedy, and Thomas—took the position that the government should be able to provide any aid to religious schools, even if it is used for religious indoctrination, so long as the government does not discriminate among religions. In fact, Justice Thomas's opinion, joined by these other justices, argued that to deny such aid to religious schools was impermissible hostility to religion and violated the Establishment Clause. Under the Thomas view, any government aid to religion is allowed, even if used for expressly religious purposes, so long as all religions are treated the same. Justice Thomas argued that the Constitution required that private religious schools receive the same aid as private secular schools.

Five justices rejected this view. Three of them—Stevens, Souter, and Ginsburg—adhered to the position that had emerged from many Supreme Court decisions: Louisiana could not give this aid to religious schools because it easily could be used for religious education. Their concern was that any monitoring would be impossible and would inevitably entail too much government entanglement with religious institutions.

Two of the justices—O'Connor and Breyer—said that the government could provide the aid to religious schools so long as it was not actually used in religious education. This then became the law: the government may provide assistance, like that supplied by Louisiana, so long as it is used only in the secular education of students.

As I wrote my brief in *Van Orden v. Perry* and stood before the justices, I knew that there were four who would surely vote against me: Rehnquist, Scalia, Kennedy, and Thomas. Their view, expressed in a number of cases, was that religious symbols on government property never violate the Establishment Clause. To prevail, I needed to get the votes of all of the remaining justices: Stevens, O'Connor, Souter, Ginsburg, and Breyer. I perceived that Justice O'Connor would be the swing vote. I know that the state of Texas, defending the Ten Commandments monument, saw it the same way. Both our briefs were shameless efforts to pander to Justice O'Connor. If we could, each of us would have placed Justice O'Connor's picture on the front of our briefs. My brief cited Justice O'Connor twenty-three times.

On the day I argued *Van Orden v. Perry*, it was one of two cases concerning Ten Commandments displays. The other case, *McCreary County v. ACLU*, involved a county in Kentucky that had passed a resolution requiring the posting of the Ten Commandments in county buildings. After the ACLU sued, the county passed another resolution requiring that the Ten Commandments be accompanied by nine other displays, all of the same size and framing, about the role of religion in American history. These were to include the religious portions of the Declaration of Independence and the words "In God We Trust," which appear on American money.

Van Orden was argued first on that Tuesday morning in March, and since my client, Thomas Van Orden, had lost in the lower courts, I was the first to be at the podium. Chief Justice Rehnquist was absent because of his surgery for thyroid cancer, a disease that would take his life six months later. As expected, Justices Scalia and Kennedy expressed their hostility to my position and to any limits on religious symbols on government property.

In hindsight, the most important question came from Justice Breyer. Immediately after the argument, it was the answer that I was most proud of. As soon as the decision came down, it was the question that I most wished I had answered differently.

Justice Breyer said to me that he found it very hard to know where to draw the line in Establishment Clause cases and that the only test he could look to was whether the government's action would be divisive in society based on religion. I replied by saying that it was essential that the Court look to the context and see that at this moment in American history Ten Commandments monuments are terribly divisive. I said that the chief justice of Alabama had been removed from office over a Ten Commandments display, that I had received hate mail before the argument, and that there were demonstrators outside the Court because people care deeply about Ten Commandments monuments and thus their presence on government property is terribly divisive.

Justice Breyer thoughtfully nodded. In hindsight, I wish that I had used my answer to explain why divisiveness can't be the test for the Establishment Clause. All efforts to enforce the Establishment Clause inherently will be divisive based on religion; all involve a court telling the majority that it cannot do something it wants to do to advance religion. Divisiveness cannot be avoided when there is a disagreement, as there always is in Establishment Clause cases, between a majority that wants the government to further religion and a minority that wants the government to remain secular.

After the oral argument ended, I had no more sense than I had before it as to how it would come out. The clerk of the Supreme Court let it be known that Monday, June 27, 2005, was to be the last day of decisions for the term. Since the two Ten Commandments cases had not been decided, it was expected that they would be announced that day. I was in Mackinac Island, Michigan, to speak to the Sixth Circuit Judicial Conference, a gathering of all the federal judges from Michigan, Ohio, Tennessee, and Kentucky. I was scheduled to speak from 8 to 9:30 A.M. The Supreme Court's decisions in all of its remaining seven cases were due at 10 A.M. My talk was a review of the major Supreme Court decisions from the prior year and what they would mean for the judges' work. After my talk ended, I was asked if I would return at 11 A.M. to report on the rulings issued that day.

I went to my room in the Grand Hotel, a large and fancy hotel on Mackinac Island, and turned on the television to CNN and my laptop to a blog that reported the decisions as they came down. The first case to be announced was the McCreary County case, and the Court ruled, 5–4, that the Ten Commandments displays in the county buildings in Kentucky violated the Establishment Clause. Justice Souter wrote for the Court, joined by Justices Stevens, O'Connor, Ginsburg, and Breyer. Justice Souter's opinion stressed that the Ten Commandments are inherently religious and that McCreary County's primary purpose was impermissibly to advance religion. Immediately I began getting e-mail messages congratulating me, with friends not realizing that it wasn't my case that had been decided. Still, it seemed a good sign for *Van Orden v. Perry* that O'Connor had gone with the more liberal justices in finding a Ten Commandments display on public property to be in violation of the First Amendment.

Five other cases were then announced. I was constantly hitting the refresh button on my laptop, but often could not get through, whether because of a poor connection from my hotel room or demand on the website. I was on the phone with my wife, who was in her office in North Carolina, and she too was anxiously searching for the ruling. Finally, after almost an hour, the last decision of the morning was announced. In a 5–4 decision, the Court held that the Texas Ten Commandments monument does not violate the Establishment Clause. Chief Justice Rehnquist, in what turned out to be his last opinion on the Court, wrote an opinion that was joined by Justices Scalia, Kennedy, and Thomas. Predictably, they found that religious symbols on government property do not offend the Establishment Clause. Justice Breyer was the fifth vote for the majority and he concurred in the judgment, which means that he agreed with the conclusion, but not the reasons given by Chief Justice Rehnquist. Justice Breyer said that the Ten Commandments monument between the Texas Capitol and the Texas Supreme Court was not a symbolic endorsement of religion. He stressed that the monument had been there since 1961 and no one had objected except for Thomas Van Orden. He noted that it had been privately donated and he emphasized that there were seventeen monuments on the Texas Capitol grounds and this was only one of them. Echoing his question at the oral argument, he said that the Ten Commandments monument did not "promote the kind of social conflict the Establishment Clause seeks to avoid."

I had spent almost a year and a half working on the Van Orden case, first seeking Supreme Court review and then briefing and arguing the case. I realized from the outset that I might lose 5–4, but always thought it would be by losing Justice O'Connor; it felt even worse to get O'Connor's vote but lose because Breyer joined the conservatives.

Almost immediately after hearing the decision, I had to return to the judges and report to them on the results in my case and the others that had just been decided. It was hard to do. It was all too soon and too raw to want to talk with people about it. It wasn't like losing the three-strikes case, which could mean a person will spend his or her life in prison for shoplifting, or like losing death penalty appeals. But it still really hurt.

After I spoke to the judges, I immediately got in a horse-drawn carriage to go back to the airport; cars are not allowed on Mackinac Island. It felt surreal to be talking from my cell phone to my co-counsel and then to reporters about the decision while riding in a horse-drawn buggy. The key question everyone wanted to talk about is how did the Court justify striking down the Kentucky Ten Commandments display while upholding the Texas one. A CNN reporter said on air that it was because the former was inside, while the latter was outside. That, of course, is a distinction that makes no sense in terms of the First Amendment.

Only one justice saw a difference: Stephen Breyer. Four justices—Stevens, O'Connor, Souter, and Ginsburg—would have declared both displays to be unconstitutional. By contrast, Rehnquist, Scalia, Kennedy, and Thomas would have upheld both the Texas and the Kentucky Ten Commandments displays. Justice Scalia's dissenting opinion in the Kentucky case was particularly disturbing. He said that the three most popular religions in the United States—Christianity, Judaism, and Islam—"account for 97.7% of all believers." He said that all of them believe that "the Ten Commandments were given by God to Moses, and are divine prescriptions for a virtuous life." He said that since this belief is recognized "across such a broad and diverse range of the population" it does not violate the Establishment Clause. As in *Lee v. Weisman*, Scalia's focus is on the majority's desire for government expression of religion; he does not recognize that the Establishment Clause is intended to protect those of minority religions, or no religion, so that they are not made to feel like outsiders. He also disregarded significant differences among the majority religions about what the Ten Commandments are.

Why did Justice Breyer see a difference between these two cases? The distinctions that he gave seemingly should make little difference. It is true that the monument had been there since 1961, but as the Court recognized in *Brown v. Board of Education*, a violation of the Constitution is not excused because it has gone on for a long time. Prayer had been part of public schools for much of American history until the Court found it to violate the Establishment Clause. Nor should it matter that the display had been donated by the Fraternal Order of Eagles and paid for by Cecil B. DeMille. The Texas legislature had expressly approved its placement at the seat of the state government. Actually, the State Preservation Board took the monument down in 1990 and put it back facing in a different, more prominent position in 1993. Other monuments that were removed at the same time were never put back on display. A reasonable observer would likely see the monument as the government's symbolic endorsement of religion.

As for the presence of other monuments on the grounds, the Ten Commandments sits by itself, in a prominent position between the Texas Capitol and the Texas Supreme Court, with no other monuments visible when standing before it. There is no other religious monument anywhere on the grounds of the state capitol. The "reasonable observer" who sees the Ten Commandments monument at literally the seat of state government can draw but one conclusion: that the state of Texas endorses the religious views expressed on it.

As I have reflected on Justice Breyer's votes in these two cases, I have speculated that he was adopting what he perceived as a practical solution. Justice Breyer prides himself on being a pragmatist. He essentially was saying that older displays, like the Texas one, would be allowed; but new ones would not be tolerated. Perhaps he was worried about the nightly news in small towns being filled with stories of Ten Commandments monuments being taken down. His approach was a compromise.

On Friday, July 1, four days after the Court released its decisions in *Van Orden* and *McCreary County*, Justice O'Connor shocked the nation by announcing her resignation from the Supreme Court. On September 3, William Rehnquist succumbed to cancer.

There seems little doubt as to where the two new justices, Roberts and Alito, will be on issues concerning church and state: they almost surely will join Justices Scalia, Kennedy, and Thomas in creating a majority to dramatically change the law and hold that the government violates the Establishment Clause only if it creates a church or coerces religious participation. Besides the fact that Roberts and Alito vote together with Scalia and Thomas about 90 percent of the time, there are strong indications that these justices share the conservative view of the Establishment Clause. As deputy solicitor general during the first Bush presidency, John Roberts was a key author of the brief urging the Supreme Court to adopt exactly this position in *Lee v. Weisman*. In his fifteen years as federal appellate court judge, Samuel Alito never found any government action to violate the Establishment Clause.

What will this shift to the right mean? I expect that religious symbols on government property, whether nativity scenes or Ten Commandments monuments or in other forms, will be allowed. Prior rulings preventing the government from acting with the purpose of advancing religion or symbolically endorsing religion, like *McCreary County*, likely will be overruled. Government likely will be able to provide any aid to parochial schools, even for religious indoctrination, so long as it does not discriminate among religions. Indeed, the Court may have five votes to hold, as Justice Thomas has urged, that the failure to provide religious schools the same aid that is given to secular private schools violates the First Amendment.

One place where the shift is less likely to matter is with regard to school prayer. Justice Kennedy, the fifth vote in this group, has consistently found that prayer in public schools is coercive. In addition to *Lee v. Weisman*, in 2000, in *Santa Fe Independent School District v. Doe*, Justice Kennedy was in the majority in finding that student-delivered prayers at public school graduations violate the Establishment Clause. Among other things, the Court noted that many students—such as football players, cheerleaders, and band members—must be at the games and they therefore are forced to experience prayer. Not surprisingly, Chief Justice Rehnquist and Justices Scalia and Thomas dissented and would have allowed the student-delivered prayers. For the foreseeable future, prayers in school will be forbidden as long as Anthony Kennedy continues to find them to be inherently coercive.

But the extent of the change in the law with regard to the Establishment Clause cannot be overstated. The view that Justice Scalia has expressed in dissent, that the Court should defer to the majority's desire for religion in government and not the minority's desire for a secular government, is likely to become the law. The wish of conservatives to eliminate the notion of a wall separating church and state, articulated by President Ronald Reagan, seems almost certain to be realized. This deference to majoritarianism will mean that little ever will be found to violate the Establish-ment Clause.

In fact, almost twenty years ago, Justice Scalia achieved exactly this result with regard to the other provision of the First Amend-ment concerning religion: the Free Exercise Clause. As mentioned, the First Amendment actually has two clauses protecting religious freedom: the prohibition of laws "respecting the establishment of religion" and the prohibition of government actions "prohibiting the free exercise" of religion. To a large extent, these provisions are complementary. Both provisions are meant to protect religious freedom from government interference. The Establishment Clause does this by keeping the government secular and ensuring that religion is left to the private realm of people's lives and places of worship. The Free Exercise Clause reinforces this principle by en-suring that people can practice their religion as they choose.

For several decades, the Supreme Court had ruled that if a government action significantly burdens religious beliefs and practices, the government would need to show that its action was necessary to achieve a compelling government interest. Free exer-cise of religion cannot be absolute; people cannot commit ritual sacrifice of human beings or impose harms on others even if they believe that their religion commands it. But the Court had ruled that for the government to significantly burden religion, it must show that a crucial interest would be served and that there was no other way to accomplish the objective.

A decision from 1963, *Sherbert v. Verner*, illustrates this prin-ciple. Adell Sherbert was a Seventh-Day Adventist who worked in the textile mills in South Carolina. She refused to work on her Sat-urday Sabbath and quit work rather than violate her religion. The state refused to give her unemployment benefits because it said that she had voluntarily left her job; unemployment benefits were limited to those who were involuntarily terminated.

The Supreme Court concluded that denying Sherbert benefits violated her free exercise of religion. Although the state was not prohibiting Sherbert from practicing her religion and observ-ing her Saturday Sabbath, the government was significantly burdening it; she was forced to choose between her religion and an income. The Supreme Court said that such government burdening of religion must be necessary to achieve a compelling interest and that the state failed to meet this heavy burden.

The law of the Free Exercise Clause changed dramatically in 1990, even though the Court did not explicitly overrule *Sherbert v. Verner*. The case was *Employment Division v. Smith*. Native Americans in Oregon wished to use peyote, a hallucinogenic substance, in their religious rituals. Many states have exemptions from their peyote laws for Native Americans; Oregon did not.

If the Court wanted to rule against the Native Americans, it could have done so without changing the law. The Court could have concluded that the government has a compelling interest in preventing the use of hallucinogenic substances and that there is no other way to achieve this result except for a ban without exceptions. This is the approach Justice O'Connor took in a concurring opinion.

But Justice Scalia, writing for the majority, used this case as the occasion to alter the law concerning constitutional protection for free exercise of religion. He said that the Native Americans could not challenge the Oregon law, because it applied to everyone in the state and because it had not been motivated by a desire to interfere with religion. The Court held that the Free Exercise Clause cannot be used to challenge a "neutral law of general applicability" no matter how much the government is burdening religion. A law is "neutral" so long as it is not motivated by the goal of interfering with religious practices; a law is of "general applicability" if it applies to everyone.

To see how radical this idea is in changing the law, imagine a county that prohibits all consumption of alcoholic beverages. There are a few in the United States. Prior to *Employment Division v. Smith*, a priest who wanted to use wine in communion or a Jewish family who wanted to use wine at a Sabbath or seder dinner surely would have prevailed; it is inconceivable that the government could have shown that preventing this use of alcohol would serve a compelling government purpose. But after *Employment*

Division v. Smith, the priest and the Jewish family would lose. The law prohibiting consumption of alcohol is neutral in that it was not motivated by a desire to interfere with religion and it is of general applicability in that it applied to everyone in the state.

Another case that I handled on appeal illustrates the impact of *Employment Division v. Smith.* Herman Resnick is an Orthodox Jew who was serving time in federal prison for embezzlement. He requested a kosher diet. Prior to *Employment Division v. Smith,* Orthodox Jewish and Muslim inmates had consistently won such claims. But after *Smith,* Resnick was one of many prisoners to lose. Prison food plans are not created to infringe on the free exercise of religion and the diets apply to all prisoners.

In *Employment Division v. Smith,* Justice Scalia stressed that religious exemptions from laws should come from the legislatures, not from the courts. He acknowledged that "leaving accommodation [of religion] to the political process will place at a relative disadvantage those religious practices that are not widely engaged in." But he said that this is the "unavoidable consequence of democratic governance." In other words, minority religions that want protection for their ability to practice their religion must rely on the majority for this protection. According to such reasoning, the central idea of the Bill of Rights, protecting minority rights from decisions of the majority, is abandoned for the Free Exercise Clause, just as it is about to be abandoned for the Establishment Clause.

There is a striking similarity in the conservative approach to these clauses: almost total deference to the government and the absence of any protection for minority religions or those who have no religion. Virtually nothing has been found by the Supreme Court to violate the Free Exercise Clause in the two decades since *Employment Division v. Smith.* The likely conservative change in the law will mean that the same will be true of the Establishment Clause.

Ironically, when the majoritarian process acted after *Employment Division v. Smith* to protect free exercise of religion, the Supreme Court declared that law unconstitutional. In 1993,

Congress overwhelmingly passed and President Clinton signed the Religious Freedom Restoration Act. The law, often called RFRA, was explicit that its goal was to overturn *Employment Division v. Smith* and to require that any government action significantly burdening religion be shown to be necessary to achieve a compelling government interest.

In 1997, in *City of Boerne v. Flores*, the Supreme Court declared RFRA unconstitutional as applied to state and local governments. The case involved a church in a city in Texas. Its membership had grown and it wanted to significantly expand its facilities. The city, however, had classified the building as a historic landmark and refused to approve the new construction. The church, through its bishop, sued under the Religious Freedom Restoration Act. It claimed that the refusal to approve the new construction was a significant burden on the religious freedom of its members. The city of Boerne responded by arguing that the Religious Freedom Restoration Act was unconstitutional as exceeding the scope of Congress's powers.

The Supreme Court, in an opinion by Justice Anthony Kennedy, agreed with the city and declared the law unconstitutional as applied to state and local governments. Congress had adopted the law pursuant to its powers under section five of the Fourteenth Amendment, which allows it to adopt laws "to enforce" the provisions of the amendment that ensure that states provide due process and equal protection. Justice Kennedy, writing for the Court, said that Congress was expanding rights and that this is not "enforcing" the Fourteenth Amendment. The Court concluded that under section five of the Fourteenth Amendment Congress cannot expand rights or create new rights.

The Court in *Smith* had said that the protection of religious freedom is up to the legislature. Yet, when Congress enacted a statute to protect religious freedom, the Court declared the law unconstitutional. *City of Boerne v. Flores* takes an unduly cramped view of Congress's powers to enforce the Fourteenth Amendment. The Court perceived Congress as overruling a Supreme Court decision and thus challenging judicial supremacy in interpreting the

Constitution. But that is not what occurred. Congress, and for that matter state legislatures and city councils, always can create more rights than the Supreme Court finds in the Constitution. In RFRA, Congress, by statute, was seeking to restore religious freedom to what it was prior to *Employment Division v. Smith.*

Justice Kennedy's majority opinion said that Congress is not "enforcing" the Fourteenth Amendment if it expands rights. But this is a limited definition of *enforce.* One dictionary defines that word as: "Urge, presume home (argument, demand); impose (action, conduct upon person); compel observance of." Another dictionary defines *enforce* as: "1. to give force or strengthen; 2. to urge with energy; 3. constrain, compel; 4. to effect or gain by force; 5. to carry out effectively." From the perspective of these definitions, Congress is "enforcing" the Fourteenth Amendment when it broadens the scope of liberty. In this sense, congressional expansion of rights, as in RFRA, is strengthening the Fourteenth Amendment.

The point is that the Court's emphasis on deference to majoritarian processes protecting religious freedom rings hollow when it then strikes down a law adopted by Congress and signed by the president to protect religious freedom. Congress responded to *City of Boerne v. Flores* and the invalidation of RFRA by adopting a new statute, the Religious Land Use and Institutionalized Persons Act. This law says that in its land use regulation and in its treatment of institutionalized persons, government actions significantly burdening religion must be shown to be necessary to achieve a compelling government interest. It is uncertain whether this narrower protection of religious freedom will survive Supreme Court review.

I do not know what happened to Thomas Van Orden. We continued to correspond by e-mail for some time after the Supreme Court's decision in June 2005. A woman wrote me that she was working with him to get his law license back and asked me to send a check to help pay the fees. I did so, but never heard from her again. After a time, my e-mail messages to Thomas bounced back as undeliverable.

The Ten Commandments monument remains at the corner between the Texas Capitol and the Texas Supreme Court. Anyone walking from one building to another sees it. It is a powerful reminder of how little is left of the wall that separates church and state.

4.

The Vanishing Rights of Criminal Defendants

My client Phillip Wilkinson is on death row in North Carolina for having committed a horrible crime, killing three people and raping one of them. But he should not be put to death, because the government violated his constitutional rights and because he did not have a competent lawyer to represent him when the jury considered whether to impose a capital sentence. His story is remarkably similar to those of many on death row in the United States, including some who are likely innocent of the crimes for which they were convicted.

The police had no suspects for the murders of Judy, Chrystal, and Larry Hudson, which occurred in Fayetteville, North Carolina, on July 29, 1991. About six months later, on January 9, 1992, Wilkinson, accompanied by his pastor, walked into the police station and confessed to the murders. Wilkinson was in the military at the time of the murders and had been stationed in the area. He had since been honorably discharged and had moved away, but he was overcome by remorse and turned himself in.

Wilkinson then was appointed a series of lawyers, as one after another found a reason to withdraw from the case. Under well-established law, prosecutors are required to disclose to a defendant any evidence that could help to show his or her innocence, or impeach prosecution witnesses, or that possibly would be helpful at the sentencing stage. In *Brady v. Maryland,* in 1963, the Supreme Court ruled that prosecutors violate due process of law if they fail to disclose to the defense such crucial, material evidence. The code of ethics for lawyers also requires that prosecutors reveal such material.

Wilkinson's lawyers repeatedly requested, among other things, any evidence concerning tests that had been done on Wilkinson regarding his level of intoxication. Wilkinson had told his attorneys that he had been very drunk when he committed his crimes and that a blood alcohol test had been done on him when he returned to the base the morning after committing the crimes. The results of the test were potentially crucial because severe intoxication can be used to negate the intent required for first-degree murder; it also is a possible basis for the defense of voluntary intoxication, which would lead to a conviction for second-degree, not first-degree murder, and thus not a possible death sentence. Despite repeated requests, prosecutors did not turn over these test results.

On August 22, 1994, without giving prior notice to his attorneys and against their advice, Wilkinson pled guilty to two counts of first-degree burglary, three counts of first-degree murder, attempted first-degree rape, four counts of first-degree sexual offense, and two counts of felonious larceny. He thus admitted that he committed crimes that could lead to a possible death sentence; all that then remained was a hearing where a jury would decide whether to recommend capital punishment.

Two days later, after Wilkinson pled guilty, the police gave Wilkinson's lawyers the reports in their files about his blood alcohol level. These demonstrated that Wilkinson was severely intoxicated, with a blood alcohol level deemed to be approximately .174 at the time of the crimes. In most states, a blood alcohol level of half this amount, .08, is sufficient for a conviction for driving while intoxicated.

The Supreme Court has said that there are three requirements for showing a violation of *Brady v. Maryland:* the evidence not disclosed must be favorable to the defendant; the evidence must have been suppressed by the government; and the evidence must be important, or as it is phrased by the Supreme Court, it must be "material." All these requirements were met in Wilkinson's case.

First, the level of intoxication was favorable to Wilkinson because it could have been used to demonstrate the defense of voluntary intoxication, or to help convince him not to plead guilty, or to plead guilty to second- rather than first-degree murder. Either result would have prevented him from being sentenced to death.

Second, the federal district court explicitly found that the material was suppressed by the government, either willfully or inadvertently. The police had these records and did not turn them over despite requests for them.

Third, information about the intoxication level was "material." The test for materiality is whether there is a "reasonable probability" that the nondisclosed material would have made a difference in the outcome. Certainly that is true here. For example, Wilkinson wanted to plead guilty to the crimes that he committed. With the knowledge of his blood alcohol level, he likely would have realized that he committed second-degree and not first-degree murder. Also, Wilkinson would have known that he had a possible defense, voluntary intoxication, and very well would have gone to trial or pled guilty to a lesser offense that did not carry with it a death sentence.

After being sentenced to death, Wilkinson appealed and the North Carolina appellate courts ruled against him. He then obtained a terrific lawyer, Mary Ann Tally, who presented this constitutional violation to the federal district court in a petition for habeas corpus. The district court ruled against Wilkinson on this and other issues. Tally then asked if I would take primary responsibility for briefing and arguing the case in the federal court of appeals. I did so believing that there were strong arguments that Wilkinson's constitutional rights had been violated.

I argued Wilkinson's case in the United States Court of Appeals for the Fourth Circuit in Richmond, Virginia, in November 2006. I thought the argument went well and the three judges seemed to agree that the police and prosecutors acted wrongly in not turning over the information about Wilkinson's level of intoxication. Several months went by after the argument before the court handed down its decision. The court unanimously ruled against

Wilkinson and upheld his death sentence. The court did not deny that the prosecutors and police acted wrongly in failing to turn over the information about Wilkinson's intoxication level. But the court declared that it "is exceedingly unlikely that having the actual test results would have made any difference to the outcome."

Wilkinson's experience is not unique. Many lawyers have observed that prosecutors and police officers frequently fail to turn over important material that the law requires to be disclosed, but courts usually respond by saying that they don't think this would have made any difference to the outcome of the case. It is such an easy response for a court that does not want to overturn a conviction despite a constitutional violation.

The even more serious problem with Wilkinson's sentence, and one typical of capital cases in the United States, was the inadequacy of his original lawyer. Wilkinson's court-appointed lawyer for the hearing on whether the death penalty would be imposed had no experience handling capital cases; in fact, he had little experience handling complex matters. He made many serious mistakes.

For example, although mental illness is an important mitigating factor in death penalty cases, Wilkinson's lawyer presented no such evidence, even though the trial court urged defense counsel to do so and there were doctors who had examined Wilkinson who would have testified about his mental condition to the jury. Billy W. Royal, M.D., and Faye E. Sultan, Ph.D., had been hired by earlier defense counsel in 1992 to perform a forensic evaluation and to conduct psychological testing of Wilkinson. Dr. Royal made eight diagnoses of mental illness, which he related to Wilkinson's lawyer. Dr. Royal stated that his opinion was and continued to be that "Wilkinson's capacity to appreciate the criminality of his conduct or to conform his conduct to the requirements of the law was significantly impaired." Dr. Sultan came to same the conclusion, that Wilkinson suffered from serious mental illnesses. These judgments would not have exonerated Wilkinson; the crimes to which he pled guilty would have led to a very long incarceration, probably imprisonment for the rest of his life. But his mental illness might have caused the jury to spare his life.

The defense counsel did not call Wilkinson's parents to testify at the sentencing hearing, even though they were still alive and had volunteered to appear. The impression for the jury had to be damaging. If so few who knew him came forward, and not even his parents testified, then why should a jury care about his fate? In fact, Wilkinson's parents were told by his lawyer that they could not come to the trial and that there were no funds available to pay their expenses for travel. This was wrong; under North Carolina law, Wilkinson, as an indigent, was entitled to have the state pay for the attendance of witnesses at the sentencing hearing.

These and other family members could have testified that Wilkinson was raised in poverty. They could have described how when he was a child, Wilkinson's mother would often desert him for long periods of time. They could have described how Wilkinson grew up in a family that had an extensive history of alcoholism, parental neglect, depression, and attempted suicide. This is exactly what the Supreme Court has recognized to be powerful mitigating evidence in death penalty cases.

At the oral argument in the federal court of appeals, Judge Roger Gregory asked the attorney for the prosecution, the state of North Carolina, how she explained the failure of Wilkinson's state-supplied lawyer to call the parents as witnesses. The state was denying that Wilkinson had ineffective assistance of counsel and should receive a new trial. The lawyer responded that it was "a strategic choice of counsel." Judge Gregory was incredulous and said that this was a southern jury; it would have wanted "to hear from the boy's mama." North Carolina's lawyer had no answer.

Perhaps the most egregious omission by Wilkinson's lawyer was the failure to present crucial evidence of Wilkinson's remorse. Remorse is an extremely important circumstance to be considered in determining punishment for the commission of a crime under North Carolina law. The North Carolina Supreme Court has stressed that remorse, or the lack of it, is crucial in death penalty cases.

Nonetheless, the defense counsel never called as a witness Pastor Randy Johnson, pastor of Word of Life Christian Assembly, to whom Wilkinson had confessed his crimes, even though he was in the courtroom and offered to testify. Given Wilkinson's relationship with Pastor Johnson, this was not a choice that any reasonable attorney would have made. Pastor Johnson said that he would have testified about the remorse shown by Wilkinson the night he gave his confession to the police. For approximately one year following Wilkinson's arrest, Pastor Johnson went to the Cumberland County Jail to visit Wilkinson. Wilkinson called Pastor Johnson at his home on a weekly basis. Based on all of this, Pastor Johnson said that he would have testified that Wilkinson was deeply and genuinely remorseful for the crimes that he had committed.

During the sentencing hearing, Pastor Johnson came to the courtroom to see if he could be of help to Wilkinson. Instead of being called as a witness, he was told by Wilkinson's lawyer to leave.

At the oral argument in the Fourth Circuit, the judges asked the lawyer for North Carolina to explain this omission. She could not. She said that it was a strategic choice by counsel, but never explained how this was so. Strikingly, the jury, in completing a form in presenting its recommendation for a death penalty, said that it found no remorse by Wilkinson for his crimes. The court of appeals even said: "The failure to call Pastor Johnson as a witness is troubling, particularly since it appears that no other witness testified at length regarding Wilkinson's remorse for the crimes, and counsel did not spend any significant time arguing that Wilkinson was remorseful."

All of this together is substantial evidence of ineffective assistance of counsel. If the court accepted this argument, that would not necessarily have meant that Wilkinson would have avoided a death sentence. It would have meant a new sentencing hearing, with competent counsel, who could have tried to convince the jury to spare Wilkinson's life. The court of appeals, though, ruled against Wilkinson and said that under the federal law governing habeas corpus—the Antiterrorism and Effective Death Penalty Act, adopted in 1996—it had to defer to the state court decision upholding Wilkinson's conviction. The court of appeals said that it could not rule that the state court was "unreasonable" in its conclusion that the jury would have imposed a death sentence even without these crucial omissions by Wilkinson's lawyer. The court of appeals stated: "[W]e cannot say that it was *unreasonable* for the [North Carolina state] court to conclude that the failure to present the additional testimony . . . would not have created a reasonable probability of a different outcome. We therefore affirm the denial of relief on this claim." In fact, I could find no case where the U.S. Court of Appeals for the Fourth Circuit had in the prior decade overturned a death sentence for ineffective assistance of counsel.

I sought Supreme Court review of the court of appeals decision. I felt that there were strong arguments that Wilkinson's constitutional rights were violated. The Court denied review. Wilkinson is on death row in North Carolina awaiting execution. Mary Ann Tally continues to represent him in the North Carolina courts, trying to save his life.

Phillip Wilkinson is not a sympathetic figure. But he should not be put to death without fair procedures and effective representation by counsel. In many ways, his story is reflective of the problems with the death penalty in this country. These problems are exacerbated by a series of decisions by the conservatives on the Supreme Court and a law enacted by the conservatives in Congress that make it much harder for individuals, even wrongly convicted ones, to gain relief from the federal courts.

There are serious problems with the criminal justice system that were evident in Wilkinson's case and that are especially evident in death penalty litigation like his. In 1994, about six months before he retired from the United States Supreme Court, Justice Harry Blackmun wrote: "Twenty years have passed since this Court declared that the death penalty must be administered fairly and with reasonable consistency or not at all, and despite the efforts of the States and courts to devise legal formulas and procedural rules to meet this daunting challenge, the death penalty remains fraught with arbitrariness, discrimination, caprice and mistake." He then said that no longer would he "tinker with the machinery of death"; he said that he would vote in every case capital case that a death sentence was cruel and unusual punishment.

Justice Blackmun's words received enormous national media attention, but they had no measurable effect on the Supreme Court for how it was handling death penalty cases. Despite Blackmun's eloquent pronouncement, the Supreme Court continued to deny review in almost all death penalty cases. When it granted review, it affirmed most of the death sentences. In 1976, the Supreme Court reversed itself and held that the death penalty was allowed. It is difficult to identify many cases over the next quarter of a century where the Court overturned death sentences or articulated rules that ensured fairness in proceedings for those on death row.

Lower courts clearly got this message. One of the most significant problems in death penalty cases, as it was in Wilkinson's case, is the lack of competent representation for those facing possible capital sentences. Justice Ruth Bader Ginsburg, in a speech, said that she has never seen a capital case without substantial evidence of lawyer incompetence.

A study that was done in Florida found that the single largest variable that would predict whether a capital defendant would be sentenced to death is whether that person had a privately retained counsel or a court-appointed lawyer. Another study in Georgia found that those who had court-appointed lawyers were 2.6 times more likely to be sentenced to death than those who had privately appointed lawyers.

A study done of 131 individuals who were executed in Texas during the governorship of George W. Bush found that forty-three had an attorney who had previously been disciplined by the Bar for misconduct. Moreover, forty of those who had been sentenced to death had a lawyer who presented no evidence on their behalf or only one witness.

Justice Thurgood Marshall lamented the frequency with which those on death row had been represented by lawyers who had no prior experience trying criminal cases or who were handling their first death penalty case. There are instances of defense lawyers in capital cases literally sleeping through the trial. In a famous case in Texas, *Burdine v. Johnson,* two of three judges on the United States Court of Appeals for the Fifth Circuit said it was not ineffective assistance of counsel when the defense lawyer slept through a good deal of the trial. The court said that it could not be shown that the lawyers slept through important parts of the trial. Thankfully, the entire Fifth Circuit reversed this decision, but five judges dissented and maintained that there was not a sufficient showing of ineffective assistance of counsel just because the lawyer had slept through much of the trial in a capital case.

One reason why so many court-appointed lawyers are incompetent is that the pay is so low that talented or even pretty good lawyers choose other work. Leading death penalty attorney Stephen Bright said that in Alabama a lawyer appointed to handle a capital case gets paid on average twenty dollars an hour. But that's better than Mississippi, where Bright says the average compensation, by his calculation, is $11.50 an hour. Moreover, there is no right to an attorney on habeas corpus, when a person convicted of a crime can go to federal court and argue that the conviction or sentence is unconstitutional.

This situation did not just happen. Here, too, the conservative vision of the Constitution has had a profound effect. In a 1984 decision, *Strickland v. Washington,* the Supreme Court made it very difficult for courts to find ineffective assistance of counsel, even when representation is very deficient, as it was for Phillip Wilkinson. Justice Sandra Day O'Connor, writing for the conservative majority, set a standard that means that only rarely will a conviction be overturned for inadequacy of representation. The Court said that a finding of ineffective assistance of counsel requires demonstrating first that the attorney's performance was so deficient "that counsel was not functioning as the 'counsel' guaranteed by the Sixth Amendment." But even gross deficiency by a defense counsel is not sufficient to overturn a conviction or a sentence for ineffective assistance of counsel. Second, the defendant must show prejudice; that is, the defendant has to demonstrate that the "counsel's deficient performance more likely than not altered the outcome in the case." In other words, relief for ineffective assistance of counsel requires that a convicted defendant show that the result of the trial likely would have been different if the attorney had acted competently.

This is usually an insurmountable burden. As in the Wilkinson case, it is so easy for later judges to say that they think that the judge or jury would have come to the same conclusion anyway. Justice Marshall explained exactly this problem in his dissent in *Strickland:* "[I]t is often very difficult to tell whether a defendant convicted after a trial in which he was ineffectively represented would have fared better if his lawyer had been competent. Seemingly impregnable cases can sometimes be dismantled by good defense counsel."

My former colleague, Yale law professor Dennis Curtis, said that under *Strickland* an attorney will be found to be adequate so long as a mirror put in front of him or her at trial would have shown a breath. Professor Curtis overstates, but not by much. I can identify only two cases in the twenty-five years since *Strickland* in which the Supreme Court has found ineffective assistance of counsel. The second of these, in 2005, was a 5–4 decision, with Justice O'Connor in the majority, reversing an opinion written by then federal court of appeals judge Samuel Alito.

The problem of finding ineffective assistance of counsel was made even more difficult by the Antiterrorism and Effective Death Penalty Act. The law, pushed through by the Republican majority that took control of the House and the Senate in 1994, dramatically altered the law of habeas corpus to make it much harder for those convicted of a crime to obtain relief from the federal courts, including for ineffective assistance of counsel.

"Habeas corpus" was derived from English law, where it was referred to as the "Great Writ." It allows a person convicted of a crime, in federal or state court, to come to federal court and argue that his or her constitutional rights were violated. One of the key changes in criminal law during the Warren Court era was to make it easier for federal courts to grant habeas corpus petitions. The Burger and the Rehnquist courts imposed substantial new hurdles on habeas petitioners, including overruling some of the Warren-era decisions. For example, during this latter time, the Supreme Court held that some constitutional violations, such as claims of illegal searches and arrests by the police, could not be raised on habeas corpus at all. The Court, in a direct reversal of Warren Court decisions, said that individuals could not raise issues on habeas corpus that had not been presented at trial. In a crucial 1989 case, the Court in a 5–4 decision, split along ideological lines, said that there is no right to counsel for habeas petitions. The vast majority are thus filed by prisoners on their own.

But the Antiterrorism and Effective Death Penalty Act, or AEDPA, went much further in limiting the availability of habeas corpus. It created a strict one-year statute of limitations for habeas petitions. Except under very rare circumstances, AEDPA restricts a person convicted of a crime to filing one habeas petition. These seemingly innocuous requirements are serious impediments to prisoners, acting without counsel, who often lack the sophistication to calculate the statute of limitations under a very complex set of rules determining when the clock starts and stops. Prisoners representing themselves often make mistakes in their petitions and need more than one chance to present their claims. This is virtually impossible under AEDPA. Most importantly, though, the 1996 act says that federal courts must give great deference to the conclusions of state courts; habeas corpus can be granted only if there was an "unreasonable application" of clearly established constitutional law as articulated by the Supreme Court.

In other words, it is not enough for a federal court to find a constitutional violation, such as ineffective assistance of counsel. It must conclude that the state court's decision to the contrary was "unreasonable." In Phillip Wilkinson's case, the United States Court of Appeals for the Fourth Circuit emphasized that this was why it was ruling against him. Although it acknowledged being disturbed by Wilkinson's lawyer's failings, it said that it could not find that the state court was unreasonable in rejecting the claim of ineffective assistance of counsel.

John Grisham, in his powerful nonfiction book *An Innocent*

Man, described the effect of this law and told the story of an innocent person who was wrongly convicted and almost put to death. Once a person is convicted in state court, the state court of appeals usually gives great deference to what occurred at trial. It is very difficult under *Strickland v. Washington* to convince a court of appeals that trial counsel was deficient, even when the lawyer's performance was grossly inadequate. The convicted individual then usually has to go to federal court on his or her own and file a habeas petition. There are enormous procedural obstacles to having the petition heard, but even when it is, AEDPA requires that the federal court give great deference to the state proceedings and applies a standard for ineffective assistance of counsel that makes relief highly unlikely.

This situation might be acceptable if there were reason to believe that the criminal justice system almost always got it right. But that is not the case. The work of Innocence Projects across the country has brought to public attention people who are wrongly convicted and then sentenced to death. In Illinois alone, the Innocence Projects were able to show that more than a dozen individuals were unquestionably wrongly convicted and then sentenced to death. As a result of these cases, the then governor of Illinois, Republican George Ryan, imposed a moratorium on the death penalty in that state and then before leaving office commuted the death sentences of all on death row in Illinois.

There is nothing uniquely bad about the procedural system or the courts in Illinois compared to any other state. The leading study on the execution of wrongly convicted individuals was done by Hugo Bedau and Michael Radelet. They found that between 1900 and 1991, 416 unquestionably innocent people were sentenced to death in the United States. They identified thirty of these cases where individuals were found to be innocent only hours or days before the scheduled execution. They have documented twenty-three of these cases where innocent people were executed by the state. For example, there has been compelling evidence that a man executed in Texas for killing his family by arson, Cameron Todd Willingham, was actually innocent;

experts have found that the fire was likely caused by an electrical problem. Recently, Frank Sterling became the 254th person in the country to be exonerated by DNA evidence.

The reality is that any human system will make mistakes, especially one with as many problems as the American criminal justice system. Sometimes innocent people are wrongly convicted because of police or prosecutorial misconduct. There are instances of police fabricating evidence and of prosecutors failing to meet their duty under *Brady v. Maryland* to turn over potentially exculpatory evidence. Sometimes faulty eyewitness identifications lead to the convictions of innocent people. Eyewitness identification is tremendously powerful in a courtroom when someone points to a defendant and says "He's the one." That has tremendous sway with the jury. But studies such as those by my colleague, psychology professor Elizabeth Loftus, show that eyewitness identifications are often flawed, especially when people are identifying those of other races. Sometimes the wrong person in the wrong place at the wrong time is convicted for a crime that he or she didn't commit. For whatever reason, there are innocent people on death row today and innocent individuals serving sentences for crimes that they did not commit.

Astoundingly, the conservatives on the Supreme Court have even gone so far as to say that the execution of an innocent person does not violate the Constitution. In *Herrera v. Collins,* Chief Justice William Rehnquist, writing for the conservative majority, said: "Claims of actual innocence based on newly discovered evidence have never been held to state a ground for federal habeas relief absent an independent constitutional violation occurring in the underlying state criminal proceeding." In other words, the chief justice said that convicting and even executing an innocent person does not itself violate the Constitution. He specifically said "a claim of 'actual innocence' is not itself a constitutional claim." Two of the justices who joined this opinion, O'Connor and Kennedy, wrote separately to say that they believed that execution of an innocent person would be unconstitutional.

But as recently as the summer of 2009, Justices Scalia and

Thomas dissented from the stay of a death sentence and declared: "This Court has *never* held that the Constitution forbids the execution of a convicted defendant who has had a full and fair trial but is later able to convince a habeas court that he is 'actually' innocent. Quite to the contrary, we have repeatedly left that question unresolved, while expressing considerable doubt that any claim based on alleged 'actual innocence' is constitutionally cognizable." Justices Scalia and Thomas are concerned about the effect of a large number of petitions from those on death row on the court system. They are willing to accept the risk of executing an innocent person to avoid these costs. But it seems unthinkable that justices on the Supreme Court could say that there is no constitutional violation in executing an innocent person.

The conservative majority of the Supreme Court also has made it impossible to challenge the racial bias that exists in the criminal justice system, including in the administration of the death penalty. Study after study has shown that whenever there is discretion in the criminal justice system, it is likely to be used to the detriment of individuals of color. A study done in Memphis, Tennessee, found that an African-American was ten times more likely to be shot by a police officer than a white individual in that city, eighteen times more likely to be wounded, and five times more likely to be killed by a police officer.

A study in Minnesota found that white criminal defendants with a past criminal record were much more likely to be released on bail than African-American criminal defendants without a prior criminal record.

A study of sentencing in the United States found that on average, an African-American defendant's sentence was 10 percent longer than a white defendant's sentence for the same crime, holding constant prior criminal records. The National Sentencing Commission found with regard to the federal courts that the average sentence for white defendants was 44.7 months and the average sentence for black defendants was 68.5 months.

In January 2010, the United States Court of Appeals for the

Ninth Circuit pointed to a study done in the state of Washington that found "African Americans in [the state] were over nine times more likely to be in prison than whites, even though the ratio of Black to White arrests for violent offenses was only 3.72:1." The court noted that a study found that "Native Americans were twice as likely to be searched as whites; African Americans were 70% more likely to be searched than whites; and Latinos were more than 50% more likely to be searched." The study found that charging and bail decisions "are infected with racial disparities"; whites are less likely to have charges filed against them, and minority defendants are less likely to be released "even after adjusting for differences among defendants in the severity of their crimes, prior criminal records, ties to the community, and the prosecuting attorney's recommendation."

In any aspect of the criminal justice system where there is discretion, racial minorities are at a significant disadvantage. And there is tremendous discretion with regard to the death penalty. Prosecutors have great discretion whether to seek the death penalty in a particular case. Juries have discretion whether to find aggravating factors that outweigh mitigating circumstances and thus recommend imposition of the death penalty. Judges have discretion whether to impose the death penalty. Not surprisingly, statistics show that at every phase, racism affects the capital sentencing system.

A study by David Baldus at the University of Iowa found that prosecutors sought the death penalty 70 percent of the time when there was a black defendant and a white victim, 15 percent of the time if there was a black defendant and a black victim, and 19 percent of the time if there was a white defendant and a black victim.

Baldus found, looking at the state of Georgia, that those who murdered whites were four times more likely to have a death sentence imposed than those who murdered blacks. In Alabama, the state's population is 24 percent African-American, but death row is 43 percent black.

A national study found that killers of whites were three times more likely across the country to have the death sentence imposed than those who killed African-Americans. In the state of Florida killers of whites were ten times more likely to have the death sentence imposed than killers of blacks.

A study of the federal death penalty found significant racial bias. In a thirty-year period beginning in the mid-1970s, the study documented that of a total of 312 defendants against whom the United States attorney general had authorized the government to request the death penalty, 78 were white, 54 Hispanic, 14 Asian/ Indian/Pacific Islander/Native American, 3 Arab, and 163 African-American. Seventy-five percent—233 of the 312—of the defendants approved for a capital prosecution by attorneys general to date were members of minority groups. Nineteen of the twenty-six defendants (73 percent) on federal death row under active death sentences are nonwhite, and all but one are black.

In light of the statistics proving racial bias in the administration of the death penalty, it was to be expected that the Supreme Court would be asked to find that there is a denial of equal protection if a defendant can show a statistical pattern so stark as to leave no other explanation than that the death penalty was administered in a racially discriminatory manner. However, in *McCleskey v. Kemp*, in 1987, the Supreme Court, 5–4, held that statistics are insufficient to prove race discrimination in death penalty sentencing. Justice Powell authored the opinion for the Court and was joined by Chief Justice Rehnquist and Justices White, O'Connor, and Scalia. Justices Brennan, Marshall, Blackmun, and Stevens dissented.

The defendant, Warren McCleskey, was an African-American sentenced to death for murder in Georgia. In his petition for a writ of habeas corpus, McCleskey argued that Georgia administered its capital sentencing process in a racially discriminatory manner and thus violated both the Eighth Amendment and the Equal Protection Clause of the Fourteenth Amendment. At the heart of his claim was the Baldus statistical study. The study examined more than two thousand homicide cases in Georgia and controlled for 230 nonracial factors. The results showed that a person accused of murdering a white individual was 4.3 times more likely to be sentenced to death than a person accused of murdering a black individual.

The Supreme Court rejected this claim and the use of statistical proof to demonstrate an equal protection violation in capital cases. The Court explained that there was no proof that the Georgia legislature had a racist purpose in adopting the laws authorizing capital punishment nor was there proof that the jury sentencing McCleskey used race as the basis for its sentencing decision. However, juries only issue a verdict, not an expression of reasons. The Court explained that the Baldus study at most proved a correlation between race and capital sentencing; the study did not prove causation—that race was actually the basis for the jury's decision. The Court emphasized that there are many checks against the manifestation of racism in capital cases, including limits on prosecutorial bias in charging decisions and aggressive questioning of prospective jurors about their racial sentiments during voir dire.

The Court concluded its opinion by expressing concern that if McCleskey's argument were accepted, the judiciary would be confronted with similar challenges to other penalties. The Court refused to open the courthouse doors to such challenges based on racially disproportionate impact in sentencing.

In other words, despite the clear statistical pattern and a study that controlled for every other variable, the Court still was unwilling to find that the data proved racial discrimination in capital decision making. Subsequently, after Justice Thurgood Marshall's death, his papers were made publicly available by the Library of Congress, and within them was a memorandum from Justice Scalia to the other justices in the McCleskey case. The memo is only a paragraph long and worth quoting in its entirety. Dated January 6, 1987, it states:

Re: No. 84—6811—McCleskey v. Kemp

MEMORANDUM TO THE CONFERENCE: I plan to join Lewis's opinion in this case, with two reservations. I disagree with the argument that the inferences that can be drawn from the Baldus

*study are weakened by the fact that each jury and each trial is
unique, or by the large number of variables at issue. And I do not
share the view, implicit in the opinion, that an effect of racial factors
upon sentencing, if it could only be shown by sufficiently strong
statistical evidence, would require reversal. Since it is my view that
unconscious operation of irrational sympathies and antipathies,
including racial, upon jury decisions and (hence) prosecutorial
decisions is real, acknowledged in the decisions of this court, and
ineradicable, I cannot honestly say that all I need is more proof.*

The memorandum was signed, in hand, "Nino," the justice's nick-name.

The implications of this memorandum are enormous. Justice Scalia recognized that unconscious racism infects the capital sentencing process. But he nonetheless concluded that there is no denial of equal protection even though statistics prove racism and even though he believes that the process is inherently racist. Justice Scalia stated that, no matter what the statistical proof, he would not find a denial of equal protection.

After *McCleskey*, statistical proof of racially disparate impact is not enough even to shift the burden of proof to the prosecutor to offer a non-race-based explanation. A defendant could challenge a death sentence as a denial of equal protection only if there was specific evidence that the jury in his or her case consciously used race as a basis for its decision making. Because juries don't explain the basis for their decisions and because racism is often uncon-scious, or at least not openly expressed, such proof will rarely be available.

In fact, cases since *McCleskey* indicate that death sentences are upheld even when there is other evidence of racism. In one Florida case, the trial judge on the record referred to the parents of the black defendant in a capital case as "niggers." The Florida Supreme Court upheld the death sentence and rejected the argu-ment that there was sufficient proof of impermissible bias by the trial court.

In a Georgia case that involved a black man sentenced to death for killing a white victim, the trial judge referred to the defendant, a grown man, as a "colored boy." Additionally, after the trial, two of the jurors admitted that during deliberations they used the slur "nigger," and two jurors said that they found blacks to be scarier than whites. Nonetheless, the federal court rejected a habeas corpus petition and found the death sentence to be constitutional.

The approach of the conservative justices on the Supreme Court reflects the conservative approach to the criminal justice system that began with Richard Nixon's campaign for the presidency. Most today think of the phrase "law and order" as the title of a successful series of long-running television programs. But it actually was a slogan used repeatedly by Richard Nixon and Spiro Agnew in their campaign in 1968. A central theme of their message was the need to be tougher on criminals and to change the Supreme Court so that its attitude toward the criminal justice system would be far more pro–law enforcement.

For example, in his speech accepting the Republican presidential nomination on August 8, 1968, Richard Nixon declared: "And tonight it's time for some honest talk about the problem of order in the United States. Let us always respect, as I do, our courts and those who serve on them, but let us also recognize that some of our courts in their decisions have gone too far in weakening the peace forces as against the criminal forces in this country." Many perceived Nixon's appeal for "law and order" as being calculated to appeal to southern voters and to keep them from defecting to third-party candidate George Wallace.

A constant message of Nixon's campaign was its attack on the Warren Court. This fit with the campaign's "southern strategy," appealing to southern voters who had generally voted Democratic since the Civil War. The Warren Court was terribly unpopular with many whites in the South because of its decisions ordering desegregation and banning school prayer. Nixon repeatedly said that he would appoint "strict constructionist" judges, which included those who would take a very different approach to criminal defendants as compared with that of the Warren Court.

Nixon's southern strategy succeeded and he made good on

his promise in the four justices he appointed from 1969 to 1971. In fact, the most immediate effect of the four Nixon appointees to the Supreme Court in those years was in the area of criminal procedure. The Supreme Court quickly created exceptions to *Miranda v. Arizona*, the ruling that requires that suspects in police custody be given warnings of their right to remain silent and of their right to an attorney during questioning. In 1971, in *Harris v. New York*, with the Nixon appointees in the majority, the Court said that statements gained in violation of *Miranda* could still be used at trial to impeach a witness's testimony. This was an important erosion of *Miranda* because it gave police a crucial incentive to violate its dictates knowing that the results of the illegal questioning could be used at trial.

Similarly, in a series of decisions in the 1970s, with the Court split along ideological lines, the conservative justices made it much easier to find that a suspect had waived his or her Miranda warnings. The result again was to allow statements to be used at trial even when police violated the law.

Ronald Reagan continued the Nixon attacks on "judicial activism" and the appeal for fewer protections for criminal defendants. In the words of his attorney general, William French Smith, Reagan aspired to nothing less than readjusting the "balance between the forces of law and the forces of lawlessness." President Reagan's efforts had very significant long-term effects on the American criminal justice system.

In a weekly radio address on September 11, 1982, President Reagan addressed the issue of crime and put the blame for the nation's problems squarely on the Supreme Court. He said that "an important part of the problem is that Americans are losing faith in our courts and our entire legal system. Nine out of 10 Americans believe that the courts in their home areas aren't tough enough on criminals. Another 8 out of 10 Americans believe that our criminal justice system does not deter crime. And these figures have gone up drastically in the last 10 or 15 years." In the speech, he specifically proposed modifying the exclusionary rule, the principle that evidence gained as a result of an illegal search or arrest must be suppressed and cannot be used by prosecutors. He explained: "Now, this is the rule that can force a judge to throw out of court on the basis of a small technicality an entire case, no matter how guilty the defendant or how heinous the crime. Our bill would stop this grievous miscarriage of justice by allowing evidence to be introduced where the police officer was acting in good faith."

Reagan proposed legislation known as the Comprehensive Crime Control Act, many of the provisions of which were adopted, continue to this day, and substantially changed the nature of the criminal justice system. For example, the Bail Reform Act, adopted in 1984, allows incarceration of suspects before trial if they are found dangerous. Previously, courts would generally deny bail only to those who were genuine flight risks or clearly posed a danger to the community. The Bail Reform Act greatly expanded pretrial detention and for the first time created substantial preventative detention. Obviously, it is good to get dangerous people off the streets, but this law allowed courts to incarcerate individuals who had never been convicted of any crime, based on a guess about future dangerousness. Often individuals such as low-level drug dealers are detained, sometimes as much as a year before trial. As the statistics presented above indicate, defendants of color are much more likely to be detained before trial than white defendants.

In the same legislative package, Reagan successfully gained passage of twenty-three other "anti-crime" bills. One of the longest-lasting effects of these laws has been a substantial increase in the length of sentences for federal crimes. Mandatory minimum sentences for gun crimes were created in 1984 and then for drug crimes in 1986. In 1984, the Sentencing Reform Act created the Federal Sentencing Guidelines, which greatly reduced the discretion of federal judges and, as implemented, substantially increased the penalties for federal crimes.

The effect of the stricter sentences at the federal level, and their being copied at the state level, has been huge in terms of the number of individuals incarcerated. In 2003, the number of people in United States jails and prisons exceeded two million for the first time, rising to 2,019,234. The problem is particularly acute for racial minorities. An estimated 12 percent of African-American men ages twenty to thirty-four are in jail or prison. By contrast, 1.6 percent of white men in the same age group are incarcerated. There are over one million African-American prisoners, constituting about half the prison population, yet African-Americans constitute only about 12 percent of the country's population. One-third of African-American men in their twenties are in some form of government custody, whether in prison, on probation, on parole, or under some other type of court-ordered supervision.

Nationally, five times more prisoners are incarcerated today than just a few decades ago. "Between 1991 and 1999, the number of children with a parent in a federal or state correctional facility increased by more than 100%, from approximately 900,000 to 2,000,000." The nation's incarceration rate is among the world's highest, and five to ten times higher than the rates in other industrialized nations.

Obviously, everyone in society wants to be protected from crime. But Presidents Nixon and Reagan and the conservative justices on the Court err in thinking that effective crimefighting requires the elimination of constitutional rights of criminal defendants and long sentences for even minor crimes. Evidence does not show that these have the slightest effect in making society safer or decreasing crime. There is a temptation to think of criminal procedure protections as just safeguarding guilty criminals. In reality, they protect everyone from the possibility of police misconduct and prosecutorial overreaching.

One place where this loss of safeguards is evident and where the conservative agenda on the criminal justice system has been very successful has been in decreasing the protections of the Fourth Amendment. The Fourth Amendment is an essential assurance of privacy for all in society. It generally requires that for the police to search or arrest a person there must be "probable cause"—reason to believe that the person has committed a crime. A weakening of Fourth Amendment protections lessens an important restraint on the police abuse and a crucial protection for everyone's privacy. Yet, in many ways, the conservative justices on the Court have carried out the Nixon and Reagan philosophy and lessened the safeguards of the Fourth Amendment.

At 7 A.M. on February 3, 1998, a SWAT team and other officers burst into the home in Los Angeles where Iris Mena was asleep in her bed. The SWAT team, clad in helmets and black vests adorned with badges and the word POLICE, entered her bedroom and placed her in handcuffs at gunpoint. Mena was not suspected of anything and was not the target of the search. The police were looking for Raymond Romero, a suspected participant in a drive-by shooting, and had warrants to search two places where he was known to stay. One of them was where Mena lived.

The police took Mena, a young woman in her early twenties, into a converted garage. She was dressed only in a thin nightgown and was not allowed to put on any additional clothes despite the cold temperature. Mena remained locked in handcuffs. Because this was an area known for having undocumented immigrants, an INS officer accompanied the police executing the warrant. During their detention in the garage, the INS officer questioned Mena about her immigration status. She ultimately produced papers showing that she is a permanent resident lawfully in the United States.

Mena spent almost two hours in handcuffs, even though she had done nothing wrong. The police found Romero, the target of their search, at his mother's house in a search done at the same time as the one of Mena's residence. Ironically, Romero was briefly questioned and released while Mena remained in handcuffs.

Mena sued claiming that the police violated her Fourth Amendment rights to be protected from unreasonable searches and seizures. A jury found in her favor and the federal court of appeals rejected the defendants' appeal.

Although I did not argue Mena's case in the Supreme Court, I worked on the brief and sat at counsel table as Paul Hoffman argued for Mena in December 2004. I thought that the argument had gone very well for our side and was confident about the results. In late April 2005, I was arguing another case in the Supreme Court. Before oral arguments in the Court, the lawyers for all of the cases to be heard that day meet with the clerk of the Court, William Suter. Among other things, he tells them what will happen before arguments begin. That day, Suter said that the Court would be announcing three cases before hearing oral arguments. I turned to my co-counsel and said that it would be great if they announced that we had won Mena's case.

The third decision to be announced that morning was *Muehler v. Mena.* The Court ruled against Mena, reversing the lower court decision and the jury verdict. The five conservative justices said that when the police search a home, they may restrain all of the occupants of the home even when there is no basis for believing that they did anything wrong or that they pose any threat to the police. For the Court, detaining Iris Mena in handcuffs, in her nightgown, for just being in the house posed no problem. As soon as Chief Justice Rehnquist completed announcing that we had lost, I immediately had to approach the podium to argue my case, which involved a First Amendment issue. I had to quickly put aside my disappointment at the results in *Mena.* But the loss in *Mena* continues to bother me. The Supreme Court long has said that the Fourth Amendment has its greatest force in protecting people in their homes. Yet the Court ruled that people can be detained in handcuffs for hours in their homes even when the police have no reason to believe that they have done anything wrong.

As the *Mena* case reflects, one of the areas where the Burger, Rehnquist, and Roberts courts have been most pro–law enforcement has been with regard to the Fourth Amendment. This has been manifest in countless decisions. The Supreme Court has held, for example, that Fourth Amendment claims of illegal searches and seizures cannot be raised on habeas corpus. Even though a federal statute expressly provides that all constitutional violations may be presented in federal court on habeas corpus by a person convicted in state court, the Supreme Court held that this does not apply to those who claim that the evidence against them was obtained or that they were arrested in violation of the

Constitution. Thus a person convicted in state court who claims that his or her Fourth Amendment rights have been violated may seek Supreme Court review, which is highly unlikely, but never may go to federal court with a habeas corpus petition raising the issue.

The Court has made it far easier for the police to stop and frisk individuals. Very little is needed to provide the reasonable suspicion needed to justify such actions. In one case, the Court found, 5–4 with the conservatives in the majority, that an individual seeing police officers and then turning to walk in the opposite direction was enough to provide reasonable suspicion for a stop. In many neighborhoods, people distrust the police and attempt to avoid them. Such behavior hardly seems to be enough to justify a stop. In another case, again 5–4 and split along ideological lines, the Court held that refusal to disclose one's identity to the police was enough to justify arresting a person.

Quite troubling, the Supreme Court has held that the police can stop and search a person even if they are doing so entirely on a pretextual ground. The case was *Whren v. United States*. Undercover police officers were driving in what they referred to as a "high drug area." The officers became suspicious of a truck when it remained at a stop sign for an unusually long time, "more than twenty seconds." I have a terrible sense of direction and often remain at stop signs more than twenty seconds to look at a map, or now my GPS. The officers decided to follow the truck and saw it make a right turn without a signal. The officers pulled over the vehicle, even though District of Columbia law was clear that undercover officers are not allowed to enforce traffic laws.

Nonetheless, the Supreme Court, in an opinion by Justice Scalia, ruled in favor of the police. The Court said that so long as police have reason to believe a crime was committed, in this instance turning without a signal, the police may stop a vehicle. Once a car is stopped, a variety of doctrines give police authority to conduct a search. The fact that the stop was entirely pretextual—the police were using the traffic violation as a pretext for a search for drugs—did not matter. Of course, if any car is followed long enough, a driver will change lanes or turn without a signal, or not stop quite long enough at the stop sign, or stop "too long" at a stop sign, or go slightly over the speed limit.

Overall, the Supreme Court ruled in favor of the police in about 90 percent of all the Fourth Amendment cases during the last decade. But the greatest success of conservatives in changing the law is in the substantial erosion of the exclusionary rule as a remedy for Fourth Amendment violations. This is exactly the change that President Reagan urged and now the justices he appointed and the lawyers from his administration who are on the Court are making that change happen.

In 1914, in *Weeks v. United States*, the Supreme Court held that if federal officers violate the Fourth Amendment, the fruits of the illegal arrest or search must be suppressed in court. The Court expressed concern that courts would be tainted if convictions were obtained on the basis of illegally obtained evidence. Judges should not be putting people in prison based on illegally obtained evidence. Over time, the Court also has emphasized that the exclusionary rule is essential to deter police violations of the Fourth Amendment. Police are much less likely to engage in an illegal search or arrest if they know that the evidence they obtain will be suppressed and excluded from use at trial. In 1961, in the landmark case of *Mapp v. Ohio*, the Supreme Court held that the exclusionary rule applied to the actions of state and local police officers as well.

Overall, the exclusionary rule has worked well, at the federal level for almost a century and against state and local police officers for almost a half century. Police are instructed about the Fourth Amendment in their academies and training manuals and work hard to comply with the requirements articulated by the Supreme Court. Nonetheless, the exclusionary rule long has been opposed by conservatives. Their understandable concern—and it is the one that President Reagan expressed—is that it can lead to guilty people going free if evidence is suppressed.

However, study after study shows that rarely does this outcome occur. One comprehensive study found that the exclusionary rule resulted in a "loss" for the prosecution, either a dropping of charges or a nonconviction, in between 0.6 percent and 2.35 percent of felony arrests. A study by the General Accounting Office of cases in federal court found that in only 1.3 percent of the cases was evidence excluded as a result of the exclusionary rule and in only 0.4 percent of cases declined for prosecution was this decision made because of the exclusionary rule.

Moreover, when evidence is suppressed because of the exclusionary rule it is almost always in drug cases and not crimes like murder, rape, or assault. One study found that "illegal search problems were given as the reason for the rejection of only 117 of more than 68,000 robbery arrests, only thirteen of more than 14,000 forcible rape arrests, and only eight of approximately 12,000 homicide arrests." Another study found that "[f]ewer than 1% of Chicago defendants accused of violent crimes have their cases thrown out because the evidence was illegally obtained." Boston University law professor Tracey Maclin observed that "the exclusionary rule has not been responsible for the release of dangerous criminals who prey on society," but that instead the "rule's greatest impact is felt in drug and weapons possession cases."

The exclusionary rule rarely leads to guilty people going free because the police know the rules for searches and arrests and try hard to conform to them. In the last few years, though, the conservatives on the Supreme Court have substantially eroded the exclusionary rule as a remedy for illegal police conduct. The Court initially signaled this change in 2006 in *Hudson v. Michigan*. For many years, the Court has held that the police usually must knock and announce their presence before entering a residence. *Hudson* involved a situation where all of the justices, and all of the judges in the lower courts, agreed that police violated this requirement. The question was whether the evidence gained had to be suppressed.

The Supreme Court ruled 5–4 that the exclusionary rule does not apply when police violate the Fourth Amendment's requirement for "knock and announce." Justice Scalia's opinion called into question the very existence of the exclusionary rule. He referred to it as a "last resort" and stressed the great costs of the exclusionary rule in terms of suppressing important evidence and potentially allowing dangerous people to go free. He argued that the exclusionary rule is unnecessary because of the availability of civil suits against the police and the increased professionalization of police forces. Justice Scalia's arguments did not address an exception to the Fourth Amendment in knock-and-announce cases; they were the arguments that conservatives have made for decades against the existence of the exclusionary rule.

After *Hudson*, there is no reason for police ever to meet the Fourth Amendment's requirements for knocking and announcing before entering a dwelling. Police know that there will be no consequences to violating this rule. Justice Scalia mentioned the possibility of civil suits against police officers as an alternative to suppressing the evidence. Such suits, though, rarely will be brought and rarely succeed. It is difficult for individuals to obtain attorneys willing to bring such cases because there is little chance of recovering enough damages to make it worthwhile to sue. Juries are far more likely to be sympathetic to police officers, especially when their actions succeeded in gaining evidence of illegal activities. Moreover, the Supreme Court has made it almost impossible to sue cities for such violations and has made it difficult to sue police officers by providing them immunity to many suits for civil rights violations. Cities can be sued only if it can be proven that their own policy caused the constitutional violation and officers are liable only if they violate clearly established law that the reasonable officer should know. Countless suits against cities and officers are dismissed on these grounds.

In 2000, after the Rampart scandal was exposed in the Los Angeles Police Department, I was asked by the Police Protective League, the officers' union, to do a study of the department. The Rampart scandal involved members of an anti-gang "crash unit" engaging in egregious violations of the law, including planting evidence to frame innocent individuals and lying in court to gain convictions. As part of preparing my report, I interviewed dozens of police officers. I was impressed in many ways, including with their sophisticated knowledge of the law. After *Hudson*, I have little doubt that many officers will ignore the requirements for knocking and announcing because they know that there will not be any adverse effects for their unconstitutional actions.

In a separate opinion, Justice Kennedy said that "the continued operation of the exclusionary rule . . . is not in doubt." But *Hudson* made clear that there are now four votes—Scalia, Roberts, Thomas, and Alito—to eliminate the exclusionary rule in Fourth Amendment cases and that it will continue to exist, or exceptions to it will be created, to the extent that Justice Kennedy wants.

This situation was evident in 2009 when the Supreme Court significantly changed the law of the exclusionary rule, again in a 5–4 decision with the most conservative justices in the majority. The case, *Herring v. United States*, is the most important change in the exclusionary rule since *Mapp v. Ohio* applied it to the states in 1961.

Police in Coffee County, Florida, learned that Bennie Dean Herring had driven there to pick up an impounded truck. The officer knew Herring and decided to check to see if there were any outstanding warrants for him from other counties. The officer, Mack Anderson, found an outstanding warrant from Dale County and arrested Herring based on it. Herring was searched incident to his arrest and methamphetamines were found in his pocket. It turns out, though, that the warrant had been lifted by the other county five months earlier; its computer system had just not been updated. Thus the arrest and the resulting search were illegal. The issue was whether the exclusionary rule applies when police commit an illegal search based on good-faith reliance on erroneous information from another jurisdiction.

Chief Justice Roberts, writing for a 5–4 majority, held that the exclusionary rule does not apply. The Court once more said that the exclusionary rule is the "last resort" and is to be used only where its application will have significant additional deterrent effect on police misconduct. The Court ruled that the exclusionary rule may be used only if there is an intentional or reckless violation of the Fourth Amendment or only if there are systemic police department violations with regard to searches and seizures. For the first time in history, the Court concluded that the exclusionary rule does not apply if the Fourth Amendment is violated by good-faith or even negligent police actions.

The Court could have come to the same result in favor of the police in a far narrower, more mimimalist holding. In an earlier case, *Arizona v. Evans*, the Court held that the exclusionary rule does not apply if police rely in good faith on erroneous information about a warrant from a court. The Court could have simply ruled that the same exception applies when the police rely on erroneous information about a warrant from another jurisdiction. Instead the Court issued a sweeping rule that the exclusionary rule never applies if the police violate the Fourth Amendment in good faith or through negligence.

Exempting all negligent violations of the Fourth Amendment from the exclusionary rule is, in itself, a very significant undermining of this protection. The reality is that many police violations of the Fourth Amendment are the result of negligence and not "systematic error or reckless disregard of constitutional rights."

Chief Justice Roberts went even further and said that the exclusionary rule applies only where the value in deterring police misconduct outweighs the costs of releasing a potentially guilty person. He concluded that "[t]o trigger the exclusionary rule, police conduct must be sufficiently deliberate that exclusion can meaningfully deter it, and sufficiently culpable that such deterrence is worth the price paid by the justice system."

In other words, the Court has created a major new exception to the exclusionary rule. Instead of it being presumptively applicable for almost all Fourth Amendment violations, the law now is that the exclusionary rule will apply only if it would deter the specific police misconduct at issue and only if, on balance, the deterrence gained outweighs the costs of possibly guilty people going free.

There are significant problems with this erosion of the exclusionary rule. As Justice Ginsburg noted in her dissent, "[t]he exclusionary rule, it bears emphasis, is often the only remedy effective to redress a Fourth Amendment violation." Rarely will a victim of a

Fourth Amendment violation, such as the one in *Herring,* be able to successfully sue the officers for money damages.

Without the exclusionary rule, there is nothing to deter police misconduct. In the context of *Herring,* without the exclusionary rule there would be no reason at all for police to check to make sure that the warrant for Herring is valid. Police are very savvy about this and they will quickly learn when they can violate the Fourth Amendment with impunity and no real consequences.

Moreover, Chief Justice Roberts's opinion errs in focusing on the exclusionary rule solely in terms of police deterrence. As Justice Ginsburg explains in her dissenting opinion, "But the rule also serves other important purposes: It 'enabl[es] the judiciary to avoid the taint of partnership in official lawlessness,' and it 'assur[es] the people—all potential victims of unlawful government conduct—that the government would not profit from its lawless behavior, thus minimizing the risk of seriously undermining popular trust in government.'"

To be sure, *Herring v. United States* does not eliminate the exclusionary rule. But it does erode it and it makes clear that there is a majority on the Court that wants to go very far in limiting it. Conservatives always have vocally opposed it and now they have a majority on the Supreme Court that will significantly undermine it. *Herring* is an unfortunate significant step in that direction.

Why does this matter? Our privacy, not just that of people who may have committed crimes, is protected by the Fourth Amendment, which limits when the police can engage in searches or arrests. Without the Fourth Amendment, there is nothing to keep the police from stopping and searching any person, or searching anyone's home, anytime they want. This surely would mean more effective law enforcement, but at a huge cost in terms of privacy. The primary incentive for the police to comply with the Fourth Amendment is their knowledge that violations will be counterproductive because illegally obtained evidence will be suppressed. The Roberts Court's dramatic erosion of the exclusionary rule in its first few years thus puts the privacy of all of us and our rights in jeopardy.

One of the areas where conservatives have been most success-ful in changing constitutional law has been in eroding protections for criminal procedure. The Warren Court's concerns for enforcing these constitutional safeguards have been abandoned. The views of Richard Nixon and Ronald Reagan have triumphed largely through the justices whom they put on the bench.

Phillip Wilkinson likely will be executed by the state of North Carolina despite serious constitutional violations and grossly in-adequate counsel. Countless others, including innocent individu-als, remain incarcerated and even face death despite egregious misconduct by police and prosecutors. This is because over the last forty years, in a series of decisions by the conservative major-ity on the Supreme Court and in a series of federal laws favored by conservatives, constitutional protections in the criminal justice system have been significantly lessened.

5.

The Erosion of Individual Liberties

Seventeen years ago, in the spring of 1993, my father was dying of terminal lung cancer. Near the end of his life, he was in the hospital, far too weak to get out of bed or even to shave. Except when sedated, he was fully conscious and completely rational. He understood that he was in the last days of his life and that he would never get out of that hospital bed.

I stood next to him as he asked a doctor to administer drugs to end his life. He cogently explained to the doctor that either he was awake and in great pain or he was drugged into unconsciousness. He told the doctor that it was his time to go and there was no point in prolonging his life a few more days. No one in my family objected to his choice.

The doctor brusquely said, "I can't do that," and quickly changed the subject. My father, though, was persistent and again asked the doctor to give him enough morphine to stop his breathing and end his suffering. The doctor said that the law did not allow that and that he would not discuss it further. The doctor then abruptly left the hospital room.

My father died four days after making that request. I will never understand what interest the state of Indiana, where he was hospitalized, had in keeping him alive for those few additional days. He was awake for ever shorter intervals and while awake he complained of great pain. The tumor had blocked blood circulation to his arm and the arm was grotesquely swollen. The doctor had suggesting amputating the arm, but my dad did not see any point in having an amputation since he was about to die. He told the doctor that at that stage it did not matter to him whether he died of gangrene spreading from the dead tissue in his arm or from the lung cancer.

I cannot approach the topic of assisted death without confronting the vivid image of my father pleading with a doctor to help end his suffering. Of all the topics of constitutional law, the issue of physician-assisted death is the hardest for me to teach. The prohibition of physician-assisted death affects those like my father who are not on life support and are physically too weak to commit suicide. Those on artificial life support can order it ended; the law is clear that competent adults have the right to refuse medical care, even lifesaving medical care. Those with the physical ability to do so can commit suicide, albeit with far greater trauma to their family and loved ones than ending life support. But a person like my father was left with no alternatives. Thankfully, he lingered for only a few days after his request; but there are many terminally ill patients who suffer for months because of the lack of a right to death with dignity.

Ironically, something so deeply personal came down to a matter of constitutional law. I strongly believe that my father, and others like him facing terminal illnesses, should have the right to assisted death. For decades the Supreme Court has recognized a right to privacy, and if privacy means anything, it should be the ability of competent terminally ill adults to make this fundamental choice.

Three years after my father died, the United States Court of Appeals for the Ninth Circuit found that the right to privacy included a right to physician-assisted death. In a lengthy and carefully reasoned opinion, the court, in a 7–4 decision, ruled in favor of terminally ill patients in the state of Washington who were challenging the law prohibiting aiding or abetting a suicide. Almost simultaneously, the United States Court of Appeals for the Second Circuit found that a similar New York law prohibiting aiding or abetting a suicide violated equal protection because those on artificial life support could end their lives by having it stopped while those not on life support could not have the same death with dignity.

A year later, in 1997, the Supreme Court reversed both of these decisions and emphatically rejected any constitutional right to physician-assisted death. The majority opinion in each of these cases was written by Chief Justice Rehnquist and joined by Justices O'Connor, Scalia, Kennedy, and Thomas. Justices Stevens, Souter, Ginsburg, and Breyer agreed to uphold the Washington law, but they would have left open the possibility that there would be instances where such a right to assisted death would exist.

How did the Court come to hold that there was no constitutional right to assisted death despite decades of decisions protecting a right to privacy? The answer reveals something often overlooked about constitutional law under the conservative Burger, Rehnquist, and Roberts courts: since *Roe v. Wade* was decided in 1973, the Supreme Court has rarely recognized new constitutional rights or extended existing rights; in fact, it often has significantly cut back on important civil liberties. The refusal to recognize a right to physician-assisted death as part of the right to privacy is an example. In fact, the major areas where the Court has been willing to recognize new rights in recent years are those that advance conservative ideology: a Second Amendment right of individuals to own firearms and a First Amendment right for corporations, labor unions, and others to spend unlimited amounts of money in election campaigns.

The story of individual rights over the last several decades must begin with *Roe v. Wade*, which held that a woman has the constitutional right to choose whether to terminate her pregnancy before the fetus is viable and capable of surviving outside the womb. Few Supreme Court cases in history have so defined the political landscape or shaped thinking about constitutional law. Conservatives have argued since *Roe* was decided in 1973 that it was an illegitimate decision. Their attack on *Roe* has led them to a jurisprudence that prevents the recognition of new rights and leads to the curtailment of existing ones.

Was *Roe* illegitimate as conservatives contend? The answer to this question goes a long way to defining the proper role of the courts with regard to individual liberties. The Court in *Roe* faced three questions. First, is there a right to privacy protected by the Constitution even though privacy is not mentioned in the document's text? Second, if so, is the right infringed by a prohibition of abortion? Third, if so, does the state have a sufficient justification for upholding laws prohibiting abortion?

The first question, is there a right to privacy protected by the Constitution, is the place where opponents of *Roe* have focused their attack, arguing that there is no such right because it is not mentioned in the Constitution and was not intended by its drafters. The most famous critique of the decision was written by then Harvard professor John Hart Ely, who declared, "It is, nevertheless, a very bad decision. . . . It is bad because it is bad constitutional law, or rather because it is not constitutional law and gives almost no sense of an obligation to try to be." Ely's objection was that abortion and privacy are not mentioned in the Constitution and therefore no such rights exist. This is the criticism that conservatives have launched at *Roe* since it was decided.

The problem with this argument is that it fails to acknowledge that it urges a radical change in constitutional law. Since early in the twentieth century, the Court has interpreted the word *liberty,* which is expressly protected from interference by the federal government by the Fifth Amendment and from interference by state and local governments by the Fourteenth Amendment, to include important aspects of personal autonomy.

Before *Roe,* the Court had recognized a right to privacy, including over matters of reproduction, even though privacy is not mentioned right in the text of the Constitution. In *Griswold v. Connecticut,* in 1965, the Court declared unconstitutional as violating the right to privacy a state law prohibiting the sale, distribution, or use of contraceptives. In *Eisenstadt v. Baird,* in 1972, the Court invalidated a state law preventing unmarried individuals access to contraceptives and declared, "If the right of privacy means anything, it is the right of the individual, married or single, to be free from unwarranted governmental intrusion into matters so fundamentally affecting a person as the decision whether to bear or beget a child."

In fact, long before these decisions, the Court safeguarded many aspects of liberty and autonomy as fundamental rights even though they are not mentioned in the text of the Constitution and were never contemplated by its drafters. In the 1920s, the Supreme Court held that parents have a fundamental right to control the upbringing of their children and used this right to strike down laws prohibiting the teaching of the German language and forbidding parochial school education. In the 1940s, the Court ruled that the right to procreate is a fundamental right and declared unconstitutional an Oklahoma law that required the sterilization of those convicted three times of crimes involving moral turpitude. In the 1960s, the Court proclaimed that there is a fundamental right to marry and invalidated a Virginia law prohibiting interracial marriage.

Unless the Court intended to overrule all of these decisions, it was clear at the time of *Roe* that the Constitution had long been interpreted as protecting basic aspects of personal autonomy as fundamental rights even though the rights to marry, procreate, and raise children are not mentioned in the text of the document. Put another way, the Court never has adopted the position of justices like Scalia and Thomas, who insist that the Constitution is limited to those rights explicitly stated or originally intended at the time of its ratification. In fact, rejecting privacy as a right because it is not in the text of the Constitution would mean repudiating other rights not mentioned that have long been safeguarded, such as freedom of association.

Of course, opponents of *Roe* could argue that all of these decisions were wrong and that there should be no protection of privacy or other rights not explicitly mentioned in the Constitution. But this would be a dramatic change in the law. Professor Cass Sunstein has explained: "[The rejection of privacy rights] is a fully plausible reading of the Constitution. But it would wreak havoc with established law. It would eliminate constitutional protections where the nation has come to rely on them—by, for example, allowing states to ban use of contraceptives by married couples."

The second question before the Court in *Roe* was whether laws that prohibit abortion infringe a woman's right to privacy.

Interestingly, no one, not even the staunchest opponents of abortion rights, disputes this. Opponents of *Roe* argue against there being a right to privacy and/or claim that the state has a sufficiently important interest in prohibiting abortion. But understandably, there is no disagreement that a prohibition of abortion interferes with a woman's autonomy.

Obviously, forbidding abortions interferes with a woman's ability to control her reproductive autonomy and to decide for herself, in the words of *Eisenstadt v. Baird*, whether to "bear or beget a child." Also, no one can deny that forcing a woman to continue a pregnancy against her will is an enormous intrusion on her control over her body. Justice Blackmun expressed this position forcefully in his majority opinion in *Roe:* "The detriment that the State would impose upon the pregnant woman by denying this choice altogether is apparent. Specific and direct harm medically diagnosable even in early pregnancy may be involved. Maternity, or additional offspring, may force upon the woman a distressful life and future. Psychological harm may be imminent. Mental and physical health may be taxed by child care. There is also the distress, for all concerned, associated with the unwanted child, and there is the problem of bringing a child into a family already unable, psychologically and otherwise, to care for it."

The third question before the Supreme Court in *Roe* was whether states have a compelling interest in protecting fetal life. Once it was decided that there is a fundamental right to privacy and that laws prohibiting abortion infringe it, then the question is whether laws prohibiting abortions are needed to achieve a compelling government interest. This is the test the government must meet whenever it burdens or infringes a fundamental right. The key issue at this stage in the analysis was whether the government has a compelling interest in protecting the fetus from the moment of conception.

The Court ruled against Texas, where *Roe v. Wade* originated, and concluded that the state has a compelling interest in prohibiting abortion only at the point of viability, the time when the fetus can survive outside the womb. Justice Blackmun, writing for the majority, stated: "With respect to the State's important and legitimate interest in potential life, the 'compelling' point is at viability. This is so because the fetus then presumably has the capability of meaningful life outside the mother's womb."

But as many commentators noted, this begs the question of why viability is deemed the point at which the state has a sufficient interest to prohibit abortion. In fact, the choice of viability as the point where there is a compelling government interest seems at odds with Justice Blackmun's earlier declaration: "We need not resolve the difficult question of when life begins. When those trained in the respective disciplines of medicine, philosophy, and theology are unable to arrive at any consensus, the judiciary, at this point in the development of man's knowledge, is not in a position to speculate as to the answer."

Ultimately, the question before the Court was who should decide whether the fetus before viability is a human person: each woman for herself or the state legislature. Harvard law professor Laurence Tribe, in an article written soon after *Roe*, put this well: "The Court was not, after all, choosing simply between the alternatives of abortion and continued pregnancy. It was instead choosing among alternative allocations of decisionmaking authority, for the issue it faced was whether the woman and her doctor, rather than an agency of government, should have the authority to make the abortion decision at various stages of pregnancy."

Why leave the choice about abortion to the woman rather than to the state? There was then, and is now, no consensus as to when human life begins. Some regard the fetus as an unborn child, but others see the fetus as a part of a woman's body at least until it can survive on its own. The argument that conception is the point at which human life begins, which underlies state laws prohibiting abortion, is based not on consensus or on science, but on religious views. Professor Tribe wrote, "And, at least at this point in the history of industrialized Western civilization, that decision in turn entails not an inference or demonstration from generally shared premises, whether factual or moral, but a statement of religious faith upon which people will invariably differ widely."

A state could offer a secular argument that there is at least potential human life at the moment of conception and that the state therefore has a compelling interest in prohibiting abortion from that point. The problem with this argument is that it has no stopping point. The argument is that absent abortion there is a significant likelihood that a human person will be born. But actually, the statistics are surprising in terms of how uncertain it is whether there will be a birth if there is no abortion. About 15 to 20 percent of known pregnancies end in miscarriage and studies have found that 30 to 50 percent of fertilized eggs are lost before a woman learns she is pregnant. In other words, there is a reasonable chance—but no more than that—that there will be a baby but for an abortion.

But the same, of course, can be said about contraception. There is the potential for life every time a couple has sex without contraception: but for contraception there is a reasonable chance that there will be a baby. Studies indicate that "[w]hen trying to conceive, a couple with no fertility problem has about a 30 percent chance of getting pregnant each month."

Thus the potential-life argument justifies a ban on contraception as much as it does a ban on abortion. This is the position of the Catholic Church. But then the power of Professor Tribe's argument becomes even more apparent: there is no nonreligious basis for the prohibition of contraception and abortion.

Put another way, in deciding when the state has a compelling interest in prohibiting abortion, the Court had three realistic choices: conception, viability, or birth. Conception is problematic because it requires the Court accepting that the state can decide that human life begins at conception when there is no consensus about this and no apparent nonreligious justification for it. Viability made sense as the point at which a state may prohibit abortion because, by definition, it is then that there is a human being that can survive outside the womb. Almost two decades after *Roe,* in *Planned Parenthood v. Casey,* in 1992, the joint opinion of Justices O'Connor, Kennedy, and Souter explained why viability is the appropriate point for finding a compelling state interest in prohibiting abortion. They wrote: "[T]here is no line other than viability which is more workable.... The viability line also has, as a practical matter, an element of fairness. In some broad sense it might be said that a woman who fails to act before viability has consented to the State's intervention on behalf of the developing child."

I realize, of course, that those who believe that human personhood begins at conception are not persuaded by this argument. My point, though, is that it is wrong to attack *Roe v. Wade* as unjustifiable constitutional law. The Court's opinion was carefully reasoned and consistent with precedent.

But since it was decided in 1973, it more than any other single issue has defined the difference between liberals and conservatives. Every Republican president has opposed abortion rights and the Court's decision in *Roe v. Wade;* every Democratic president has supported abortion rights and the Court's decision in *Roe v. Wade.*

Richard Nixon, for example, declared: "From personal and religious beliefs I consider abortion unacceptable.... Abortion on demand, I cannot square with my personal belief in the sanctity of life." Ronald Reagan was even stronger in his opposition to abortion and supported both a constitutional amendment and a federal law, the Human Life Bill, to ban abortions. On countless occasions, President Reagan criticized the Court's decision in *Roe* and urged its overruling, including by a constitutional amendment. In a typical speech he said: "More than a decade ago, a Supreme Court decision literally wiped off the books of fifty states statutes protecting the rights of unborn children. Abortion on demand now takes the lives of up to one and a half million children a year."

Both Presidents Bush took the same position. In the first weekly radio address after his inauguration, President George H. W. Bush stated: "I think that the Supreme Court's decision in *Roe v. Wade* was wrong and should be overturned. I think America needs a human life amendment." President George W. Bush spoke repeatedly of the need for building a "culture of life" that did not tolerate abortions and his opposition to abortion led him to ban almost all stem cell research.

Not surprisingly, many of the justices that these presidents have appointed have taken the same position and want to overturn *Roe v. Wade*. But it has not happened because some of the Republican appointees have not been willing to go that far, though they have substantially cut back on abortion rights.

The critical moment when it appeared that *Roe* would be overruled was in *Planned Parenthood v. Casey* in 1992. The case involved a Pennsylvania law that did not ban abortions, but that imposed restrictions such as a twenty-four-hour waiting period before abortions and a requirement for a husband's consent for a married woman's abortion. The administration of President George H. W. Bush, in a brief written by Solicitor General Kenneth Starr and Deputy Solicitor General John G. Roberts, Jr., urged the Supreme Court to use this as the occasion to overrule *Roe*.

It appeared that there were at least five votes to do so. Chief Justice William Rehnquist and Justice Byron White had been the only two dissenters in *Roe* and had consistently voted to over-rule it. Three years earlier, in a case involving a Missouri law, Justice Anthony Kennedy joined an opinion by Rehnquist and White that effectively called for the overruling of *Roe* and said that the Court should find that a state has a compelling interest in protect-ing fetal life from the moment of conception. In that case, Justice Antonin Scalia, in a strongly worded opinion, called for the imme-diate and express overruling of *Roe;* he wrote a scathing opinion attacking Justice Sandra Day O'Connor for not being willing to be the fifth vote to end abortion rights.

Between that decision in 1989 and the Court's considering *Casey* in 1992, President Bush had made two appointments to the Court: David Souter and Clarence Thomas. No one knew Souter's views on abortion. As a justice on the New Hampshire Supreme Court and briefly as a federal court of appeals judge, he had never dealt with abortion issues. Nor had he ever written or publicly spoken about them. Thomas, by contrast, had authored articles before going on the Court that attacked *Roe* and called for its overruling. I knew no one who had the slightest doubt as to how Thomas would vote on the question of whether *Roe v. Wade* should be overruled. So that meant that there seemed to be five clear votes to overrule *Roe:* Rehnquist, White, Scalia, Kennedy, and Thomas, with Souter a possible sixth vote.

We know now, thanks to the papers of Justice Harry Blackmun being made public after his death and the reporting of David Savage and Linda Greenhouse, that when the justices first voted in their private conference after the oral arguments in *Casey*, it was 5–4 to effectively overrule *Roe.* Chief Justice Rehnquist assigned to himself writing the majority opinion. Over the succeeding weeks, Justice Kennedy changed his mind. No one knows exactly what caused this shift. He joined with Justices O'Connor and Souter in a joint opinion to reaffirm *Roe.* In a ruling that startled abortion rights supporters and foes alike, by a 5–4 margin the Court reaffirmed that states cannot prohibit abortions before viability. Justices Blackmun and Stevens agreed with the joint opinion, though they would have gone further in protecting abortion rights than O'Connor, Kennedy, and Souter. Chief Justice Rehnquist and Justices White, Scalia, and Thomas dissented and urged the immediate overruling of *Roe.*

Less than six months after *Casey*, Bill Clinton won the White House and not surprisingly his two nominees to the Supreme Court, Ruth Bader Ginsburg and Stephen Breyer, consistently have voted in favor of abortion rights. *Roe*'s immediate survival was secure. But by the 2008 presidential election, it was clear that once more abortion rights were in jeopardy. I have no doubt that John Roberts and Samuel Alito will join Antonin Scalia and Clarence Thomas in voting to overrule *Roe v. Wade* as soon as there is the chance to do so. There is nothing in the background or record of either Roberts or Alito that provides any reason to believe otherwise.

If John McCain had won the presidency in November 2008 and had been the one to replace David Souter, there is every reason to believe that his nominee would have been the fifth vote to overrule *Roe.* McCain was clear during the campaign that he believed that *Roe* was wrongly decided and that he wanted to appoint justices in the mold of Scalia and Thomas. Although no one knows for sure how Justice Sonia Sotomayor will vote on abortion issues, the conventional wisdom is that she will be the same as the justice she replaced, David Souter: a reliable vote in favor of abortion rights.

So the current Court is likely 5–4 to continue *Roe:* Stevens, Kennedy, Ginsburg, Breyer, and Sotomayor to uphold a woman's right to choose; Roberts, Scalia, Thomas, and Alito to overrule *Roe* and end constitutional protection for abortion rights. Everyone expects that Elena Kagan will vote, like the justice she is replacing, to uphold a constitutional right to abortion. But the continued protection of this right remains fragile in that it depends on a single vote on the Supreme Court. Moreover, although Justice Kennedy has been clear that he will not vote to overrule *Roe*, he has been equally clear that he is willing to join with the four most conservative justices to allow the government to restrict abortion rights short of a complete ban.

Actually, in *Casey* and in subsequent cases the Court has done exactly this. The Supreme Court long has held that the government may infringe fundamental rights only if it meets what is called "strict scrutiny"—that is, if the government proves that its action is necessary to achieve a compelling purpose. Strict scrutiny is a legal test that is used to ensure that the courts carefully examine government actions that burden fundamental rights and that the government can prevail only if its action is needed to accomplish a crucial goal. In *Roe*, Justice Blackmun's majority opinion for the Court expressly used strict scrutiny in evaluating the Texas law prohibiting abortion.

In *Casey*, though, the joint opinion of Justices O'Connor, Kennedy, and Souter scrapped strict scrutiny and said that instead a law limiting pre-viability abortions should be declared unconstitutional only if it imposes an "undue burden" on a woman's right to choose. It is still not clear what "undue burden" means, but there is no dispute that it is less protective of abortion rights and more deferential to the government than strict scrutiny. In *Casey*, for example, the Court held that a twenty-four-hour waiting period for abortions is not an undue burden and therefore is constitutional. Every prior case concerning waiting periods for abortions had applied strict scrutiny and had invalidated the waiting periods.

Justice Kennedy's willingness to join with the conservative bloc of Roberts, Scalia, Thomas, and Alito to allow the government to limit abortions was most evident in a 2007 decision, *Gonzales v. Carhart*. In this case, the Supreme Court upheld the constitutionality of the federal Partial-Birth Abortion Ban Act of 2003.

In 2000, in *Stenberg v. Carhart*, the Court struck down a Nebraska law prohibiting so-called "partial birth abortion." There is actually no medical procedure termed partial birth abortion; it is a phrase coined by anti-abortion activists. The Nebraska statute at issue in *Stenberg* prohibited the removal of a living fetus or a substantial part of a living fetus with the intent of ending the fetus's life. Justice Breyer wrote the opinion for the Court and was joined by Justices Stevens, Souter, Ginsburg, and O'Connor. The Court stressed that the Nebraska law was unconstitutional because it did not have an exception allowing the procedure when the health of the woman warranted it and because it was broadly written and likely prohibited many types of abortion procedures. As Justice Ginsburg explained in a concurring opinion, a prohibition of partial birth abortion does not save a single fetus. Nor is it "more humane." Partial birth abortion has some or all of the fetus removed from the womb before it is killed. The alternative is to kill the fetus in the uterus and then dismember it, removing it piece by piece, with each intrusion into the uterus running the risk of perforating the uterus and increasing the danger of infection.

President Clinton vetoed prior bills that banned partial birth abortions and expressly praised the Supreme Court's decision in *Stenberg v. Carhart*. He declared: "I am pleased with the Supreme Court's decision today in *Stenberg v. Carhart* striking down a Nebraska statute that banned so-called partial birth abortions. The Court's decision is consistent with my past vetoes of similar legislation. . . . A woman's right to choose must include the right to choose a medical procedure that will not endanger her life or health. Today's decision recognizes this principle and makes an important victory for a woman's freedom of choice."

President George W. Bush, though, strongly favored the Partial-Birth Abortion Ban Act. He declared, for example, "Partial-birth abortion is an abhorrent procedure that offends human dignity, and I commend the Senate for passing legislation to prohibit it." The bill that he signed was plainly inconsistent with what the Supreme Court said was permissible in *Stenberg;* it has no health exception, and though narrower than the Nebraska law, it is more broadly written than the Court said it would allow.

Nonetheless, the Court in *Gonzales v. Carhart,* a 5–4 decision, upheld the Partial-Birth Abortion Ban Act. Justice Kennedy wrote the opinion for the Court and was joined by Roberts, Scalia, Thomas, and Alito. The key to the case was not in the difference in the wording between the federal law and the Nebraska act; it was Justice Alito having replaced Justice O'Connor. During the confirmation hearings for Chief Justice Roberts and Justice Alito, there was so much talk about "precedent" and "super precedent" in the area of abortion rights, but the new justices had no difficulty in abandoning a precedent that was just seven years old.

Justice Kennedy said that the federal law is constitutional because it is not an undue burden for a "large fraction of women." This is a significant change in the standard with regard to evaluating the constitutionality of laws regulating abortion. In *Stenberg* and in *Planned Parenthood v. Casey,* the Court said that laws regulating abortion are unconstitutional if they are an undue burden for *some* women. For example, in *Casey,* the Court invalidated a provision in a Pennsylvania law that required married women to notify their husbands before obtaining an abortion. The justices noted that some women are in abusive relationships and a requirement for spousal notification would be an undue burden on them. The joint opinion by Justices O'Connor, Kennedy, and Souter explained that it did not matter whether this stipulation affected a large number of women; it was enough to invalidate the law that it was an undue burden for those women who were in abusive relationships.

But after *Gonzales v. Carhart*, laws regulating abortion will be struck down only if they are an undue burden for a significant fraction of women. This test is obviously far more deferential to legislatures and will allow much more government regulation of abortion.

Morever, the Court clearly changed the rhetoric of abortion rights. Justice Kennedy's majority opinion repeatedly referred to the fetus as the "unborn child." He wrote: "[r]espect for human life finds an ultimate expression in the bond of love the mother has for her child. . . . While we find no reliable data to measure the phenomenon, it seems unexceptionable to conclude some women come to regret their choice to abort the infant life they once created and sustained. Severe depression and loss of esteem can follow."

This statement is at odds with prior Supreme Court decisions protecting the right to reproductive freedom. It also is demeaning to women. *Roe v. Wade* is based on the fundamental premise that it is for a woman to decide how to regard the fetus before viability and whether to have an abortion. Women—not the legislature or five men on the Supreme Court—are in the best position to decide whether continuing an unwanted pregnancy is best for their psychological and physical well-being.

As Justice Kennedy candidly admitted, there is no reliable data to support the notion that the ban on so-called "partial birth" abortions will improve the psychological health of women. The majority ignored the fact that the banned procedure is in many cases the safest for the woman. Alternative procedures last longer and involve increased risks of perforation of the uterus, blood loss, and infection.

Thus the conservative attack on abortion rights has come close to overruling *Roe*. It has succeeded in changing the law of abortion to allow much more government regulation.

The attack on *Roe* has had another, more far-reaching effect. Conservatives needed to develop a judicial philosophy that explains why *Roe* is wrongly decided. In the decades since *Roe*, many conservatives, including Supreme Court justices, have argued that the Court should protect rights only if they are supported by the Constitution's text or original meaning. This is an approach to constitutional interpretation that was rarely articulated before *Roe v. Wade*. This philosophy, which is discussed in more detail in the concluding chapter, has led the Court to refuse to recognize new constitutional rights and often to narrow existing rights. Certainly it is not just *Roe* that is responsible for this change; conservatives have generally opposed expanding most, though not all, individual rights. But the rhetoric of the conservative attack on *Roe* has contributed to the refusal to provide constitutional protection for additional liberties and to the cutback on many existing rights.

A few examples illustrate this shift in the Court's thinking. A 1989 decision, *DeShaney v. Winnebago County Department of Social Services*, is particularly troubling and also very revealing. Joshua DeShaney was born in 1979. In 1980, a Wyoming court granted his parents a divorce and awarded custody of Joshua to his father, Randy DeShaney. The father moved to Winnebago County, Wisconsin, taking the infant Joshua with him. There Randy entered into a second marriage, which also ended in divorce.

Over a two-year period, Winnebago County authorities were told that Randy was seriously abusing Joshua. The Department of Social Services first learned that Joshua might be a victim of child abuse in January 1982, when his father's second wife complained to the police, at the time of their divorce, that he had previously "hit the boy causing marks and [was] a prime case for child abuse." The Winnebago County Department of Social Services (DSS) interviewed the father, but he denied the accusations, and the department did not pursue them further.

In January 1983, Joshua was admitted to a local hospital with multiple bruises and abrasions. The examining physician suspected child abuse and notified DSS, which decided that there was not enough evidence to remove Joshua from the home. For the next six months, a caseworker made monthly visits to the

DeShaney home, during which she noted in her files that she observed a number of suspicious injuries on Joshua's head. She noted her continuing concern that someone in the DeShaney household was physically abusing Joshua, but she did nothing more. In November 1983, DSS was notified by the hospital emergency room that Joshua had been treated again for injuries that they believed to be caused by child abuse. This was the third time that the emergency room had reported likely abuse of Joshua to the department. On the caseworker's next two visits to the DeShaney home, she was told that Joshua was too ill to see her. Nonetheless, she and the Department of Social Services took no action.

The Supreme Court summarized what happened next: "In March 1984, Randy DeShaney beat 4-year-old Joshua so severely that he fell into a life-threatening coma. Emergency brain surgery revealed a series of hemorrhages caused by traumatic injuries to the head inflicted over a long period of time. Joshua did not die, but he suffered brain damage so severe that he is expected to spend the rest of his life confined to an institution for the profoundly retarded. Randy DeShaney was subsequently tried and convicted of child abuse."

Joshua's mother sued the Department of Social Services for violating Joshua's rights; for two years it had received complaints of child abuse and had done almost nothing. The Supreme Court in an opinion by Chief Justice Rehnquist ruled against Joshua and his mother. Chief Justice Rehnquist said that the government had no duty to protect Joshua from his father, even when the government had every reason to believe that there was danger and could have prevented it. More generally, the Court said that the government has no duty to protect people from privately inflicted harms. The Court declared: "But nothing in the language of the Due Process Clause itself requires the State to protect the life, liberty, and property of its citizens against invasion by private actors. . . . As a general matter, then, we conclude that a State's failure to protect an individual against private violence simply does not constitute a violation of the Due Process Clause."

Justice Blackmun wrote a powerful dissent, displaying emotion rarely seen in Supreme Court opinions. He concluded by lamenting: "Poor Joshua! Victim of repeated attacks by an irresponsible, bullying, cowardly, and intemperate father, and abandoned by [the Department of Social Services] who placed him in a dangerous predicament and who knew or learned what was going on, and yet did essentially nothing.... It is a sad commentary upon American life, and constitutional principles—so full of late of patriotic fervor and proud proclamations about 'liberty and justice for all'—that this child, Joshua DeShaney, now is assigned to live out the remainder of his life profoundly retarded. Joshua and his mother, as petitioners here, deserve—but now are denied by this Court . . . constitutional protection."

The Court's decision in *DeShaney* has had tragic consequences. The Court so easily could have held that there is a constitutional right when the government has a legal duty to provide protection, as the Department of Social Services did, and has knowledge and the ability to act. If such a right existed, government agencies would be motivated to perform their jobs competently. Subsequent cases show the impact of *DeShaney*'s refusal to recognize such a right.

On the evening of March 10, 1989, Officer Donald Johnson responded to a call reporting a domestic disturbance at the home of Carol Pinder. Pinder's former boyfriend, Don Pittman, had broken into her home. Pittman had just been released from prison for having attempted to set fire to Pinder's home ten months earlier. After breaking into Pinder's home on that March night, he beat Pinder and threatened to kill her and her children. A neighbor subdued Pittman until the police arrived.

The officer arrested Pittman. The officer repeatedly promised Pinder that he would keep Pittman locked up overnight. Pinder explained that she was afraid for herself and her children and wanted to know whether it was safe for her to return to work that evening. The officer assured Pinder that Pittman would remain in jail and that she could go to work. Pittman, though, was taken to the police station and quickly released on his own recognizance. He immediately returned to the Pinder house and lit it on fire.

Carol Pinder was at work, but her three children were home and died of smoke inhalation. Pittman was convicted of three counts of first-degree murder and sentenced to life in prison without possibility of parole.

Carol Pinder sued the police saying that she had relied on their promise and her reliance on them led to the death of her children. She won at trial, but the United States Court of Appeals for the Fourth Circuit reversed the lower courts and based on *DeShaney* found that Pinder had no constitutional right to protection by the police.

One more recent example: Jessica Gonzales had received a court restraining order limiting the time that her husband, from whom she was separated, could spend with their three daughters. Based on past events, she believed that her husband was unstable and capable of violence. Colorado law was strict in creating a duty for police officers to enforce such restraining orders; the back of the restraining order that Gonzales was given by the court stated this duty. On June 22, 1999, the three daughters were playing in front of the house and the husband picked up the girls, even though this violated the terms of the court order.

Jessica Gonzales called the police to ask their help four times that night, at 7:30, 8:30, 10:10, and 12:10. At 8:30, her husband called to tell her that he had the girls at an amusement park. Jessica told this to the police, but they told her to wait until 10 P.M. When she called at that hour, they told her to wait until midnight. Finally, at 12:50 she went to the police station. An officer took an incident report, but did nothing about it; he went to dinner.

At approximately 3:20 A.M., Gonzales's husband arrived at the police station and opened fire with a semiautomatic handgun he had purchased earlier that evening. Police shot back, killing him. Inside the cab of his pickup truck, they found the bodies of all three daughters, whom he had already murdered. In a 2005 decision, the Supreme Court, in an opinion written by Justice Scalia, ruled against Jessica Gonzales and reaffirmed that under *DeShaney* the government had no constitutional duty to provide protection, even when state law requires it.

A constitutional right is important so that there is a legal remedy when government officials fail to do their job and cost people their lives without due process of law. In all of these cases, government employees made egregious errors and innocent children died or were gravely injured as a result. Usually, the law provides a remedy when someone's negligence causes a death. But government officials are protected in these instances and as a result there is not a remedy available which might provide some compensation to the families and even more important, a deterrent to such improper behavior by government officials in the future.

The refusal of the Court to recognize new constitutional rights on life-and-death issues is also apparent in other contexts where vulnerable individuals were denied essential constitutional protection. It is illustrated by the story of my father's death at the beginning of this chapter. As explained earlier, in 1997, in *Washington v. Glucksberg,* the Supreme Court held that the right to privacy does not include a right of terminally ill patients to assisted death; the Court ruled that laws prohibiting aiding and assisting a suicide are constitutional even when applied to prevent assistance to terminally ill patients. The tragedy of the Supreme Court's decision is that countless other individuals in my father's situation needlessly suffer every day across the country. They are denied the most basic aspect of their autonomy: the power to decide to end their life with dignity and on their own terms.

In *Glucksberg,* Chief Justice Rehnquist's majority opinion formulated an approach to identifying fundamental rights that is at odds with the Supreme Court's approach in its earlier privacy cases. Rehnquist wrote that the Court would protect rights not mentioned in the Constitution only if they were "objectively, 'deeply rooted in this Nation's history and tradition.' " The Court said that there was no tradition of protecting assisted death and thus no constitutional right.

However, this statement that a fundamental right exists only if there is a tradition of protecting it is wrong both as a description of what the law is and as a statement of what the law should be.

Descriptively, the Court has been willing to recognize and safeguard rights even though there has not been a tradition of protection. For example, laws prohibiting interracial marriage were far more "deeply rooted in this Nation's history and tradition" than the right to interracial marriage, but in *Loving v. Virginia* the Court declared anti-miscegenation laws to be unconstitutional. And there obviously was no deeply rooted tradition of protecting a right to abortion before *Roe v. Wade;* abortion was illegal in forty-six states when *Roe* was decided.

Of course, conservatives can argue that these decisions were wrong. But that misses the point: Chief Justice Rehnquist purports to describe how the Court has acted in determining when a right is protected by the Constitution. His description is inaccurate. There could be a different discussion about whether the Court should protect such rights, but as a descriptive matter he was incorrect in saying that due process has been limited to protecting those rights that are "objectively, 'deeply rooted in this Nation's history and tradition.' "

The fact that laws have long existed does not answer the question whether the personal choice involved, death with dignity, is so integral to personhood as to be worthy of being deemed a fundamental right. Oliver Wendell Holmes expressed this matter well: "It is revolting to have no better reason for a rule of law than that so it was laid down in the time of Henry IV. It is still more revolting if the grounds upon which it was laid down have vanished long since, and the rule simply persists from blind imitation of the past."

The real question that should have been addressed by the Court is whether the right to physician-assisted death is so basic to autonomy that it should be deemed a fundamental right. Put another way, is this right sufficiently analogous in its importance to the privacy rights that the Court has previously protected that it should be deemed a fundamental right?

Judge Stephen Reinhardt, writing for the federal court of appeals in the case, answered these questions persuasively: "[B]y permitting the individual to exercise the right to choose we are following the constitutional mandate to take such decisions out of the hands of the government, both state and federal, and to put them where they rightly belong, in the hands of the people. We are allowing individuals to make the decisions that so profoundly affect their very existence—and precluding the state from intruding excessively into that critical realm." The court of appeals explained that the matter of life and death was so "central to personal dignity and autonomy" that the Constitution left it to the individual. Judge Reinhardt wrote: "Those who believe strongly that death must come without physician assistance are free to follow that creed, be they doctors or patients. They are not free, however, to force their views, their religious convictions, or their philosophies on all the other members of a democratic society, and to compel those whose values differ with theirs to die painful, protracted, and agonizing deaths."

The Ninth Circuit was correct in that the Supreme Court long has recognized the constitutional right of individuals to have the autonomy to make crucial decisions concerning their lives, such as the right to marry, the right to raise one's children, and the right to reproductive autonomy. Certainly, the choice of whether to live or to die is of equal importance. Indeed, it is difficult to imagine any aspect of autonomy more basic than the ability to choose whether to continue one's life.

The government has a vital interest in protecting life and preventing abuses if assisted death is allowed. But the state's general interest in safeguarding life is hollow when it is a terminally ill patient who will soon die and wishes to do so with dignity and less suffering. States can regulate to prevent abuses, as Oregon has done.

Every competent adult facing a terminal disease should be able to choose to die with dignity. The Supreme Court was wrong in *Glucksberg* and countless individuals and their families have suffered from the decision ever since. The ruling must be seen, in part, as a reflection of the unwillingness of the Court since *Roe v. Wade* to protect new rights, or to extend existing rights such as privacy.

It would be an overstatement, though, to say that no new constitutional rights have been recognized since *Roe*. There are not many, but it has happened in a couple of instances. In *Lawrence v. Texas*, in 2003, over the vehement dissents of Chief Justice Rehnquist and Justices Scalia and Thomas, the Court held that the right to privacy protects a right of adults to engage in private consensual homosexual activity.

In 1986, in *Bowers v. Hardwick*, the Supreme Court had come to an opposite conclusion. A police officer came to Michael Hardwick's apartment to deliver a bench warrant for his appearance in court. A roommate answered the door and said that he did not know if Hardwick was there, but that the officer should check Hardwick's room. The officer said that the door to the room was open slightly and he peered in and saw Hardwick and another man engaged in sex. They were arrested for violating a Georgia statute that prohibited oral-genital or anal-genital contacts.

Hardwick challenged the constitutionality of this law as violating the right to privacy. The federal court of appeals agreed and struck it down. In a 5–4 decision, the Supreme Court reversed and upheld the Georgia statute. Justice Byron White wrote for the Court and was joined by Chief Justice Burger and Justices Rehnquist, Powell, and O'Connor. The Court said that it was unwilling to find "a fundamental right to engage in homosexual sodomy." The Court stated that "[p]roscriptions against that conduct have ancient roots. Sodomy was a criminal offense at common law and was forbidden by the laws of the original thirteen States when they ratified the Bill of Rights." The Court said that in 1868 when the Fourteenth Amendment was ratified, criminal laws prohibited homosexual conduct in 32 of the 37 states, and that as recently as 1961, all fifty states and the District of Columbia had statutes making homosexual activity a crime.

The five most conservative justices then on the Court thus held that the government could punish adults for consensual sexual activities in their own bedroom. But seventeen years later the Court expressly overruled *Bowers v. Hardwick*. Police officers in Houston, Texas, responded to a report of a weapons disturbance in a private residence. They entered John Lawrence's apartment and observed Lawrence and another man, Tyron Garner, engaging in a sexual act. The two men were arrested for violating a Texas law prohibiting "deviate sexual activity," which was defined as sex acts between individuals of the same sex. The men were held in custody overnight, charged, convicted, and fined two hundred dollars each.

Justice Kennedy wrote the opinion for a five-person majority overturning the conviction and overruling *Bowers v. Hardwick*. Justices Stevens, Souter, Ginsburg, and Breyer joined. Justice Kennedy wrote eloquently and stated: "It suffices for us to acknowledge that adults may choose to enter upon this relationship in the confines of their homes and their own private lives and still retain their dignity as free persons. When sexuality finds overt expression in intimate conduct with another person, the conduct can be but one element in a personal bond that is more enduring. The liberty protected by the Constitution allows homosexual persons the right to make this choice."

Lawrence is an important exception to the Court's refusal to protect additional rights in the years since *Roe*. But *Lawrence* is a less strong precedent than at first it seems. The Court never said that the right to engage in adult homosexual activity is a fundamental right or that government laws regulating private adult sexual activity must meet strict scrutiny and thus be shown to be necessary to achieve a compelling government interest. Generally, the courts uphold laws so long as they are reasonable; almost any government action can meet this test and be found reasonable. But when there is a fundamental right involved, or discrimination against a racial minority, the government must meet strict scrutiny and convince the Court that its actions are necessary to achieve a compelling purpose. The government is far less likely to win under this test.

The Court's key failing in *Lawrence* is that it did not indicate that more than a reasonableness test is to be used when the government regulates adult sexual conduct. As a result, lower courts have read the decision and its constitutional protections very narrowly. A federal court of appeals upheld an Alabama law that prohibits the sale or distribution of sex toys, items intended primarily for stimulation of the genitals. The court explicitly said that *Lawrence* was using only a reasonableness test, though it is hard for me to imagine what legitimate government interest is served by a prohibition on vibrators. The same federal court of appeals upheld a Florida law that prohibited gays and lesbians from adopting children, though this is discrimination based on the worst and most inaccurate stereotypes about gays and lesbians. The Ohio Supreme Court held that two adults who engaged in sex and were not related by blood could be punished under the state's incest law because they were stepbrother and stepsister. The court stressed that *Lawrence* used only reasonableness review. Hopefully, in the future the Court will address this problem and recognize a fundamental right of consenting adults to engage in private sexual activity, but it has not happened yet.

The other instance in which the Court recognized a new right concerns the Second Amendment. The provision has enigmatic language. It says: "A well regulated militia, being necessary to the security of a free state, the right of the people to keep and bear arms shall not be infringed." One way to interpret the amendment is that it protects a right of individuals to have guns for the purpose of militia service. An alternative interpretation would be that it protects the right of individuals to have firearms, even apart from militia service.

Throughout American history, the Court chose the former interpretation. It seems most consistent with the text's statement of the purpose for possessing guns; otherwise the amendment would mean the same as if it just said "the right of the people to keep and bear arms shall not be infringed." Also, the original version of the Second Amendment drafted by James Madison had an exemption from militia service for conscientious objectors, a strong indication that the provision was addressing militia service.

I am not sure when it was that views on guns came to track political ideology so closely, with liberals favoring gun control and conservatives favoring gun rights. But that is the social reality today and it explains the Supreme Court's decision in 2008 in *District of Columbia v. Heller*. The case involved a thirty-five-year-old District of Columbia ordinance banning private ownership or possession of handguns and imposing restrictions on long guns. Justice Scalia wrote for the Court and was joined by Roberts, Kennedy, Thomas, and Alito. Conservatives who have long preached the need for judicial restraint and deference to the democratic process showed no hesitation about striking down this law. Conservatives, who for the last several decades have taken a narrow approach to individual liberties and refused to recognize new rights, had no difficulty in finding a Second Amendment right of individuals to have handguns.

The case left open many questions concerning when and under what circumstances the government may regulate firearms. Justice Scalia, writing for the Court, was clear that it is not an absolute right. He said, for example, that the government can regulate where people have guns, such as in preventing guns in schools or airports. He said that the government can keep those with a history of serious mental illness or a prior felony conviction from having firearms. But unlike the Court in *Lawrence*, Justice Scalia's majority opinion was explicit that more than a reasonableness test will be used in evaluating government regulation of firearms. He stated, "[I]f all that is required to overcome the right to keep and bear arms was a rational basis, the Second Amendment would be redundant with the separate constitutional prohibitions on irrational laws, and would have no effect."

Although much remains uncertain as to which gun laws will survive after *Heller*, it is accurate to say that the Second Amendment is the only new right that the Court has recognized in the last thirty-five years where it has approved more than rational basis review. It is hardly coincidental that this interpretation meshes with conservative political ideology.

Thus, with only very limited exceptions, the conservative approach to constitutional law has meant that new constitutional rights have not been recognized. At the same time, conservatives on the Court have narrowed many existing rights. In the introductory chapter, I told the story of how the Court has made it far more difficult to find a sentence to be cruel and unusual punishment in violation of the Eighth Amendment, upholding the sentence Leandro Andrade received of fifty years to life in prison for stealing $153 worth of videotapes. In Chapter 3, I discussed how the Supreme Court in a 1990 opinion by Justice Scalia essentially negated the protection of free exercise of religion in the First Amendment. The Court held that laws burdening religion, even very substantially burdening religion, cannot be challenged under the Free Exercise Clause so long as that was not their purpose and so long as they apply to everyone. In Chapter 4, I discussed how the Court has narrowed the rights of criminal defendants, such as in making it more difficult to prove ineffective assistance of counsel, in greatly limiting the availability of habeas corpus, and in significantly reducing the application of the exclusionary rule to police violations of the Fourth Amendment.

There are a great many other instances in which the Court has split along ideological lines with the conservatives voting to limit long-standing constitutional rights. I will cite two examples, involving privacy rights and freedom of speech.

The privacy decision, from 1989, is *Michael H. v. Gerald D.* It is a case that has facts on which a made-for-television movie, or at least an episode of *Desperate Housewives*, could be based. Carole D. (no last names were used in the case) was an international model. She was married to Gerald, but she had an affair with Michael. Biological evidence showed to more than a 98 percent certainty that Michael was the father of her child.

After the birth of the child, Carole lived with Michael and the baby, Victoria, for many months. Ultimately, Carole returned to Gerald and took Victoria with her. Michael sued for visitation rights; he was almost unquestionably Victoria's father and had formed a relationship with her when they had lived together. California law, though, created a conclusive presumption that a married woman's husband was the father of her child in these circumstances. The California court applied the state law to deem that Carole's husband, Gerald, was Victoria's father and to deny Michael all visitation and all parental rights.

This should have been an easy case for the Supreme Court under existing precedents. The Court had previously held that parents have a fundamental right to custody of their children and that this right includes unmarried fathers. In four prior decisions, the Court had been clear that the constitutional rights of an unmarried father are protected if he had established a substantial relationship with the child. By this test, Michael was constitutionally entitled at least to visitation rights.

But Justice Scalia, writing for a five-person majority composed of the most conservative justices then on the Court, upheld the California law and its application to deny Michael all parental rights. Justice Scalia said that while prior cases involved the parental rights of unmarried fathers, none had involved a mother who was married to someone else. The Court rejected both Michael's right to custody *and* Victoria's right to see her father. It was a narrowing of a fundamental right that the Court had long recognized.

Most of the examples in this chapter concerning individual liberties have involved aspects of privacy. But it is important to note that the same is true in other areas of rights as well: the Court has narrowed constitutional liberties except when it serves the conservative ideological agenda to do otherwise. Two First Amendment cases, one where the Court significantly curtailed protection for freedom of speech and one where the Court expanded it, illustrate this.

A case that involved narrowing speech rights was the decision in 2006 in *Garcetti v. Ceballos,* denying free speech protection to public employee whistle-blowers. In a 5–4 decision, the Supreme Court held that the government does not violate the First Amendment when it punishes an employee for exposing wrongdoing on the job. This was an enormous loss of rights for the millions of people who work for the government, but even worse, it meant that the public is much less likely to learn of serious misconduct by their government.

The case involved Richard Ceballos, a supervising district

attorney in Los Angeles County, who concluded that a witness in one of his cases, a deputy sheriff, was not telling the truth. He wrote a memo to his supervisors expressing his doubts about the veracity of the officer's story, but was told by his supervisor to soften its tone and content. Ceballos refused and felt that he was required by the Constitution to disclose the memo to the defense; as explained in Chapter 4, prosecutors are compelled to turn over to the defense evidence that might show the defendant's innocence or that can be used to impeach prosecution witnesses.

As a result of his memo, Ceballos said, his employers retaliated against him, including transferring him to a less desirable position and denying him a promotion. Although the Supreme Court long has held that there is constitutional protection for the speech of government employees, it ruled against Ceballos and concluded that he could not bring a claim for the violation of his First Amendment rights. It was a 5–4 decision with Justice Kennedy writing a majority opinion joined by Roberts, Scalia, Thomas, and Alito.

The Court drew a distinction between speech "as a citizen" and "as a public employee"; the Court said that only the former is protected by the First Amendment. The majority opinion by Justice Anthony Kennedy stated: "[W]hen public employees make statements pursuant to their official duties, the employees are not speaking as citizens for First Amendment purposes, and the Constitution does not insulate their communications from employer discipline."

This is a false and unprecedented distinction between individuals speaking as "citizens" and as "government employees." Never before has the Supreme Court held that only speech "as citizens" is safeguarded by the First Amendment. For example, in prior decisions holding that speech by corporations is constitutionally protected, the Court emphasized the public's interest in hearing the speech. The fact that corporations are not "citizens" did not matter because it is the right of listeners, according to the Supreme Court, that is paramount. The Court said that "[t]he inherent worth of the speech in terms of its capacity for informing the public does not depend upon the identity of its source, whether corporation, association, union, or individual."

The same, of course, is true when government employees, especially whistle-blowers, speak out. The public receives valuable information that otherwise might not be available about wrongdoing within the government. Without First Amendment protection, many fewer whistle-blowers are likely to expose government misconduct.

Moreover, an individual who exposes misconduct is acting both as a citizen and as a government employee; it is a false dichotomy to say that a person is in one role or the other. A public employee does not relinquish his or her citizenship on entering a government office building.

In this case, Ceballos was revealing a serious problem: misconduct by a deputy sheriff that he believed led to an invalid warrant for a search in violation of the Fourth Amendment. The long history of misconduct by police within Los Angeles shows why it is so important that people like Ceballos be protected when they reveal wrongdoing. Ceballos suffering adverse consequences from speaking out surely means that other government employees, in similar situations, will be chilled from exposing misconduct.

Several years ago, when I did a study of the Los Angeles Police Department, I learned that officers who reported misconduct by other officers often suffered reprisals, including being transferred to precincts far from their homes. This practice even had a name: "freeway therapy." In fact, the Christopher Commission, in its report after the beating of Rodney King in 1991, said that the "code of silence" in the department was the single largest obstacle to effective discipline. *Garcetti v. Ceballos* means that there is no First Amendment protection for such officers or other government employees exposing wrongdoing on the job, even when their speech is truthful and of great public concern.

Nor was the Supreme Court's decision restricting protection of government employees needed to safeguard the efficient functioning of the workplace. Almost forty years ago, the Court held that employees could be disciplined for their speech if the government's interests in protecting the efficient operation of the workplace outweighed the speech rights of the government employee. The Court's decision in *Garcetti v. Ceballos* is terribly misguided because it says that the speech of government employees within their jobs is not protected even if the speech involves a matter of public concern and even if the government's interests are outweighed by the public benefits.

Government employees like Ceballos who expose wrongdoing should be rewarded, not punished. The Constitution and courts should be there to provide protection when government, whether because of bureaucratic defensiveness or malevolence, lashes out against the speaker. The decision is representative of the conservatives' curtailment of liberties.

There is a stunning contrast between *Garcetti*'s narrowing of free speech protection and the Supreme Court's recent ruling expanding free speech rights of corporations. For decades, the Court ruled that the government could limit the ability of corporations to spend money in election campaigns. In a 1990 decision, the Court upheld a state law restricting corporate campaign expenditures, explaining that this action was justified to prevent corporate wealth from distorting elections and to protect shareholders from having their money used for political purposes with which they disagree.

In 2003, the Court reaffirmed this principle and upheld a provision of the McCain-Feingold Bipartisan Campaign Finance Reform Act, which limited corporate and union spending on broadcast advertisements before primary and general elections. But on January 21, 2010, in *Citizens United v. Federal Election Commission*, the Supreme Court in a 5–4 decision overruled this recent precedent and held that corporations have the First Amendment right to spend money in election campaigns. What changed in seven years? In the 2003 ruling, Justice O'Connor was in the majority with Justices Stevens, Souter, Ginsburg, and Breyer. Her replacement, Justice Alito, voted the other way and tipped the balance to overturn the earlier decision.

The decision will have a significant effect in federal, state, and local elections as corporations can spend as much as they want to elect their candidates of choice and defeat the candidates they oppose. In the cases described earlier in this chapter, conservatives opposed rights such as for abortions or for assisted death because they were not mentioned in the text or intended by the framers. But the framers did not intend to protect speech rights of corporations nor did they believe that spending money in election campaigns was speech; there is no unbroken tradition of protecting such a right. The contrast to *Garcetti v. Ceballos* is important because it shows that conservatives are willing to expand speech rights when it serves their agenda, such as giving more power to corporations to influence the outcome of elections.

When I was a freshman in college at Northwestern I became friends with a woman who lived down the hall in my dorm. We used to eat meals together sometimes and occasionally would study together. One night in the spring of our freshman year, we were alone after dinner in the dorm's cafeteria and I mentioned that she seemed upset. I asked if everything was all right. She broke into tears and said that she thought that she might be pregnant; she told me a story of what today would be regarded as date rape, of being at a party at her sorority, of having too much too drink, and of a senior who refused to take no for an answer.

She talked of needing to go to the student health center to have a pregnancy test. This was April 1972, before home pregnancy tests. At the time abortion was illegal in Illinois. I offered what little comfort I could. I tried over the following days to check in on her, but I always felt that she was embarrassed for what she had confided in me. I learned from her, though, that she was indeed pregnant, that she felt that she could not have the child, and that she could never tell her parents. She expressed panic and was searching desperately for a way to have an abortion. I also learned that the man who raped her refused to talk to her or to help her in any way. Within a couple of weeks, she told me that a girl in her sorority took her to a doctor who performed the abortion, though it was illegal. Thankfully, unlike for many women, as far as I know this abortion was done safely and my friend finished her classes and took her exams that spring.

I wrote her occasionally over the summer and my letters were not answered. Finally in September she wrote back to me and said that she was transferring from Northwestern to the state university near where she grew up; she said that the horrible spring left too many bad memories.

As I teach the abortion cases each year in my constitutional law class, I always think of her. I realize that the women (and men) in my classes have lived only at a time when abortions have been legal. It is something that they have come to take for granted.

This right was almost ended in 1992. Today it rests on a single vote in the Supreme Court. *Roe* and the cases about individual rights discussed in this chapter show that constitutional law affects people in the most intimate and important aspects of their lives: contraception, abortion, sexual activity, custody of one's children, death with dignity. In all of these areas, conservatives vehemently reject the notion of constitutional rights. The same conservatives who for so long have preached the need to get the government off the backs of the American people reject the privacy protections that achieve precisely that.

6.

Closing the Courthouse Doors

Valerie Plame Wilson and Joseph C. Wilson IV are best known as victims of an abuse of power at the highest levels of the administration of President George W. Bush. Vice President Dick Cheney, his chief of staff, I. Lewis "Scooter" Libby, presidential advisor Karl Rove, and Deputy Secretary of State Richard Armitage disclosed that Ms. Wilson was a secret operative for the CIA. They did this to retaliate against her husband for revealing that President Bush spoke falsely in his State of the Union address in claiming that Iraq was seeking to buy uranium from Africa. Exposing the identity of an undercover government agent is a felony.

What is less well-known, though, is that when the Wilsons sued for their injuries, their case was dismissed on procedural grounds of the sort that keeps many others from having their day in court. In fact, their experience reflects one of the most pernicious aspects of the conservative assault on the Constitution: the closing of the courthouse doors to those with serious injuries. In a series of decisions over the last few decades, the conservatives on the Supreme Court have made it far more difficult to sue the government, government officials, and businesses. These rulings and the doctrines that they have created are particularly insidious because they are largely invisible to the general public. The media provides little coverage of Supreme Court decisions about procedural issues. Yet these seemingly technical decisions matter enormously in who can come to court, who can recover damages or obtain injunctions, and whether those violating the law are held accountable.

The experience of the Wilsons is illustrative of this situation. I unsuccessfully represented them in their lawsuit, arguing their case in both the federal district court and the United States Court of Appeals. My attempt to gain Supreme Court review was denied in June 2009.

My involvement began with a phone call in March 2006 from a lawyer in Washington, D.C., Chris Wolfe. I knew Chris, though not well, and thought very highly of him. He said that he was representing Valerie Plame Wilson and Joseph Wilson in their civil suit for money damages and he wanted to know if I was interested in helping. He apologized that it was pro bono, without compensation. I eagerly agreed and we immediately began to discuss our legal theories and the obstacles we would face in getting the case past a motion to dismiss. We calculated that because of the statue of limitations, the complaint had to be filed in federal court by July 14, three years to the day after the revelation of Ms. Wilson's status as a secret operative.

Soon after the complaint was filed, Wolfe withdrew from involvement in the case. I never quite understood what happened, though I had the sense that there was a disagreement between him and Joe and Valerie. I agreed that I would remain involved and would work with two excellent lawyers, Melanie Sloan and Anne Weismann, at Citizens for Responsibility and Ethics in Washington. I agreed to take primary responsibility for handling the likely motion to dismiss by defendants Cheney, Libby, Rove, and Armitage. If I succeeded and the case went to discovery and trial, a renowned trial lawyer, Joe Cotchett, would take over. My experience is almost entirely in handling appellate matters, not in trying cases.

As I learned the details of what happened to Joe and Valerie my outrage grew. Valerie Plame Wilson was an employee of the CIA until January 2006. Her employment status was classified and was not publicly known until July 14, 2003, when a press report precipitated by leaks by top government officials revealed her status and exposed her.

From 1976 through 1998, Mr. Wilson was a member of the United States Diplomatic Service. From 1988 to 1991, he was the deputy chief of mission at the United States Embassy in Baghdad, Iraq. In that position, he was recognized as "truly inspiring" and "courageous" by President George H. W. Bush after he shielded more than fifty Americans at the embassy in the face of threats from Saddam Hussein to execute anyone who refused to turn over foreigners. Mr. Wilson later served as United States ambassador to Gabon and São Tomé and Príncipe under President George H. W. Bush and as senior director for Africa at the National Security Council under President Clinton.

In 2002, Joseph Wilson was sent at the request of the CIA to Niger to investigate reports that Saddam Hussein was trying to buy uranium there. He learned that the allegations were incorrect.

Even though Wilson reported what he found to the CIA and the State Department, in the State of the Union address on January 28, 2003, President George W. Bush stated that "[t]he British government has learned that Saddam Hussein recently sought significant quantities of uranium from Africa." That March, the United States invaded Iraq, in part because of its belief that Hussein was attempting to acquire weapons of mass destruction.

On May 6, the *New York Times* published a column by Nicholas Kristof that disputed the accuracy of the "sixteen words" in the State of the Union address in which the president made the assertion about Hussein. The column reported that as a result of a request from the vice president's office for an investigation of allegations that Iraq sought to buy uranium from Niger, an unnamed former ambassador—now known to have been Mr. Wilson—was sent on a trip to Niger in 2002 to look into the matter. According to the column, the former ambassador reported back to the CIA and the State Department in early 2002 that the allegations were unequivocally wrong and based on forged documents.

On May 29, 2003, in the White House, Lewis Libby asked an undersecretary of state for information concerning the unnamed former ambassador's trip to Niger. The undersecretary provided Libby with interim oral reports in late May and early June, and advised Libby that Wilson was the former ambassador who took the trip.

A short time later, on June 11 or 12, the undersecretary of state told Libby that Wilson's wife worked at the CIA and that State Department personnel were saying that Wilson's wife was involved in the planning of his trip (which was later found to be untrue). About the same time, Libby was advised by Vice President Cheney that Mrs. Wilson worked at the Central Intelligence Agency in the Counterproliferation Division.

On July 6, the *New York Times* published an op-ed article by Wilson titled "What I Didn't Find in Africa." On that same day, the *Washington Post* published an article, which was based in part on an interview with Wilson, about his 2002 trip to Niger. Wilson also appeared as a guest on July 6 on the television interview show *Meet the Press*. In his op-ed, and in interviews with print reporters and on television, Wilson explained what he had found on his trip. He stated that he believed, based on his understanding of government procedures, that the Office of the Vice President had been advised of the results of his trip.

In a May 12, 2006, court filing in the criminal case of *United States v. Libby*, the government proffered a copy of the July 6 op-ed annotated shortly after its publication in the handwriting of Vice President Dick Cheney. The government told the court that it believed those notes of the vice president "support the proposition that publication of the Wilson Op-Ed acutely focused the attention of the Vice President and [Libby]—his chief of staff—on Mr. Wilson, on the assertions made in his article, and on responding to those assertions."

Following the publication of Mr. Wilson's op-ed piece and statements in the national media, Cheney, Libby, Rove, and Armitage engaged in a concerted effort to retaliate against him by exposing his wife's employment as an operative for the CIA. On July 8, 2003, Vice President Cheney advised Libby that the president of the United States specifically had authorized Libby to disclose to *New York Times* reporter Judith Miller certain information from an October 2002 National Intelligence Estimate concerning Iraq and weapons of mass destruction in order to rebut Mr. Wilson. Three days after this, on July 11, Director of Central Intelligence George Tenet conceded that claims about Iraqi attempts to buy uranium from Africa in the State of the Union address were a mistake and that the "16 words should never have been included in the text written for the President," an acknowledgment that the substance of Mr. Wilson's criticism was legitimate and correct.

Rather than admit the validity of Wilson's criticisms, on the morning of July 8, 2003, Libby met with Judith Miller. When the conversation turned to the subject of Joseph Wilson, Libby asked that the information Libby provided on the topic of Wilson be attributed to a "former Hill staffer" rather than to a "senior administration official," as had been the understanding with respect to other information that Libby provided to Miller during this meeting. Libby discussed Wilson's trip and criticized the CIA report concerning it. During this discussion, Libby advised Miller of his belief that Wilson's wife worked at the CIA.

Around the same time, on July 10 or July 11, Libby spoke to a senior official in the White House, believed to be Karl Rove, who advised Libby of a conversation earlier that week with columnist Robert Novak in which Wilson's wife was discussed as a CIA employee involved in Wilson's trip. Libby was advised that Novak would be writing a story about Ms. Wilson.

Libby also spoke by telephone to *Time* reporter Matthew Cooper, who asked whether Libby had heard that Wilson's wife was involved in sending Wilson on the trip to Niger. Libby confirmed to Cooper, without elaboration or qualification, that he had heard this information, too. On the same day, Libby spoke by telephone with Miller and discussed Wilson's wife, and that she worked at the CIA.

Others in the White House similarly revealed Ms. Wilson's employment at the CIA in an attempt to punish her and Mr. Wilson. For example, on Friday, July 11, Cooper telephoned Karl Rove, and in the ensuing conversation, Rove instructed Cooper that the conversation was to be on "deep background," which Cooper has stated he understood to mean that he could use the information

Rove was giving to him, but not quote it, and that Cooper must keep the identity of the source confidential.

In the telephone conversation, Rove told Cooper that Ms. Wilson worked "at the agency," which Cooper understood to mean the CIA. Rove also told Cooper that Ms. Wilson "worked on 'WMD' [weapons of mass destruction]" issues and that she was responsible for sending Mr. Wilson to Niger. This was the first time that Cooper had heard anything about Wilson's wife. Cooper has said he has a distinct memory of Rove ending the call by saying, "I've already said too much."

Shortly after Novak's column appeared, in July Rove called Chris Matthews, host of the MSNBC program *Hardball,* and told him that Mr. Wilson's wife was "fair game." "Fair game" is a hunting term used colloquially to describe a person who may legitimately be attacked. Valerie Plame (the name she went by at the CIA) titled her autobiography *Fair Game.*

Cheney, Rove, Libby, and Armitage thus acted to punish Mr. Wilson for exposing a significant error by the Bush administration. On October 28, 2005, Special Counsel Patrick Fitzgerald explained at a press conference announcing the indictment against Mr. Libby: "In July 2003, the fact that Valerie Wilson was a CIA officer was classified. Not only was it classified, but it was not widely known outside the intelligence community. Valerie Wilson's friends, neighbors, college classmates had no idea she had another life. The fact that she was a CIA officer was not well known for her protection and for the benefit of all of us. It is important that a CIA officer's identity be protected, that it be protected not just for the officer, but for the nation's security." Libby was indicted and ultimately convicted in March 2007 for perjury in answering questions from the FBI about violations of the federal law which makes it a crime to reveal publicly the identity of an undercover agent.

At the same press conference, Special Counsel Fitzgerald stated: "Valerie Wilson's cover was blown in July 2003. The first sign of that cover being blown was when Mr. Novak published a column on July 14th, 2003. But Mr. Novak was not the first reporter to be told that Ambassador Wilson's wife, Valerie, worked at the CIA. Several other reporters were told [by Libby]."

I have no doubt that Joe and Valerie Wilson were seriously injured by what occurred. Valerie's career at the CIA was effectively ruined. No longer could she be a secret operative. In talking with them, I realized their great fear for their safety and the safety of their children. They believed that the disclosure of Valerie's covert identity made them a target, including by those she may have dealt with as an operative.

I thought the Wilsons had strong constitutional claims for their lawsuit. The defendants—Cheney, Libby, Rove, and Armitage—had violated Joe Wilson's freedom of speech by their effort to punish him for his speaking out and revealing the inaccuracies in the president's State of the Union address. Both Joe and Valerie had claims for invasion of their constitutional right to privacy, including the revealing of very private information about their lives. Valerie also had lost her job, a property interest recognized under a long series of Supreme Court decisions, and her life had been placed in jeopardy.

The hurdles they faced were procedural; over recent years, the conservative justices on the Supreme Court have made it more difficult than before for injured individuals to gain recovery. Those whose constitutional rights have been violated by the federal government and its officers generally cannot sue the United States government itself. The United States has sovereign immunity and cannot be sued for money damages without its consent. Usually the only recourse is to sue the government officers who violated the Constitution. There is no federal statute expressly authorizing such suits against federal officers, although there is a law adopted in 1871 that allows state and local government officers to be sued when they violate the Constitution and federal laws. In 1971, in *Bivens v. Six Unknown Named Federal Agents*, the Supreme Court held that federal officers who violate constitutional rights may be sued for money damages.

Webster Bivens had been subjected to an illegal and humiliating search in violation of the Fourth Amendment by agents of the

Federal Bureau of Narcotics. He could not sue the United States because of its sovereign immunity, so he instead sought to sue the agents themselves. The Supreme Court ruled in his favor and said that a right to sue federal officials for money damages could be inferred directly from the United States Constitution. Justice John Marshall Harlan in an eloquent concurring opinion explained that for someone in Bivens's circumstances such a damages remedy must be available or there is no recourse against improper behavior.

In the last two decades, the Supreme Court has repeatedly rejected such suits and greatly narrowed the circumstances where government officers can be sued for violating the Constitution. The Court has said that such *"Bivens* actions" will not be available when there are "special factors counselling hesitation." The Court has been very willing to find these special factors. One of the most egregious examples of this was in *Stanley v. United States.* James Stanley had served in the military in the 1950s and had been subjected to human experimentation without his knowledge or consent. He and other soldiers were told that they were trying out new protective gear, but in reality they were given LSD so that the military could observe its effects. Stanley said that LSD caused him serious subsequent lifelong harms, including flashbacks and psychosis.

The Supreme Court did not deny that this occurred, but instead said that there were "special factors counselling hesitation": military officers should not be able to be sued for violating the rights of those under their command. There certainly are instances where such suits would not make sense. Decisions in the midst of a battle generally should not be amenable to judicial review. But Stanley's injuries were not suffered in the battlefield or even in a foreign country. He was the victim of planned human experimentation. As Justice O'Connor forcefully argued in her dissent, this was exactly the type of human experimentation that was condemned by international law and that had been universally decried since the Nazis engaged in such reprehensible behavior. Stanley, though, was left without any remedy for the injuries he suffered.

Decisions like *Stanley* create problems for any plaintiffs bringing such constitutional claims and I knew from the beginning of handling the Wilsons' case that so much would depend on the identity of the judge. Judges in both the federal district court and the United States Court of Appeals are selected at random to hear particular cases. In the district court, our judge was John Bates, a young, conservative appointee of President George W. Bush. After he dismissed our case, we appealed to the United States Court of Appeals for the District of Columbia Circuit. As soon as I saw our panel of three judges, I realized that we had little chance to prevail. The panel consisted of two conservative judges, David Sentelle and Karen Henderson, and one liberal judge, Judith Rogers.

Predictably, we lost 2–1. In an opinion by Judge Sentelle, the court found two special factors counseling hesitation and barring the Wilsons' lawsuit. First, the court said that the Privacy Act provided a remedy for violations of privacy and thus there could not be a suit for constitutional violations. But the absurdity of this statement is that the Privacy Act has no application in these circumstances, something which neither the defendants nor the judges denied. The Supreme Court previously had held that the offices of the president and the vice president were not covered by the Privacy Act and thus it did not apply to defendants Cheney, Libby, and Rove. Moreover, Joe Wilson had no claim under the Privacy Act since nothing about him had been revealed; the law was absolutely clear that he could not sue under this statute. His First Amendment rights had been violated by the reprisal against him for his speech and the Privacy Act had no application whatsoever to this situation. At most, the Privacy Act applied to Valerie's claim against Richard Armitage, a State Department employee, for invasion of privacy. Yet the district court and then the federal court of appeals used this statute to bar all of the constitutional claims.

The other special factor counseling hesitation was even more troubling: the possibility that the Wilsons' suit might lead to the revelation of secret information. The irony in this judgment was enormous. Cheney, Libby, Rove, and Armitage revealed

Valerie Plame Wilson's secret status as a CIA operative in violation of federal law. They surely should not be able to have her claim against them dismissed on the ground that her secret status might implicate sensitive information. This is the equivalent of the child who kills his or her parents and then begs the court for mercy on the grounds of being an orphan.

Besides, after the criminal prosecution and conviction of Libby, it is hard to imagine what sensitive information remained to be disclosed. Almost everything about the revelation of Valerie Plame's covert status and the circumstances of its revelation had been proven in open court at the Libby trial. Most importantly, at the early stage of our lawsuit it was purely speculative whether any sensitive information would be implicated. Some of the claims, such as Joe Wilson's claim that his speech had been violated by the retaliation against his wife, involved no secret information since the government repeatedly admitted to the fact that Valerie had been a secret agent. Yet both the district court and the court of appeals said that the entire case should be dismissed on this basis.

I was tremendously impressed by Joe and Valerie. Throughout the litigation they could not have been kinder or more gracious to me, though they were puzzled by the grounds for their lawsuit being dismissed. When I first met Valerie, I was immediately charmed. One of my first thoughts was how hard it was to imagine her as a spy. I realized that is probably why she was very good at her job.

I thought that we had strong grounds for Supreme Court review. An important legal issue was presented: Can a federal statute that provides no remedy be a basis for precluding constitutional claims under *Bivens*? Whether a federal statute ever can preclude a constitutional claim seems dubious, but certainly a statute that does not apply and can provide no recourse should not bar a suit for constitutional violations. Unfortunately, on June 22, 2009, the Supreme Court denied review. Joe Wilson and Valerie Plame Wilson never will get their day in court; nor will they receive any compensation for the constitutional violations and harms that they suffered.

* * *

For the last several decades, the conservative justices on the Court have fashioned a series of procedural devices to close the courthouse doors to those with injuries. These include restrictions on who can bring a lawsuit, much greater requirements for factual details in complaints to get into court, the tremendous expansion of sovereign immunity that prevents suits against state governments, a strong preference for arbitration over adjudication before juries, and strict limits on the size of punitive-damage awards. Each of these restrictions warrants explanation, but the whole is even more than the sum of these parts. All of these doctrines together make it harder for injured plaintiffs to get into court and to recover once they are there. Each and every one of them undermines accountability by strongly favoring defendants, governments, government officials, and businesses.

Standing

"Standing" simply refers to who is allowed under the law to bring a matter to court. Like so much in this book, the restrictions on standing began with the Nixon administration and the justices that it appointed to the United States Supreme Court. During the Warren Court era, the justices had made it easier for those with constitutional claims to have access to the federal courts. For example, in *Flast v. Cohen*, in 1968, the Court said that taxpayers could sue to challenge a federal program that gave aid directly to parochial schools in alleged violation of the Establishment Clause of the First Amendment. Even though no taxpayer suffered a measurable injury, the Court stressed the need to ensure that the Constitution was enforced.

In the early 1970s, the Nixon Justice Department urged the Supreme Court to greatly narrow or even overrule *Flast v. Cohen* and other Warren Court decisions opening the courthouse doors. In two cases in 1973, the Supreme Court accepted this invitation. In *Schlesinger v. Reservists Committee to Stop the War*, the Supreme Court considered whether taxpayers and citizens could sue to enforce a provision of the Constitution that prohibited members of Congress from holding positions in the executive branch of government. During the Vietnam War, some members of Congress remained members of the armed forces reserves in clear violation of this constitutional provision.

The Nixon administration asked the Supreme Court to dismiss the case and the Court agreed and ruled that no one had standing to sue to challenge this unconstitutional practice. The Court said that no one suffered a sufficiently personal and concrete injury to allow the lawsuit to go forward. The government thus could violate the express language of the Constitution and no court could provide a remedy, because the Court ruled that no person was sufficiently injured to be able to come to court to sue.

In another case, decided the same day, *United States v. Richardson*, the Court said that no one could sue to enforce a provision of Article I of the Constitution, which requires that Congress give a regular statement and account of all expenditures. Richardson sued to challenge the federal law that provides for the secrecy of the CIA budget; he said that this secrecy violated the requirement for a statement and account of all expenditures. As in *Schlesinger*, the Supreme Court agreed with the Nixon administration and held that no one had standing to bring such a lawsuit. In both of these cases, the Court was not just rejecting the claims of these particular plaintiffs; the Court was explicit that no one would be able to come to court to challenge these constitutional violations.

The implications of these decisions are enormous: the government can violate provisions of the Constitution and no one can bring a lawsuit to stop it. Long ago, in 1803 in *Marbury v. Madison*, the Supreme Court explained that judicial review to enforce the Constitution is essential because otherwise the limits within the Constitution would be rendered meaningless. Yet in the decades since *Schlesinger* and *Richardson*, the Supreme Court has continued to greatly limit standing.

Just a few years ago, in *Hein v. Freedom from Religion Foundation*, in 2006, the Supreme Court held that no one could sue to challenge the Bush administration's giving money directly to religious institutions—churches, synagogues, mosques—to provide social services. In a 5–4 decision, with Justice Samuel Alito writing for the conservative majority, the Court said that *Flast v. Cohen* was distinguishable from *Hein* because it involved the expenditure of money pursuant to a federal statute, whereas the Bush program spent money from general federal revenues. It is hard to imagine a more specious or less relevant distinction. The Establishment Clause of the First Amendment long has been found to apply to the executive branch as well as to the legislature. More importantly, under the Constitution, all spending is pursuant to a federal statute. Six of the justices agreed that the distinction of *Flast* made no sense. Justices Scalia and Thomas voted with the majority, but said that they would expressly overrule *Flast v. Cohen* and hold that taxpayers never can challenge the constitutionality of federal expenditures. Justices Stevens, Souter, Ginsburg, and Breyer dissented.

Since *Schlesinger* and *Richardson* were decided in 1973, the Supreme Court has imposed many limits on who has standing to sue. One of the most disturbing, and one with far-reaching consequences, was the decision in *City of Los Angeles v. Lyons*, in 1982.

On October 6, 1976, at approximately 2 A.M., Adolph Lyons, a twenty-four-year-old African-American man, was stopped by four Los Angeles police officers for driving with a burned-out taillight. The officers ordered Lyons out of his car and greeted him with drawn revolvers as he emerged from it. Lyons was told to face his car and spread his legs. He did this and was then ordered to clasp his hands and put them on top of his head. He again complied. After one of the officers completed a pat-down search, Lyons dropped his hands, but was ordered to place them back above his head. One of the officers grabbed Lyons's hands and slammed them onto his head. Lyons complained about the pain caused by the ring of keys he was holding in his hand. Within five to ten seconds, the officer began to choke Lyons by applying a forearm against his throat. As Lyons struggled for air, the officer handcuffed him, but continued to apply the choke hold until he blacked out. When Lyons regained consciousness, he was lying facedown on the ground, choking, gasping for air, and spitting up blood and dirt. He had urinated and defecated. He was issued a traffic citation and released. He suffered an injured larynx as a result of being choked by the officer.

The chokehold was commonly used by Los Angeles police officers, as well as by police departments across the country, to subdue suspects. Indeed, a survey in 1980 revealed that 90 percent of departments authorized the carotid hold and 53.33 percent authorized the bar arm hold. Los Angeles Police Department policy manuals expressly authorized officers to use the choke hold as a way to subdue suspects. Officers were trained in its use at the police academy.

Lyons did some research and learned that to that point, sixteen people had died from the use of the choke hold by Los Angeles police officers; almost all, like him, were African-American men. This led to one of the more infamous moments during Daryl Gates's tenure as chief of the LAPD. When asked why almost all of those who died had been African-American, Gates responded that it was because of physiological differences between black people and "normal people," stating that "veins or arteries of Blacks do not open up as fast as they do in normal people."

Lyons sued the city of Los Angeles for an injunction to keep police officers from using the choke hold except where necessary to protect the officers' lives or their safety. In a 5–4 decision, with the justices split along ideological lines, the Supreme Court ruled that Lyons's suit should be dismissed for lack of standing. The Court explained that Lyons could not show that he, personally, was likely to be choked again in the future. Justice White, writing for the five most conservative justices, declared that "[a]bsent a sufficient likelihood that he will again be wronged in a similar way, Lyons is no more entitled to an injunction than any other citizen of Los Angeles; and a federal court may not entertain a claim by any or all citizens who no more than assert that certain practices of law enforcement officers are unconstitutional." The Court articulated a rule that plaintiffs seeking an injunction must show a likelihood of being harmed again in the future.

I have been part of countless discussions with civil rights lawyers who have concluded that they could not sue to halt specific constitutional violations because no one could sue for an injunction since no one could show that he or she personally would be injured in the future. There are hundreds and hundreds of reported instances of cases being thrown out of court because of *Lyons*. For example, two federal district courts ruled that women who had been strip-searched when stopped by police for routine traffic violations did not have standing to sue for an injunction. These women could sue the officers for money damages, but they could not sue for an injunction because they could not show a likelihood of their personally being subjected to this illegal and terribly degrading practice in the future. There are countless instances where the government is alleged to engage in an unconstitutional practice and individuals are injured, but no one can show that it is likely to happen to him or her again.

Heightened Pleading Requirements

The Supreme Court recently has made it much harder for injured individuals to get into federal court by significantly increasing the facts that must be stated in the complaint in order for the lawsuit to go forward. This is a perfect example of how a seemingly technical decision about court procedures can have a profound effect in keeping plaintiffs from being able to sue and in systematically favoring defendants who have allegedly violated the Constitution and federal laws.

As long as there have been courts and civil suits for relief, there has been the issue of how much detail should be required in a complaint in order for a lawsuit to go forward. If a great deal of detail is required, then many plaintiffs with meritorious claims will be unable to proceed because they do not have all of the facts until there is the opportunity to do discovery. In many instances, key facts are in the control of the defendants and cannot be obtained until there is a lawsuit and the chance to take depositions, ask interrogatories, and request documents. On the other hand, making it easier for plaintiffs to get into court means subjecting some defendants to nonmeritorious suits and all of the costs attendant to them.

American courts initially copied the English rules for pleading, which were quite strict in terms of their requirements for pleading detailed facts in order to get into court. In the mid-nineteenth century, American courts began to devise their own rules for pleadings, but again they required great specificity in alleging facts to support the claims presented. In the late 1930s, the adoption of the Federal Rules of Civil Procedure ushered in a new system of court procedures, which came to be called "notice pleading." This system strongly favored the ability of plaintiffs to have their day in court. All that was required to get into federal court was a short, plain statement of the facts, enough to give notice to the defendants and the court as to the nature of the claim, and enough so that it could not be said that it was impossible that the plaintiff could recover. In 1957, the Supreme Court explained that under the Federal Rules of Civil Procedure and notice pleading, a complaint was not to be dismissed unless there was no set of facts upon which relief could be granted.

Admittedly, this subjected some defendants to needless litigation. But the philosophy of notice pleading and the Federal Rules was that those asserting injuries should be able to get their chance at discovery to find the facts to prove their claims. Screening of suits would not be done on a motion to dismiss before discovery, but only after the opportunity for each side to gather relevant information so that a court could decide if there was a dispute over the facts that a jury should resolve.

This was the law for seventy years, until the Supreme Court dramatically changed the standard for pleading in federal court. The key case was *Ashcroft v. Iqbal*, in 2009. Iqbal was a man of Pakistani descent who claimed that he was illegally detained in New York after September 11, 2001. He sued fifty-three defendants, among them then attorney general John Ashcroft, and asserted that his detention and treatment violated the United States Constitution.

In a 5–4 decision, the Supreme Court concluded that Iqbal's complaint should be dismissed because he failed to allege sufficient facts for a court to conclude that it was "plausible" that he might recover. Justice Kennedy wrote for the Court, joined by Chief Justice Roberts and Justices Scalia, Thomas, and Alito. No longer could plaintiffs go forward unless there was no set of facts upon which they could recover. No longer did courts have to accept the allegations of the complaint as true; the Court said that conclusory allegations of fact should be ignored by federal courts. To see how radical this decision is in changing the law, one need only pick up a copy of the Federal Rules of Civil Procedure, the rules that govern the procedures in all civil cases in federal court. Every sample complaint within it would have to be dismissed because they lack adequate facts under the new standard adopted by *Ashcroft v. Iqbal.*

No longer do the federal courts follow the notice pleading standard of the last seventy years. The new standard is "plausibility": a plaintiff must allege enough facts that a court can say that it is plausible for the plaintiff to recover. It is unclear exactly what this means. Justice Kennedy, in his majority opinion, simply said that courts should decide what is plausible based on the context and by relying on common sense. Obviously, what is plausible to one district court judge might not be to another. By April 2010, just eight months after the Supreme Court's decision, there already were more than eight thousand lower federal court cases citing *Ashcroft v. Iqbal.* Hundreds of cases already had been dismissed that otherwise would have been able to go forward.

It will take years and maybe decades for the Supreme Court to clarify what it means by "plausibility." Senator Arlen Specter has introduced a bill into Congress to change the pleading rules back to the notice pleading standard that had been followed for seventy years. One staff member of the House Judiciary Committee told me that it would be difficult to get it enacted because it is hard for members of Congress to understand why pleading rules matter so much. But these rules matter tremendously because they determine who can get into federal court at all.

It is striking that the five most conservative justices on their own changed the law in a way that greatly protects defendants from lawsuits. Congress could have, but didn't, change the pleading rules at any time over the last seven decades. The Federal Rules Advisory Committee, which promulgates the Federal Rules of Civil Procedure, could have, but didn't, change the pleading rules. No studies showed any problems with the approach that had been followed for seventy years. But there is no doubt that the Supreme Court now has closed the courthouse doors to many with meritorious lawsuits by requiring many more facts to be included in the complaints that initiate litigation.

Sovereign Immunity

Michael Hason is a graduate of Yale College and New York Medical School. He speaks quickly with a New York accent. He has suffered serious depression at various stages of his life and the California Medical Licensing Board used this as a basis for denying him a license to practice medicine in the state. He sued the board and its members, claiming that this was discrimination based on disability and thus violated his rights under equal protection and Title II of the Americans with Disabilities Act, which prohibits state and local governments from discriminating against people with disabilities in government programs, services, and activities. Hason could not afford a lawyer and filed the complaint in federal court on his own. The federal district court dismissed his case based on the state government's sovereign immunity. Sovereign immunity is a principle derived from English law that prevents suits against the government, even when it violates the Constitution or acts illegally.

Hason appealed to the United States Court of Appeals for the Ninth Circuit and the court asked me to represent him. I accepted and was immediately impressed by Hason in my conversations with him. He was obviously very articulate and intelligent and had mastered a great deal of the arcane law of sovereign immunity.

One of the important changes in the law during William Rehnquist's tenure as chief justice was the substantial expansion of sovereign immunity for state governments. All of these cases were 5–4 rulings, with the conservatives in the majority. These decisions have had a significant effect in keeping many who have been injured from being able to sue state governments. The federal district court relied on these recent decisions in dismissing Hason's suit.

In 1996, in *Seminole Tribe v. Florida*, the Supreme Court expressly overruled an earlier decision and held that Congress could authorize suits against state governments to enforce federal laws only under very narrow circumstances. The Court declared unconstitutional a provision of the federal Indian Gaming Law that required that state governments negotiate in good faith with Native American tribes to allow gambling on reservations and authorized suits against states that refused to do so.

In 1999, in *Florida Prepaid Postsecondary Education Board v. College Savings Bank*, the Court ruled that a state could not be sued for patent infringement. A New Jersey company devised and patented a system for parents to use to save money for their children's college education. The state of Florida simply copied this system for use by parents in that state and was sued for patent infringement. The Supreme Court held that a federal law expressly authorizing suits against state governments for patent infringement was unconstitutional because of the sovereign immunity of state governments. Since federal law provides that only federal courts may hear patent cases, the result is that the College Savings Bank was left without any remedy for violations of its patents.

Not long ago, I was giving a speech for judges in another state and was using copyrighted material. In talking with the director of judicial education in the state, I offered to get a copyright release. She said that she did not bother with that anymore because she knew that the state could not be sued for copyright infringement.

In explaining the impact of the decision in *Florida Prepaid* to my students, I ask them to imagine a constitutional law professor who has written several textbooks and is using the royalties to pay for his four children's college education. What if some law school at a state university copied these books, digitized them, and made them available free for all law students in the country? After the Supreme Court's decision in *Florida Prepaid*, the poor law professor would be left without any remedy.

One of the most important decisions expanding the scope of state sovereign immunity was *Alden v. Maine*, in 1999. Probation officers in Maine sued the state, claiming that they were owed overtime pay under the federal Fair Labor Standards Act. Earlier, the Supreme Court had ruled that this law constitutionally applies to state governments. The probation officers sued in federal court for their money and the case was thrown out because of state sovereign immunity. The probation officers then sued in state court. The Supreme Court, again in a 5–4 decision with the five conservatives in the majority, held that state governments cannot be sued in state court, even on federal claims, without their consent. This is the first time in American history that the Supreme Court held that sovereign immunity bars suits against states in state court.

In 2000, in *Kimel v. Florida Board of Regents,* the Court said that state governments cannot be sued for violations of the federal Age Discrimination in Employment Act. A year later, in *Garrett v. University of Alabama*, the Court concluded that a nurse who lost her job at a state hospital when she took time off for treatment for breast cancer could not sue under Title I of the Americans with Disabilities Act. These cases, too, were 5–4, with the five most conservative justices—Rehnquist, O'Connor, Scalia, Kennedy, and Thomas—in the majority.

As I wrote the briefs for Michael Hason and argued his case in the federal court of appeals in the fall of 2001, all of these decisions were new and were obviously creating a substantial obstacle to suing state governments. Yet this expansion of sovereign immunity had no basis in the Constitution and, indeed, undermines basic constitutional values.

The principle of sovereign immunity is derived from English law, which assumed that "the king can do no wrong." Since the time of Edward I, the crown of England has not been suable unless it has specifically consented to suit. A doctrine derived from the premise "the king can do no wrong" deserves no place in American law. The United States was founded on rejection of monarchy and royal prerogatives. American government is based on the fundamental recognition that the government and government officials *can* do wrong and must be held accountable. Sovereign immunity undermines that basic notion.

The doctrine also is inconsistent with the U.S. Constitution. Nowhere does the document mention or even imply that state governments have complete immunity to suit. Sovereign immunity is a doctrine based on a common law principle borrowed from the English common law. However, Article VI of the Constitution states that the Constitution and laws made pursuant to them are the supreme law and, as such, should prevail over claims of sovereign immunity. Yet, according to these Supreme Court decisions, sovereign immunity, a common-law doctrine, trumps even the U.S. Constitution and bars suits against government entities for relief when they violate the Constitution and federal laws.

Sovereign immunity is inconsistent with a central maxim of American government: no one, not even the government, is above the law. The effect of sovereign immunity is to place the government above the law and to ensure that even individuals who have suffered egregious harms will be unable to receive redress for their injuries. The judicial role of enforcing and upholding the Constitution is rendered illusory when the government has complete immunity to suit. Sovereign immunity undermines the basic principle, announced in *Marbury v. Madison,* that "[t]he very essence of civil liberty certainly consists in the right of every individual to claim the protection of the laws, whenever he receives an injury."

Conservatives are fond of professing a belief in strict construction, saying that they follow the text and the original understanding of the Constitution. But sovereign immunity cannot be justified under a faithful adherence to the text or the original understanding of the Constitution. The text of the Constitution is silent about sovereign immunity. Not one clause of the first seven articles even hints at the idea that the government has immunity from suits. No constitutional amendment has bestowed sovereign immunity on the federal government.

A claim might be made that the Eleventh Amendment provides sovereign immunity to state governments. Yet, if this is a textual argument, a careful reading of the text does not support the claim. The Eleventh Amendment states, "The Judicial power of the United States shall not be construed to extend to any suit in law or equity, commenced or prosecuted against one of the United States by Citizens of another State, or by Citizens or Subjects of any foreign state." It should be noted that the Eleventh Amendment applies only in federal court; it is a restriction solely on "the judicial power of the United States." Yet, in *Alden v. Maine*, in 1999, the Supreme Court found that state governments cannot be sued in state courts. Justice Kennedy, writing for the majority, stated: "[S]overeign immunity derives not from the Eleventh Amendment but from the structure of the original Constitution itself."

Moreover, the text of the Eleventh Amendment restricts only suits against states that are based on what is called "diversity of citizenship"; it says that the federal judicial power does not extend to a suit against a state by a citizen of another state or of a foreign country. Nothing within it bars a suit against a state by its own citizens. In 1890, the Supreme Court found that the Eleventh Amendment bars suits against a state by its own citizens, but that is not what the provision says and that is not what it was intended to do.

Nor can sovereign immunity be justified based on the intent of the Constitution's framers. There was no discussion of sovereign immunity at the Constitutional Convention in Philadelphia in 1787. The issue did arise in the state ratifying conventions in a dispute over whether Article III authorized suits against unconsenting states in federal court. Two of the clauses of Article III, §2, specifically deal with suits against state governments. These provisions permit suits "between a State and Citizens of another state" and "between a State ... and foreign ... Citizens." The question was whether the above-quoted language of Article III was meant to override the sovereign immunity that kept states from being sued in state courts. Justice Souter, after a detailed recounting of this history, observed: "[T]he framers and their contemporaries did not agree about the place of common-law state sovereign immunity.... [A]t most, then, the historical materials show that ... the intentions of the Framers and Ratifiers were ambiguous."

Sovereign immunity also cannot be based on the contemporary practices at the time the Constitution was ratified. In fact, charters in several colonies, including Massachusetts, Connecticut, Rhode Island, and Georgia, expressly specified that the governments could be sued.

As a result, in *Alden v. Maine*, Justice Kennedy was reduced to defending sovereign immunity as implicit in the framers' silence about the issue. The problem with this argument is that silence is inherently ambiguous. Perhaps Justice Kennedy is correct that the framers were silent because they thought it obvious that states could not be sued in state court. Alternatively, maybe they were silent because they thought it clear that states *could* be sued in state court. Most likely, though, the framers were silent because the issue did not come up and they never thought about it. Silence is inherently uncertain and a highly questionable basis for determining intent.

My point is that if the conservatives on the Supreme Court were true to their professed interpretive methodology, looking to the Constitution's text and its original meaning, they would never find sovereign immunity to be a constitutional principle. But their desire to close the courthouse doors and protect state governments from constitutional litigation has led to a tremendous expansion of sovereign immunity in recent years.

The costs of closing the courthouse doors are substantial. Sovereign immunity undermines government accountability and frustrates the supremacy of federal law by preventing the enforcement of the Constitution and federal statutes. How can the supremacy of federal law be assured and vindicated if states can violate the Constitution or federal laws and not be held accountable? The probation officers in *Alden* have a federal right to overtime pay. But there is no way of forcing the states to meet their federal obligation. College Savings Bank has a federal patent right that was allegedly infringed by the state of Florida, but there is no way to hold the state liable for patent infringement. In *Kimel*, the Court did not declare unconstitutional the application of the Age Discrimination Act to state governments. Instead, it said that states cannot be sued for violating it. In other words, the states are left free to disregard federal law.

At the oral argument in *Alden*, the solicitor general of the United States, Seth Waxman, quoted to the Court from the supremacy clause of Article VI, which says that the Constitution and laws and treaties made pursuant to it are the supreme law of the land, and contended that suits against states are essential to assure the supremacy of federal law. Justice Kennedy's response to this argument is astounding. He wrote:

> The constitutional privilege of a State to assert its sovereign immunity in its own courts does not confer upon the State a concomitant right to disregard the Constitution or valid federal law. The States and their officers are bound by obligations imposed by the Constitution and by federal statutes that comport with the constitutional design. We are unwilling to assume the States will refuse to honor the Constitution or obey the binding laws of the United States. The good faith of the States thus provides an important assurance that "[t]his Constitution, and the Laws of the United States which shall be made in Pursuance thereof . . . shall be the supreme Law of the Land." U.S. Const., Art. VI.

What, then, is the assurance that state governments will comply with federal law? Trust in the good faith of state governments. It is inconceivable that fifty years ago, at the height of the civil rights movement, the Supreme Court would have issued such a statement that state governments simply could be trusted voluntarily to comply with federal law. James Madison said that if people were angels there would be no need for a Constitution, but there would be no need for a government, either. The reality is that state governments, intentionally or unintentionally, at times will violate federal law. To rely on trust in the good faith of state governments is no assurance of the supremacy of federal law at all.

Sovereign immunity allows the government to violate the Constitution or laws of the United States and not be held accountable. It means that constitutional and statutory rights can be violated, but individuals are left with no remedies. The probation officers in *Alden*, the company with the patent in *Florida Prepaid*, and the state employees in *Kimel* all have federal rights, but due to sovereign immunity, they have no remedies. Sovereign immunity makes the laws of the United States subordinate to the will of the men and women making government decisions.

Conceptions of civil suits have changed dramatically from the time that the U.S. Constitution was written and ratified. Today, liability is justified primarily based on two rationales: the need to provide compensation to injured individuals and the desire to deter future wrongdoing. Sovereign immunity frustrates compensation and deterrence. Individuals injured by government wrongdoing are left without a remedy.

I won Michael Hason's suit in the Ninth Circuit Court of Appeals. The Court relied on long-standing precedent that state government officials can be sued even when state governments are not liable and on an earlier Ninth Circuit decision, which preceded the more recent Supreme Court rulings, holding that state governments may be sued under Title II of the Americans with Disabilities Act. The state of California sought review in the U.S. Supreme Court, and in November 2002, the Court agreed to hear the matter. It scheduled oral argument for late in March 2003.

I spent most of December and January writing my brief. In February, I learned that the disabilities rights community in California was pressuring Attorney General Bill Lockyer to dismiss the case before the U.S. Supreme Court. Since California had sought Supreme Court review it could change its mind and ask the Court to dismiss the case. Disability rights advocates were understandably worried that the Supreme Court would use this case to preclude suits against state governments for discrimination based on disabilities. Lockyer was contemplating a run for governor in 2006 (no one at that time foresaw the recall election of Governor Gray Davis and the election in 2004 of Arnold Schwarzenegger). The disabilities community delivered an unequivocal message to Lockyer: dismiss the case before the Supreme Court or there will be no hope of support from this important political constituency.

Three weeks before the scheduled oral argument, Lockyer asked the Court to dismiss the case. I called the Supreme Court and a wonderful clerk told me that he had been there for twenty years and never had seen such a thing. Michael Hason rightly did not perceive this as a victory. The issue of whether the state could be sued in his case was unresolved by the Supreme Court. The dismissal of his case by the Supreme Court would mean that the case would go back to the federal trial court. He might litigate there for years only to see the Court later in another case hold that such suits were barred by sovereign immunity. His case would then be dismissed. He said that he'd rather know sooner than later whether he could sue the state. He asked me to request the Supreme Court to keep and decide the case. I did so and said that at the very least, California should pay my attorney's fees. Although I was working pro bono, I had expended a tremendous amount of time on the matter before the Supreme Court. The attorney general did not need to seek Supreme Court review, and once he gained it, he did not need to wait until three weeks before the oral arguments before dismissing the matter. The Court dismissed the case and denied any fees.

In 2004, in *Tennessee v. Lane*, the Court ruled that a man who was paralyzed from the waist down and had to crawl on his hands and knees to get to a second-floor courtroom could sue the state under Title II of the Americans with Disabilities Act. The Court stressed that the suit could go forward because the fundamental right of access to the courts was implicated. This certainly left the implication that Michael Hason would have lost had the Court decided the case in 2003; no similar fundamental right was violated in his case. Moreover, it is quite questionable whether *Tennessee v.*

Lane will still be followed today. It was a 5–4 decision, with Justice O'Connor joining Justices Stevens, Souter, Ginsburg, and Breyer. From every indication, Justice Alito is more likely to agree with the conservative dissenters and to create a majority to overrule this decision, further expanding the scope of sovereign immunity and closing the courthouse doors.

Michael Hason has never gotten his medical license from California.

The Preference for Arbitration over Jury Trials

Not long ago I went to see a doctor I had not seen before and the receptionist gave me a whole stack of papers that I had to fill out before the physician would see me. I usually do not pay much attention to what I sign, but I noticed that one of the forms said that if I had any dispute with the doctor, the matter would go to arbitration, and that I was waiving my ability to go to court. I went to the receptionist and I said, "I don't want to sign this form. Will the doctor still see me?" She said, "I don't know; nobody has ever refused to sign it before." She said, "I have to check with the doctor." She came back and fortunately said that the doctor would see me. I imagine this is a doctor who sees a large number of patients every day and apparently I am the first one to question signing the form. Since then I have learned that malpractice insurance carriers are increasingly requiring physicians to insist that their patients agree to go to arbitration and waive any right to go to court.

Several years ago, I bought a new computer from Dell. I was about to teach the material on arbitration to my first-year civil procedure class and decided to read the fine print that came with the agreement accompanying the computer. There was a clause that said that by buying the computer and by turning it on, I was agreeing that any dispute that I would have with Dell would go to arbitration and not to a jury trial. I sent a letter back to Dell saying, "I do not consent to this and by opening my letter you hereby consent that I can take you to court." I am pleased to report the computer worked fine and that I had no occasion for suing Dell.

These two examples are illustrations of a national trend toward businesses demanding arbitration whenever possible and rejecting courts and jury trials. Why? Businesses would much prefer that suits against them by injured consumers or aggrieved employees never get before a jury. Juries are perceived as pro-plaintiff and too likely to be swayed by emotions. Professional arbiters are strongly favored by defendants as more likely to rule in their favor and likely to award less in damages when ruling for plaintiffs.

Yale law professor Judith Resnik has documented another reason why businesses prefer arbitration: an institutionalized bias among arbiters in favor of repeat players in the system. Resnik explains that professional arbiters depend for their work on being selected, or at least not being rejected by, the parties. Arbiters know that if they develop the reputation of being pro-plaintiff, businesses will be sure not to use them in the future. The corollary is that those arbiters who develop a reputation of being pro-business are much more likely to be high on the defendants' list of possible arbiters. The repeat players in the system, the businesses, thus gain a real advantage.

Arbitration has other costs as well. The American system places great, and I believe deserved, faith in juries. Every study of the jury system confirms this confidence. Arbitration, by definition, takes matters away from juries. Key procedural protections, such as the ability to appeal, are generally not present with arbitration. Arbitration, unlike court adjudication, rarely produces written opinions that develop the law and provide guidance for future cases.

To be clear, I am not against arbitration. It often has advantages over adjudication in its efficiency and simplicity. Disputing parties, of course, should be able to choose arbitration if they prefer. My concern is the aggressive way in which the Supreme Court has been pushing matters to arbitration when there is no such agreement between the parties.

A key Supreme Court decision earlier this decade was *Circuit City Stores, Inc. v. Adams.* Saint Clair Adams worked for a Circuit

City store in Southern California. When he applied for work, the application said that any grievances, including discrimination claims, with Circuit City would go to arbitration. Two years after being hired, Adams sued Circuit City for discrimination. Adams's lawyer decided it was best to keep the case in California state courts and sued entirely under California law, eschewing any claims under federal civil rights.

Circuit City then filed a separate action in federal district court to compel arbitration under the Federal Arbitration Act. This law was adopted in 1925 and says that federal courts should enforce clauses in contracts that require arbitration. There is an exception to the Federal Arbitration Act that says that arbitration is not required for claims by "contracts of employment of seamen, railroad employees, or any other class of workers engaged in foreign or interstate commerce." The United States Court of Appeals for the Ninth Circuit said that the Federal Arbitration Act did not apply to Adams's claim. Under the literal language of the statute, Adams was an employee engaged in interstate commerce. The Federal Arbitration Act plainly says that arbitration is not required in the case of an employment dispute for somebody who is working in interstate commerce.

The Supreme Court, 5–4, reversed the court of appeals. Justice Kennedy wrote the opinion, which was joined by the four most conservative justices then on the Court: Rehnquist, O'Connor, Scalia, and Thomas. The Court interpreted the statute to say that "employees in interstate commerce" refers only to transportation workers. In other words, under the Court's interpretation, contractual clauses requiring arbitration are not enforceable for those working in the transportation industry, but all other employees are compelled to have their employment disputes, including discrimination claims, resolved through arbitration. This is inconsistent with the plain language of the statute. Moreover, it is hard to see how there was a contractual agreement between Adams and Circuit City. A clause on an employment application that the employee had no choice but to sign is not a contract in any meaningful sense of the word.

This decision, of course, does not just apply to Saint Clair Adams. It means that countless other employees with claims of race or gender or age discrimination will be deprived of their chance to go to court. As Justice Stevens lamented in his dissenting opinion, the Supreme Court has "pushed the pendulum far beyond a neutral attitude and endorsed a policy that strongly favors private arbitration."

One more recent example illustrates the Court's strong push toward arbitration over court adjudication. In 2009, in *14 Penn Plaza LLC v. Pyett*, the Court considered whether Steven Pyett could bring his age discrimination claim to federal court. Pyett worked as a night watchman. He was a member of Service Employees International Union, Local 32BJ. Under the National Labor Relations Act, the union is the exclusive bargaining representative of employees within the building-services industry in New York City, which includes building cleaners, porters, and doorpersons. The union has exclusive authority to bargain on behalf of its members over their "rates of pay, wages, hours of employment, or other conditions of employment."

The union had decided not to pursue with Pyett's employer Pyett's claim that he was reassigned to less desirable tasks because of his age. Pyett filed suit in federal court under the federal Age Discrimination in Employment Act. The issue was whether the union's refusal to pursue his claim in arbitration with the employer precluded Pyett from suing. The Court, in a 5–4 decision, ruled that Pyett was barred from bringing his discrimination claim to federal court. Justice Thomas wrote, joined by Chief Justice Roberts and Justices Scalia, Kennedy, and Alito. An earlier Supreme Court decision had declared that features of arbitration made it a forum "well suited to the resolution of contractual disputes," but "a comparatively inappropriate forum for the final resolution of rights created by [federal antidiscrimination laws]." The Supreme Court repudiated that language and strongly endorsed the desirability of arbitration for resolving disputes, including claims under federal antidiscrimination laws. Employees in unionized workplaces will now need to take their discrimination cases to arbiters and not to courts and juries.

It is not coincidental that most of the decisions pushing matters to arbitration and away from courts and juries are split exactly along ideological lines. The conservative justices on the Court are systematically favoring business over injured patients, consumers, and employees. It is a profound change in American law and one that most people don't realize until they are injured and try to go to court.

Constitutional Limits on Punitive Damages

One of my most frustrating losses as a lawyer occurred in representing the Romo family. In the summer of 1992, Ramon Romo bought a 1978 Ford Bronco because he thought it was "a strong, safe car" that was "ideal for the family to ride in." About a year later, on June 20, 1993, Juan Romo, Ramon's eldest son, was driving the 1978 Bronco just south of Modesto, California, on a straight interstate freeway. Juan was traveling within the speed limit. The entire family was in the car: Ramon, Juan's father, was in the front passenger seat; Juan's mother, Salustia, and his brother, Ramiro, were in the backseat; and Juan's younger sisters, Evangelina and Maria, were sleeping in the farthest backseat of the vehicle.

Juan had been driving for a couple of hours when the family's Bronco approached a slow-moving truck that unexpectedly moved into the Romos' lane. Juan avoided a collision, but because of the Bronco's lack of stability (made worse merely by the presence of multiple occupants), the Bronco swerved across the roadway, and at less than fifty miles per hour started to roll. As the Bronco rolled (two and a half times), the two-thirds of the roof that was plastic broke off completely at the roof pillars and crashed into the occupant compartment; the front steel portion flattened to the dashboard.

When the plastic portion of the roof (weighing more than one hundred pounds) broke off, it inflicted massive head trauma to Juan's mother and his brother as they sat seat-belted in the rear seat. When the front part of the roof flattened, it crushed Juan's father's head as he sat seat-belted in the front seat. All three were properly seat-belted. All three died at the scene.

Expert testimony at the trial showed that if Ford had put steel reinforcement in the roof (as it later did in the 1980 and later-model Broncos) to maintain "adequate survival space" and to keep the plastic section of the roof from breaking off, the three seat-belted decedents would have "walked away" from this accident.

Juan survived only because as the Bronco rolled, he fell to his side below the crushing roof. Evangelina and Maria survived because they were lying asleep below the breaking rear plastic roof. But all three were seriously hurt. Juan, Eva, and Maria not only suffered their own injuries, they witnessed their parents' and brother's gruesome deaths.

The evidence at trial showed that the 1978 Bronco is an un-stable sport utility vehicle that Ford marketed for American fami-lies with a roof that is two-thirds plastic/one-third steel and has no roll bar. Ford knew before selling the 1978 Bronco that its roof would "fail" to protect its occupants in a rollover. Automotive ex-perts called the Bronco a "piece of junk" and the "absolute worst" vehicle ever in a rollover. As Ford formally admitted, never in its entire history had it built a hardtop vehicle without steel in the vehicle's rearmost roof pillar to protect passengers. The extreme danger of the Bronco was shown by statistics Ford itself compiled for the trial that revealed that once the 1978 Bronco rolls over, it kills more occupants per rollover than any other SUV.

Well before marketing the 1978 Bronco, Ford had acquired ex-tensive knowledge of rollover and roof crush hazards from testing, research, and safety engineering evaluations it conducted during the 1960s and 1970s. But in the mid-1970s, when the "large SUV" market suddenly took off, Ford saw it had no "entry" in that market and would have none until 1980. Ford's top management reacti-vated and "expedited" a once-shelved "stop gap" 1978 Bronco (in-tended to exist only two years), knowingly sacrificing roof safety in the rush. Henry Ford II personally cut $9 million from the vehicle's production budget, and despite its own safety engineering consen-sus on roof crush and occupant safety, Ford deleted the integral roll bar from the original one-third steel roof design, and omitted steel reinforcement in the plastic rear two-thirds of the roof.

Despite deleting the integral roll bar, Ford left a deceptive empty hump in the steel part of the roof to make it appear as if a rollover bar were inside. Ford then advertised the vehicle for family use, promoting it as "Ford Tough."

A Ford *post*-production test on the 1978 and 1979 Bronco showed the "roof crush problem," but Ford only addressed the problem in the planned, tested, and unrushed 1980 Bronco by putting steel in the plastic roof's pillar, thereby cutting rollover deaths by 60 percent. Ford did nothing about the hazards it knew existed in the 1978 Bronco.

The Romos sued Ford, and after five days of deliberations, the jury awarded $6,226,793 in compensatory damages and $290 million in punitive damages. The jury allocated 78 percent fault to Ford, 12 percent to the driver of the second vehicle, and 10 percent to plaintiff Juan Romo. Judgment for $294,935,709.10 was entered against Ford.

Ford appealed the verdict to the California Court of Appeal. In strong language, the court of appeal affirmed the judgment and ruled against Ford. The court of appeal concluded that the evidence was sufficient to permit the jury to "clearly and convincingly conclude" that Ford "acted with malice" and that it was "frivolous" for Ford to contend that its conduct was not sufficiently "vile" or "loathsome" to support the punitive-damage award. The court thoroughly examined the record and found Ford's misconduct comparable to "involuntary manslaughter" and "grossly reprehensible."

However, subsequent to the California Court of Appeal's decision, the United States Supreme Court imposed new constitutional limits on punitive-damage awards. Prior to 1996, never in American history had the Supreme Court found a punitive-damage award to be unconstitutional. In 1996, in *BMW v. Gore*, in a 5–4 decision, the Supreme Court ruled that "grossly excessive punitive damages violate due process." The case involved an award of $2 million in punitive damages for repainting cars and not disclosing that fact to consumers.

After the jury issued its award against Ford in the Romo case and after it was affirmed by the California Court of Appeal, the U.S. Supreme Court decided *State Farm v. Campbell* in April 2003. Curtis Campbell, a longtime policyholder of automobile insurance with State Farm Insurance Company, was in a serious automobile accident. Despite his insurance policy, State Farm refused to pay. At one point the agent told Campbell that he should sell his house to pay the costs he incurred because State Farm was not paying them. Campbell sued State Farm for bad faith. Campbell died before trial, but his estate continued with the suit. At trial, the estate's lawyer presented evidence of State Farm having a systematic practice of identifying vulnerable individuals and refusing to pay their claims as a way of saving the company money. The jury awarded Campbell's estate $1 million in compensatory damages and $145 million in punitive damages. The Utah Supreme Court upheld the verdict.

The Supreme Court reversed, with Justice Kennedy writing the opinion. The Court said, among other things, that punitive damages generally should be no more than nine times the size of the compensatory damages. As the phrases imply, "compensatory damages" are designed to compensate a plaintiff for the injuries suffered; "punitive damages" are intended to punish egregious wrongdoing. The Court observed that there is no clear rule, but that punitive damages that are greater than single digits in their ratio to compensatory damages are constitutionally suspect.

What is striking about this holding is its arbitrariness. There is no apparent basis for a constitutional rule that punitive damages must be no more than nine times the size of the compensatory damages. I was in the audience at the Supreme Court when this case was argued. I recall Justice Kennedy asking the attorney for Campbell, Harvard law professor Laurence Tribe, whether there should be a constitutional rule limiting punitive damages to no more than nine times the size of the compensatory damages. Professor Tribe said that there was no constitutional basis for such a rule, though legislatures could impose this if they wished. Nonetheless, that is exactly what the Court did in its decision in *State Farm v. Campbell.*

The California Court of Appeal then asked for new briefing and new arguments in *Romo* in light of *State Farm v. Campbell*. I argued the case in the California Court of Appeal in November 2003 and tried to explain that the jury's $290 million punitive-damage award against Ford should stand even though the compensatory damages were $6 million. In *State Farm v. Campbell* the Supreme Court acknowledged that there would be instances where ratios greater than nine to one would be allowed. *State Farm* was a case involving fraud; *Romo* involved the deaths of three people and serious injuries to three others. Ford's conduct put tens of thousands of lives at risk. More importantly, punitive damages are meant to deter wrongdoing and punish egregious conduct. To be effective, they thus must be calibrated to the wealth of the defendants. In its initial ruling, the California Court of Appeal noted that "[a]t the time of trial, defendant had daily after-tax profits of $20 million and its net worth was $25 billion, of which $14 billion was in cash on hand." The court noted that the "damages award is 1.2 percent of defendant's net worth and nine days of its profit at the time of trial." The punitive-damage judgment against Ford was large but appropriate given its wealth and the egregiousness of its conduct.

Ten days after the oral argument, the California Court of Appeal ruled that the judgment against Ford should be reduced from $290 million to $23.7 million. The court said that based on *State Farm v. Campbell*, the ratio between compensatory and punitive damages should be four to one. Although the court claimed that this ratio was based on the U.S. Constitution, the foundation for this judgment as a rule of constitutional law still eludes me. The California Court of Appeal also said that punitive damages should be allowed only to punish a defendant for the harms suffered by that plaintiff. This was a radical change in the law and went much further than anything the Supreme Court had held. However, four years later, in *Philip Morris v. Williams*, the U.S. Supreme Court came to the same conclusion and found that due process required that punitive damages be used to punish a defendant only for the harms suffered by the plaintiff in that lawsuit.

These rules sharply limiting punitive-damage awards obviously greatly favor defendant businesses over injured plaintiffs. Conservatives constantly object to the Supreme Court finding rights, like privacy, that are not mentioned in the Constitution. But the Constitution does not say anything about punitive-damage awards. In fact, Justices Scalia and Thomas have consistently dissented from these rulings restricting punitive damages on the grounds that there is no constitutional right in this area. But the other conservative justices—Rehnquist, O'Connor, Kennedy, Roberts, and Alito—have consistently been part of the majority in the Supreme Court's decisions imposing constitutional limits on punitive damages.

The Supreme Court's creation of constitutional limits on punitive damages also is inconsistent with the traditional conservative claim of deference to the political process. Many states, through statutes and initiatives, have imposed limits on punitive damages. Some states, like Nebraska, do not allow punitive damages at all. Other states have imposed caps on punitive damages, such as Ohio, which says that punitive damages generally cannot be more than double compensatory damages. Virginia provides that punitive damages cannot be more than three times the compensatory award. In Alaska, punitive damages cannot be greater than the larger of either $1.5 million or three times the size of the compensatory damages. California's voters through an initiative or legislators through a statute could have created a rule that punitive damages may never be more than four times greater than compensatory damages.

Businesses, especially insurance companies, have tried to convince the American public that juries are out of control in awarding punitive damages. They illustrate this claim by pointing to instances such as the woman who received a large punitive-damage award after being scalded by hot coffee from a McDonald's restaurant. Ironically, there was a strong basis for punitive damages against McDonald's, though that part of the story is rarely told. The company made the choice to sell its coffee at a dangerously high temperature that could cause serious burns.

Study after study has documented that large punitive damages are rare and that juries are generally quite restrained in their awards. Justice Souter, writing for the Court in a 2008 decision that greatly reduced a punitive-damage award against Exxon arising out of the *Exxon Valdez* oil spill, in Alaska, carefully reviewed the scholarly literature and concluded: "A survey of the literature reveals that discretion to award punitive damages has not mass-produced runaway awards, and although some studies show the dollar amounts of punitive-damages awards growing over time, even in real terms, by most accounts the median ratio of punitive to compensatory awards has remained less than 1:1. Nor do the data substantiate a marked increase in the percentage of cases with punitive awards over the past several decades. The figures thus show an overall restraint."

Nonetheless, the Supreme Court has imposed significant limits on punitive-damage awards. It means that those injured, like the Romos, are greatly limited in their ability to recover. It means that the effect of punitive damages in deterring wrongdoing is significantly reduced.

The Romos could have appealed the reduction of the punitive-damage award from $290 million to $23.7 million, but decided to accept that amount and not prolong the legal proceedings any further. It is still a large award, but it hardly seems sufficient to deter a company like Ford from making the type of economic choices that it did with the Bronco (and earlier with the Pinto) that put so many innocent lives at risk.

The day the California Court of Appeal announced its decision reducing the punitive damages against Ford from $290 million to $23.7 million, I could not help but compare the ruling to another case that I lost earlier that year in the U.S. Supreme Court. In that case, discussed in the introductory chapter, the Court ruled that it was not cruel and unusual punishment to sentence Leandro Andrade to life in prison with no possibility of parole for fifty years for stealing $153 worth of videotapes. I could not resist the cynical observation that the underlying principle seemed to be that too much money in punitive damages from a corporation that killed people through its recklessness violates the Constitution, but fifty years in prison for shoplifting is acceptable.

The Supreme Court has closed the courthouse doors to those suffering injuries, including violations of constitutional rights: limiting the ability to sue federal officers, restricting who has standing to sue, requiring more facts for complaints for cases in federal court, expanding sovereign immunity, pushing cases to arbitration rather than adjudication, and greatly limiting punitive-damage awards. The Court has also imposed significant limits on when lawyers can recover fees for representing plaintiffs in civil rights cases, placed great restrictions on the ability to sue to enforce federal civil rights laws, and increased immunity from suit for cities and also for government officers.

At the same time, Congress passed statutes limiting access to the federal courts. The Prison Litigation Reform Act has made it far more difficult for prisoners to sue, even when they suffer serious harms while in government custody. The Antiterrorism and Effective Death Penalty Act, discussed in Chapter 4, creates major new obstacles to those convicted of crimes being able to have their constitutional claims heard in federal court.

All of these major changes in the law have the effect of tremendously favoring defendants—businesses, governments, government officers. The conservative justices on the Supreme Court have been responsible for major changes in the law, almost always in 5–4 decisions. These are the types of changes in the law that rarely make headlines, but individually and cumulatively they make it far more difficult for courts to enforce the law, including the Constitution, and to provide remedies to injured individuals. Countless individuals will be denied their day in court or an adequate recovery because of these significant conservative shifts. To so many injured individuals, from Joe and Valerie Wilson to others mentioned in this chapter, the courthouse doors have now been closed.

Conclusion

RECLAIMING THE CONSTITUTION

I was home trying to finish an overdue manuscript on the Thursday morning before Thanksgiving in November 2000 when I received a call from a top official in the campaign of Al Gore for president. She explained that the next day a state trial court judge in Florida would be hearing an oral argument on whether the so-called "butterfly ballot" that was used in Palm Beach County was illegal and whether to order a new election. The campaign thought that a law professor might be an effective advocate for this judge and she wanted to know if I could go to Florida to argue the case on Friday. Like a number of law professors and lawyers across the country, I had been informally helping the Gore campaign, so the request was not entirely out of the blue.

The 2000 presidential election was one of the closest in American history. By early the next morning it was clear that the Democratic candidate, Vice President Al Gore, had won the national popular vote, but the outcome of the electoral vote was uncertain. The presidency turned on Florida's twenty-five electoral votes. Early on election night, the networks called Gore the winner in Florida, only to retract their prediction later in the evening. In the early hours of Wednesday, November 8, the networks declared Bush the winner of Florida and the presidency, only to recant that a short time later and conclude that the outcome in Florida, and thus of the national election, was too close to call.

The punch card ballot in Palm Beach County was constructed in a misleading manner: the hole next to Gore's name was actually a vote for Patrick Buchanan, who was also running for president. The result was that it was estimated that approximately four thousand Palm Beach voters mistakenly cast votes for Buchanan that they intended for Gore. This was far more than the margin of Bush's victory—at that point he led Gore statewide by 537 votes— and more than enough to have made Gore the clear winner in Florida. Dozens of affidavits had been collected from individuals who said that they thought that they had voted for Gore, but then realized that they had voted for Buchanan. Many of these individuals were elderly Jewish voters who never would have dreamed of voting for Pat Buchanan. Even Buchanan said that he was sure that these votes were meant for Gore.

I immediately agreed to go to Florida to argue the case the next day. I had followed the issue closely and would have the cross-country plane ride to prepare for the argument. I decided to take my then seventeen-year-old son, who was a senior in high school. The hearing had the chance to be historic. I picked him up at his school and we flew to Florida.

The hearing was the next morning. I needed to begin by asking for permission to argue since I am not a member of the Florida bar. Surprisingly, the Bush campaign's lawyer, Barry Richards, objected. I did not expect this because judges routinely allow out-of-state lawyers to appear and rarely do attorneys object. The judge overruled the objection and said that he always had wanted to question a law professor.

The hearing lasted a couple of hours. It was broadcast live. The core of my argument was that the design of the butterfly ballot was illegal because it misled voters and that a new election should be held in Palm Beach County with a properly designed ballot. Only those who voted on November 7 would be allowed to vote in the new election. There were precedents in Florida law as well as in the election laws of other states for ordering a new election as a remedy for serious violations that could not be cured in any other way.

The judge was concerned about whether he had the power to do this. He asked, "Doesn't the Constitution require a uniform day for choosing electors and wouldn't allowing a new election violate this constitutional provision?" I replied that this constitutional provision doesn't concern election day but rather the day that electors are chosen by each state—December 18, 2000, this time—under federal law.

I said that it was possible to imagine other situations in which elections could be held after November 7. If a hurricane in Florida on presidential election day prevented the polls from opening or an earthquake in California had the same effect, surely the election could be held on a later date. There must be the opportunity for different days of voting in extraordinary circumstances.

The judge was superbly prepared and peppered both Richards and me with hard questions. After my rebuttal and after the judge had left the bench, I was gathering my things at counsel table when my son came up to me. He put his arm around my shoulder, something I don't recall him doing before or since, and said, "Dad, you did a good job, but you're going to lose." I asked why and he said, "When you were up there at the end, the judge kept saying that if he had to rule against you that would be the hardest thing he ever did as a judge. The more he said that, the more I knew that you would lose."

A few days later, the judge ruled against us, holding that the Constitution requires a uniform day of elections. I knew—and the Gore campaign knew—that winning this lawsuit was a long shot. It was hard to hold a new election that likely would decide the presidential election, however much it was justified by the circumstances.

The Gore campaign's major focus in the courts was on asking that the uncounted ballots be counted in several Florida counties. I played a far more minor role in this litigation, but throughout it, from the time it was in the Florida trial court to the time it went before the U.S. Supreme Court, I received calls from the Gore campaign to draft particular sections of briefs that they needed to file.

On the Monday after Thanksgiving, November 27, Gore filed suit in Florida under the Florida law providing for "contests" of election results. Under Florida law there can be a contest if there is a dispute over enough votes "to change or place in doubt the result of the election." The statute authorizes a court, if it finds that there are successful grounds for a contest, to "provide any relief appropriate under such circumstances."

On Saturday and Sunday, December 2 and 3, a Florida state trial court held a nationally televised hearing as to whether Gore had met the statutory requirements for a successful contest. On Monday, December 4, the Florida trial court ruled against Gore on the grounds that Gore failed to prove a "reasonable probability" that the election would have turned out differently if not for problems in counting ballots.

The Florida Supreme Court granted review and held oral arguments on Thursday, December 6. On Friday afternoon, December 7, the Florida Supreme Court, by a 4 to 3 decision, reversed the trial court. The Florida Supreme Court ruled that the trial court had used the wrong standard in insisting that Gore demonstrate a "reasonable probability" that the election would have been decided differently. The Florida Supreme Court said that the statute requires only a showing of "[r]eceipt of a number of illegal votes or rejection of a number of legal votes sufficient to change or place in doubt the result of the election."

The Florida Supreme Court ordered the immediate counting of any uncounted ballots in counties across the state. Just hours after the court's decision, on Friday night, December 7, a Florida trial court judge, Terry Lewis, ordered that the counting of the uncounted votes commence the next morning and that it be completed by Sunday afternoon, December 9, at 2 P.M. The judge said that he would resolve any disputes concerning particular ballots and whether and how they were to be counted.

On Saturday morning, counting commenced as ordered. At about 4 A.M. California time that morning, I received a call from a lawyer in the Gore campaign saying that they expected Bush to go to the U.S. Supreme Court and asking if I could write a section of a brief concerning a jurisdictional issue. I was told that they needed it from me within a few hours. I was one of many lawyers across the country whom they were turning to for the drafting of brief sections on a very short timetable.

I was writing my part of the brief with a television on in the background that was tuned in to C-SPAN, which was showing the counting in Florida. Toward the end of the morning, California time, it was announced that the U.S. Supreme Court had granted Bush's request to hear the case and had stopped the counting in Florida. The Court's granting review was not a surprise, but its stopping the counting of the uncounted ballots made no sense. The order to stop the counting was by a 5–4 margin, with the five conservative justices—Rehnquist, O'Connor, Scalia, Kennedy, and Thomas—composing the majority.

The law is clear and long established that the Supreme Court may halt another court's order only if the person seeking the stay demonstrates that he or she would suffer an "irreparable injury" without one. This is especially important when the Supreme Court is reviewing the decisions of a state court because of the tradition of deference to the autonomy of state judges when possible. There was no plausible basis for the Supreme Court to have found such an irreparable injury to Bush in allowing the ballots to be counted while the case was pending before it.

Justice Antonin Scalia released a short concurring opinion stating that there would be "irreparable harm." His reasons, though, are dubious. First, Justice Scalia said "the counting of votes that are of questionable legality does in my view irreparable harm to [Bush] by casting a cloud on what he claims to be the legitimacy of his election." What, then, according to Scalia, was the harm to Bush from allowing the ballots to be counted? The claim was that if the recount put Gore ahead, but the Supreme Court invalidated the recount, then Bush's victory would lack legitimacy.

But ironically Bush's election was robbed of its legitimacy—at least in the eyes of 49 million people who voted for Al Gore— because it resulted from a Supreme Court order that kept many votes from ever being counted. Stopping the recount to enhance the public's opinion of a candidate's victory is not an appropriate role for the Supreme Court. No prior Supreme Court decision—or from any other court—ever found that such a harm could be the basis for finding irreparable injury.

Second, Justice Scalia argued that allowing the recount to occur while the case was pending could prevent a proper recount later because "it is generally agreed that each manual recount produces a degradation of the ballots, which renders a subsequent recount inaccurate." This was a factual question decided by Justice Scalia without any evidence whatsoever. There was nothing in the record of the case to support this assertion. More importantly, this argument ignored the reality that it was then or never for a recount; a few days later, on December 12, the Court said that the recount had to be done by that date and stopped any counting after that. It was the Court's stay that prevented the count from being completed by December 12.

On Monday, December 11, the Court held oral arguments. Although the Court adhered to its long-standing rule that prohibits the broadcast of oral arguments, audio tapes of the argument were released by the Court immediately after its completion and then played on C-SPAN. Ted Olson argued for Bush and David Boies for Gore; both were excellent.

On Tuesday night, December 12, at approximately 10 P.M., Eastern Time, the Court released its opinion in *Bush v. Gore*. In an unsigned majority opinion, the Supreme Court ruled 5 to 4 in favor of Bush and held that there could be no further counting of ballots in Florida. The Court split exactly as it had a few days earlier on the stay issue. The Supreme Court's opinion was unsigned and was joined by Chief Justice Rehnquist and Justices O'Connor, Scalia, Kennedy, and Thomas. Each of the other four justices wrote dissenting opinions.

The Court said that the central problem was that the Florida Supreme Court ordered the counting of the uncounted ballots but failed to prescribe standards for how to determine whether a ballot was valid and to be included in the tally. The Court said that this would result in similar ballots being treated differently and would deny equal protection.

The Court then confronted the key question: Should the case

be remanded to the Florida courts for them to cure the equal protection problem by setting standards for the counting or should the Supreme Court order an end to the counting process? The Court said that Florida indicated that it wished to observe the December 12 "safe harbor" date set by federal law. A federal statute provided that states that designated their electors by that date were ensured of having them recognized. This, though, was not required in order for a state's electors to participate in the Electoral College; a state choosing its electors later, and in the past some states had done so, still could have its electors participate in the Electoral College vote. In 1960, Hawaii chose its electors several weeks after the "safe harbor" date and its electors were allowed to vote in the Electoral College. But the Supreme Court said that the Florida Supreme Court had indicated a few weeks earlier that it wanted that state's electors designated by December 12. Since it was now December 12, the Court said that there was no time for further counting and it ordered an end to the recount in Florida.

The activism in the majority's decision in *Bush v. Gore* was stunning. First, as mentioned earlier, there was no basis for the Court to stay the counting of the uncounted votes while the case was being heard in the Supreme Court. Second, it was premature for the Court to find a violation of equal protection in the counting of the uncounted votes. The Supreme Court said that the central issue was whether the counting of votes would deny equal protection. There would be a constitutional violation only if similar ballots were treated differently in the counting process. But it could not be known if this would occur until the counting was done and the trial judge in Florida, Judge Terry Lewis, ruled on all of the challenges. Judge Lewis was to hear all of the disputes and potentially could eliminate any inequalities by applying a uniform standard. Until then, it was purely speculative as to whether there would be a problem with similar ballots being treated differently.

Justice Stevens stressed exactly this point in his dissent. He wrote: "These concerns are alleviated—if not eliminated—by the fact that a single impartial magistrate will ultimately adjudicate all objections arising from the recount process." The Supreme Court long has ruled that federal courts may not hear cases until they are ripe for review and the dispute in *Bush v. Gore* was not yet ripe.

Third, the Court had no business ending the counting in Florida; it should have sent the case back to the Florida courts to decide whether to end the counting or to proceed with uniform standards for tallying the uncounted ballots. Assuming that there were inequalities in the counting that violated the Constitution, there were two ways to remedy this problem: count none of the uncounted ballots or count all of the ballots with uniform standards. The latter remedy would involve remanding the case to the Florida Supreme Court for development of standards and for such relief as that court deemed appropriate. The standards did not have to be complex; the standard basically concerned how many corners of the paper "chad" had to be detached from the punch card in order for the vote to count.

It must be emphasized that the Supreme Court did not hold that federal law prevented the counting from continuing. The only reason for not remanding the case was the Court's judgment that *Florida law* prevented this recount because the state wanted to comply with the December 12 safe harbor deadline. However, no Florida statute stated or implied that the counting had to be done by December 12. The sole authority for the Supreme Court's conclusion was one statement by the Florida Supreme Court in an opinion a few weeks earlier.

That statement, however, was made in a very different context. The Florida Supreme Court was not then faced with the issue posed by the Supreme Court's ruling. After the Supreme Court decided on December 12 that the counting without standards violated equal protection, the issue was what remedy was appropriate under Florida law: continue the counting past December 12 or end the counting to meet the December 12 deadline. The Supreme Court could not possibly know how the Florida Supreme Court would resolve this issue because it never had occurred before. Prior Florida decisions emphasized the importance of making sure that every vote is accurately counted. The Florida

Supreme Court might have relied on this precedent to continue the counting past December 12 just as it might have ended the counting, treating December 12 as a firm deadline in Florida.

Indeed, after *Bush v. Gore* was decided, the Florida Supreme Court issued a decision dismissing the case. Justice Leander Shaw, in a concurring opinion, declared: "[I]n my opinion, December 12 was not a 'drop-dead' date under Florida law. In fact, I question whether any date prior to January 6 is a drop-dead date under the Florida election scheme. December 12 was simply a permissive 'safe-harbor' date under the Florida election scheme. It certainly was not a mandatory contest deadline under the plain language of the Florida Election Code."

One of the most basic and well-established principles of constitutional law is that state courts get the last word on questions of state law. From that perspective, it is inexplicable why the five justices in the majority—usually the foremost advocates of states' rights on the Court—did not remand the case to the Florida Supreme Court to decide under Florida law whether the counting should continue. The Supreme Court impermissibly usurped the Florida Supreme Court's authority to decide Florida law in this extraordinary case.

There is no way, of course, to know what would have happened if the Supreme Court had allowed the counting to occur in Florida. Perhaps George W. Bush would have won anyway. But what is striking about *Bush v. Gore* is the activism of the Supreme Court; the five most conservative justices ignored well-established principles to hand the presidency to Bush.

The irony is enormous. Ever since Richard Nixon ran for president in 1968, conservatives have railed against judicial activism. But it was the conservatives on the Court who played a key role in deciding the presidential election. Although this is an obvious and important example, throughout this book I have shown many other instances of what can only be regarded as conservative judicial activism.

Although there is no precise definition of judicial activism—it often seems to be a label people use for the decisions that they don't like—it seems reasonable to say that a court is activist if it overturns the actions of the democratically elected branches of government and if it overrules precedent. In fact, conservatives, including on the Supreme Court, often have labeled decisions striking down the will of popularly elected legislatures as "activist." It is more restrained if it follows precedent and defers to the elected branches of government.

The conservative judges have had no hesitation in striking down desegregation plans adopted by popularly elected school boards, reversing decisions creating a wall separating church and state, changing constitutional rules that have been followed for decades controlling the exclusion of illegally obtained evidence, using the Second Amendment to invalidate democratically created gun control laws, and overturning seventy years of precedent to make it harder for injured plaintiffs to get into federal court. And these are only a few examples of the many discussed that can be understood as conservative judicial activism.

Popular rhetoric makes it seem that judicial activism is an evil to be avoided. But judicial activism in the sense of invalidating laws and overruling precedents can be good or bad. *Brown v. Board of Education* was very much an activist decision because the Court struck down laws requiring segregation in dozens of states and overruled a fifty-eight-year-old precedent upholding "separate but equal." Few today, thankfully, would question the legitimacy of *Brown.*

Still conservatives rail against "judicial activism," even though the major judicial activism of recent decades, as in *Bush v. Gore*, is in a politically conservative direction. At times, the attacks on "liberal judges" get ugly. After the federal courts refused to order the feeding tube restored to Terri Schiavo, in March 2005, House Majority Leader Tom DeLay promised reprisals against the federal judges involved. At around the same time, Texas senator John Cornyn gave a disturbing speech in which he linked recent violence, which included a shooting in a Georgia courtroom and the murder of an Illinois federal judge's mother and husband, to public frustration with judicial activism. Senator Cornyn said that frustration with "political decisions" by judges "builds to the point where some people engage in violence." Instead of decrying violence, Senator Cornyn legitimated it and used it to attack judicial activism.

Like so much in this book, the conservative attack on judicial activism starts with Richard Nixon's campaign for president in 1968. Nixon declared: "I want men on the Supreme Court who are strict constructionists, men that interpret the law and don't try to make the law." Ronald Reagan continued this rhetoric in his campaigns and in his presidency. He said: "We've had too many examples in recent years of courts and judges legislating. They're not interpreting what the law says and whether someone has violated it or not. In too many instances they have been actually legislating by legal decree what they think the law should be."

When George H. W. Bush ran for president he continued this conservative rhetoric. During a presidential debate in October 1988, he said that he would "appoint people to the federal bench that will not legislate from the bench, who will interpret the Constitution." In his acceptance speech at the 1992 Republican convention, President Bush said that "Clinton and Congress will stock the judiciary with liberal judges who write laws that they can't get approved by the voters."

George W. Bush echoed the same themes. In a presidential debate in 2000, he said that he would appoint judges "who will strictly interpret the Constitution and not use the bench for writing social policy." Bush said that "judges ought not to take the place of the legislative branch of government. . . . I don't believe in liberal activist judges. I believe in strict construction." When President Bush nominated John Roberts to the Supreme Court, he said that Roberts would "strictly apply the Constitution and laws, not legislate from the bench." Similarly, in nominating Samuel Alito to the Court, President Bush said that Alito "understands that judges are to interpret the laws, not to impose their preferences or priorities on the people." The 2008 Republican platform declares: "Judicial activism is a grave threat to the rule of law because unaccountable federal judges are usurping democracy, ignoring the

Constitution and its separation of powers, and imposing their personal opinions upon the public. This must stop."

This rhetoric has had great impact. Those who seek confirmation for the Supreme Court feel that they must echo it. When John Roberts was before the Senate Judiciary Committee at his confirmation hearings, he proclaimed: "Judges are like umpires. Umpires don't make the rules, they apply them. The role of an umpire and a judge is critical. They make sure everybody plays by the rules, but it is a limited role. Nobody ever went to a ball game to see an umpire." The power of this conservative rhetoric also was seen in Justice Sonia Sotomayor's confirmation hearings; she repeatedly told the members of the Senate Judiciary Committee that judges must "apply not make the law."

Each of these brilliant jurists gave a terribly misleading impression of judging on the Supreme Court. Unlike umpires, justices on the Supreme Court create the rules. Anything the Supreme Court decides makes the law. In *Bush v. Gore*, the Supreme Court was much more than an umpire. The Court did not apply settled law; it made new law and decided a presidential election.

Bush v. Gore is thus important because it shows the hypocrisy of the conservative rhetoric about judicial restraint. Conservatives are just as willing to be activist, by any definition of that word, when it serves their ideological agenda. For example, as discussed in Chapter 5, it was the five most conservative justices on the Court who in 2008 found a thirty-five-year-old District of Columbia handgun control ordinance to violate the Second Amendment. From 1791 when the Second Amendment was ratified until June 26, 2008, not one law ever had been found to violate that constitutional provision. The Supreme Court had always held that the Second Amendment protects only the right of people to have guns for the purpose of militia service. The amendment says: "A well regulated militia, being necessary to the security of a free state, the right of the people to keep and bear arms shall not be infringed." This is the rare constitutional provision that explicitly states its purpose, though its text can be read to emphasize either the first or the second clause of the amendment.

But the conservatives in *District of Columbia v. Heller* showed no judicial restraint in overturning two hundred years of precedent and in striking down a law adopted by the D.C. City Council thirty-five years earlier. Two quite conservative federal court of appeals judges, Richard Posner and J. Harvie Wilkinson (who had been seriously considered by President George W. Bush for appointment to the Supreme Court), in separate articles sharply criticized the *Heller* decision for its judicial activism.

Another stunning example of conservative judicial activism is the decision in January 2010, *Citizens United v. Federal Election Commission,* in which the five most conservative justices overruled precedent and struck down a federal law limiting corporate spending in federal election campaigns. For the first time in American history, the Court ruled that corporations and unions can spend as much as they want to get their candidates of choice elected or others defeated. There was no deference to Congress or to precedent; the activism of the decision was startling. The Court dramatically changed federal, state, and local elections by holding that corporations and unions can expend unlimited sums of money in election campaigns.

The difference between liberals and conservatives, then, is not in their willingness to overrule precedent or in their degree of deference to popularly elected officials or to make momentous decisions affecting society. The divergence is entirely about when they want the Court to do this and for what purpose. The other difference is in their rhetoric; conservatives continue to rail against judicial activism and profess judicial restraint even though they are every bit as willing to be activist as liberals.

The first step then in reclaiming the Constitution from the conservative assault is to put to rest the misleading talk about judicial activism and strict construction and about judges as umpires and about judges applying but not making the law. The first step must be to recognize that all justices, liberal and conservative, want the Court to be activist in some areas. The disagreement is substantive, not about the judicial role.

Why, though, does the conservative rhetoric against judicial activism survive, even at a time when most activism by the Supreme Court is in a conservative direction? Why does even a Democratic nominee for the Supreme Court feel the need to echo it? I think that getting past this rhetoric requires a recognition of its power.

Conservatives claim that they are following a method of judicial decision making that is neutral, while liberals are imposing their personal preferences in constitutional interpretation. This would be a laughable claim, except for its tremendous rhetorical force. I have participated in countless debates about constitutional decision making over the years and inevitably conservatives argue that they have a theory of constitutional interpretation, that the Court must follow the original meaning of the Constitution, while liberals have no theory or consistent methodology.

It is here that *Bush v. Gore* is so important: it is a powerful example of how decision making actually occurs in constitutional cases. Although unusual in its national significance, *Bush v. Gore* is typical in two crucial respects: first, justices have tremendous discretion in deciding constitutional cases; and second, how that discretion is exercised is frequently, if not inevitably, a product of the justices' life experiences and ideology. Neither of these propositions should be the least bit controversial, except that they are vehemently denied by conservatives, such as the Republican senators who opposed and voted against Justice Sonia Sotomayor. Because *Bush v. Gore* shows that all justices, liberal or conservative, come to results at least in part based on their views and ideology, it should forever bury silly adages like "judges are umpires who don't make the rules, but apply them" and "judges should apply the law, not make it."

To reclaim the Constitution from conservatives, we must realize that there is no such thing as a neutral method of interpreting the Constitution. All justices, liberals and conservatives, have to make value choices about the meaning of the Constitution and how it applies in particular cases. Throughout this book, I have tried to show that for the last several decades conservatives have dramatically changed constitutional law to further their ideological agenda. A key step in reclaiming the Constitution is to understand that the conservative rhetoric about judicial restraint and a neutral methodology is an emperor without clothes.

Conservatives, both on and off the Court, have claimed for a generation that they are following the Constitution's original meaning and not making value choices. There are many flaws in this claim. It is clear that conservatives often abandon the original-meaning approach when it does not serve their ideological purposes. For example, in the area of affirmative action, historians have persuasively demonstrated that the framers of the Fourteenth Amendment, which prevents states from denying equal protection, also approved many programs that would be regarded as affirmative action today. Yet avowedly originalist justices like Scalia and Thomas ignore this history and follow instead their conservative ideological opposition to affirmative action.

As mentioned above, the conservative justices on the Court recently found a First Amendment right for corporations to spend unlimited amounts of money in election campaigns. It is dubious at best that the original understanding of the First Amendment included rights for corporations or a protection for spending money in election campaigns. The conservative justices, albeit in dissent, were willing to allow Congress to end habeas corpus for Guantanamo detainees even though Article I of the Constitution expressly states that "the privilege of the writ of habeas corpus shall not be suspended, unless when in cases of rebellion or invasion the public safety may require it." Not even the Bush administration claimed that there had been a rebellion or invasion that would allow this suspension of habeas corpus.

There are many reasons why the search for original meaning is an inherently futile method of interpretation. First, in the cases that come before the Supreme Court there generally is neither an answer to be found in the text of the Constitution nor a clear original meaning to the Constitution. Again, *Bush v. Gore* is a powerful example of this. The problem is common throughout constitutional law. So many people were involved in drafting and ratifying the Constitution and its subsequent amendments that it is rare that there is a clear intent to be found. Also, the problems of the modern world are so vastly different from those of the late eighteenth century when the Constitution was ratified that for most issues there is no clear answer to be found in the original meaning of the Constitution.

Over a decade ago, I had an experience that powerfully illustrated this situation. In 1997, I ran for election to a Los Angeles commission to draft and propose to the voters a new city charter. One person was elected from each of the city's fifteen city council districts. I won election from a field of seven candidates in my district and then was chosen by my fellow commissioners to be our chair.

For two years, I and the fourteen other commissioners worked to draft a new charter. In California, as in many states, a charter has many similarities to a constitution. It creates the institutions of city government and divides powers among its branches. It defines many aspects of governance in the city. A city's charter can protect additional individual rights beyond those found in the federal or state constitutions. The primary difference from a constitution is in detail and length. The charter we drafted is more than 150 pages long and includes detailed rules for matters such as civil service and the pensions of city workers.

As a result of a battle for control between then mayor Richard Riordan and the city council, there actually were two charter commissions working simultaneously: our elected commission and a commission appointed by the city council. In the end, we reconciled our differences in one proposal for a new charter, which was approved by the voters in June 1999.

Within weeks of its adoption, an issue of interpretation arose. The provision for term limits in the prior charter said that it did not apply to those who were elected before 1993, when term limits were adopted. The new charter continued the term limits, but omitted the exemption for those elected prior to 1993; it just said that a person could serve no more than two terms in the city council. Mike Woo, who had served two terms before 1993, wanted to run again. Under the old charter he could, but under the language of the new charter he couldn't.

I was asked by both sides in the litigation what our commission intended in a situation like this. The honest answer was that we had never thought about it. It did not occur to us that there might be someone who had served two terms before 1993 who might want to run again. Ultimately, the California Court of Appeal ruled in favor of Woo's being able to run and said that it was the intent of the voters who approved the Los Angeles City Charter to allow this. I am certain that none of the voters who ratified the 150-page document had given any thought to this question. The intent of the voters was purely a fiction invoked by the court.

Over and over in the last decade, issues have arisen about the meaning of the charter. Almost always the question is one that did not occur to us and that we did not discuss. Occasionally there have been instances in which issues have arisen that we did discuss. But frequently those who had been involved in the drafting of the charters have different recollections and different views about what was intended.

The same was true of the United States Constitution. Most modern constitutional issues never occurred to the framers. And even when there was discussion of such a question in 1787, there often was a sharp difference of opinion. Alexander Hamilton and James Madison, the primary authors of the *Federalist Papers*, are regarded as the preeminent framers. They disagreed about many matters. Early in the presidency of George Washington an issue arose as to whether he could issue a neutrality proclamation for the United States in the war between England and France. Hamilton said it would be constitutional; Madison argued the opposite. Later an issue arose about the purposes for which Congress can spend federal money. Hamilton took a broad view, while Madison took a very narrow one.

A second problem with trying to follow the original intent of the framers is that the world of 1787, or of 1868 when the Fourteenth Amendment was adopted, is so vastly different from our own that it often would be unthinkable to be bound by the original understandings of the earlier time. My favorite example of this is the fact that Article II of the Constitution speaks of the president and vice president with the pronoun "he." It is clear that the framers believed that only men could hold these offices; women did not receive the right to vote until 1920, when the Nineteenth Amendment was adopted. To follow literally the original understanding of the Constitution would mean that it is unconstitutional to elect a woman as president or vice president until the document is formally amended.

This example is representative of so many instances where following the original meaning would lead to unacceptable results. Under the original meaning of the Constitution, there would be no limit on the ability of the federal government to discriminate. The equal protection clause of the Fourteenth Amendment applies only to "states," and there is no indication that its framers ever thought that it would apply to the federal government. Conversely, if the original understanding were determinative, none of the Bill of Rights would apply to state and local governments. The Bill of Rights, the first ten amendments to the Constitution, were meant to limit only the federal government. The most persuasive historical analysis refutes the interpretation that the drafters of the Fourteenth Amendment meant to apply the Bill of Rights to state and local governments. So if the original understanding of the Constitution were followed, states could infringe on free speech or execute people without counsel or inflict the most barbaric punishments without constitutional limits.

A particularly powerful example of the undesirability of following the original meaning of the Constitution is that it would make *Brown v. Board of Education* illegitimate. In *Brown*, of course, the Court declared unconstitutional state laws that required segregation of the races in public schools and paved the way for subsequent decisions that ended segregation in every area of southern life. But the same Congress that ratified the Fourteenth Amendment also voted to segregate the District of Columbia public schools. There is no indication of an original intent to limit segregation; quite the opposite is true.

Of course, those who profess a belief in original meaning as the touchstone of constitutional interpretation could say that the

Court should follow the more abstract goals of the framers, not their specific intentions. But the problem with this principle is that anything can be justified then; the constraint on judging promised by conservatives who believe in the Court following original meaning is lost. If the original meaning of a provision is stated at a sufficiently abstract level, anything can be justified. Ultimately the original goal of the Constitution was to advance freedom and equality; this hardly limits the ability of justices to read their own preferences into the Constitution.

This situation points to a problem inherent in trying to have the Court follow the original meaning of the Constitution: the intent behind any constitutional provision can be stated at many different levels of abstraction. For example, who was the equal protection clause intended to protect? The intent could have been solely to protect African-Americans, or to protect all racial minorities, or to shelter all groups that have been historically discriminated against, or to defend all individuals from arbitrary treatment by the government. Each of these potential answers is a reasonable way of describing the drafters' intent for the Fourteenth Amendment. Yet a judge must eventually select among these answers and a great deal depends on that choice. Whether sex discrimination or affirmative action violates equal protection depends entirely on the choice among levels of abstraction. Here, too, there is no way to avoid having justices make choices. Their choices will depend on their ideology and views.

Finally, and quite crucially, constitutional decision making apart from the ideology and values of the justices is impossible because balancing competing interests is a persistent feature of such decision making. How should the president's interest in executive privilege and secrecy be balanced against the need for evidence at a criminal trial? How should a defendant's right to a fair trial be balanced against the freedom of the press? No constitutional rights are absolute and the Supreme Court has said that even the most precious rights can be infringed if government action is necessary to achieve a compelling government interest. Even race discrimination by the government is allowed if this test is met. But there is no way for justices to decide what is "compelling" except by making a value choice.

In deciding whether colleges and universities have a compelling interest in affirmative action and in using race as one factor in admissions decisions, all nine justices agreed that the issue was whether diversity in the classroom is a compelling government interest. The answer cannot be found in the text of the Constitution or the original understanding of that document or any other source. The justices had to make a choice about the importance of diversity, and not surprisingly, they split 5–4, with the five most liberal members then on the Court (Stevens, O'Connor, Souter, Ginsburg, and Breyer) voting that affirmative action serves a compelling interest and the four most conservative justices (Rehnquist, Scalia, Kennedy, and Thomas) dissenting.

Constitutional law constantly asks, as does so much of law, what is reasonable. Under the Fourth Amendment, which limits searches and arrests, courts routinely focus on whether the actions of police officers are reasonable. Under the "takings" clause of the Fifth Amendment, courts examine whether the government in taking private property for public use acted out of a reasonable belief that its action would benefit the public. What is reasonable requires a choice by the justice or judge; it cannot be determined based on the text of the Constitution or its original meaning.

Reclaiming the Constitution from the conservative assault requires showing that all justices—liberals and conservatives—are making value choices. I have heard Antonin Scalia say to an audience of federal judges that his decisions are not a product of his ideology and that his votes against abortion rights have nothing to do with his religious or political beliefs. This is absurd; no theory of law allows judges to deduce answers without tremendous discretion. No matter which theory one employs, constitutional interpretation inevitably involves value choices: balancing competing interests; deciding what is reasonable; selecting the appropriate amount of abstraction; and choosing among plausible readings of constitutional history, to name a few such choices.

What then does a justice base his or her decision on? I am not arguing that justices decide based on whim or their personal preferences. Throughout American history, the Supreme Court has based its constitutional decisions on many sources: the Constitution's text, its framers' intent, the Constitution's structure, the Court's prior decisions, society's traditions, and contemporary social policy considerations. All of these have been the bases for Supreme Court decisions throughout American history. A conscientious judge interpreting the Constitution will look to all of these sources in deciding cases and in explaining the rationale for his or her conclusions.

Of course, the fact that many sources are considered helps to explain why the Supreme Court has enormous discretion in deciding cases. This is what constitutional decision making always has been and always will be about. It is exactly what the conservative majority did in *Bush v. Gore*, as it looked at the text and prior decisions concerning equality in voting and considerations of fairness and equity.

Why then do conservatives who should know better, such as Chief Justice Roberts and Justice Scalia, talk in terms that they know are so clearly at odds with what they do as judges? Why did even Justice Sotomayor do this at her confirmation hearing? I imagine the justices do so because they believe their rhetoric holds political appeal. They believe the idea of judicial restraint and of judicial deference to democratic decision making resonates with how people want the system to be. Perhaps they fear that courts would lose legitimacy if people knew that the ideology of unelected jurists so often determines the results of decisions that have a direct, important impact on their lives.

I disagree. The rhetoric of discretion-free judging grossly underestimates the public. Even a cursory reading of the Constitution reveals that it does not mention abortion; yet opinion polls show that more than 75 percent of Americans believe that abortion should be legal in some circumstances. People know that abortion is not mentioned in the Constitution, but they also believe that it should be protected as a constitutional right.

Once it is recognized that judges have tremendous discretion in deciding cases and that rulings are often a product of the judges' ideology and views, there is then another key step in reclaiming the Constitution: changing the judicial confirmation process. Once the inevitable role of ideology in judging is recognized, it then becomes silly to say that individuals should be confirmed without focusing on what they are likely to do on the bench. Throughout American history, presidents have selected justices who reflect their ideologies. More ideologically defined presidents, such as Franklin Roosevelt and Ronald Reagan and George W. Bush, have done this more than less ideologically defined presidents like Dwight Eisenhower.

The Senate in its confirmation process also can and should look to ideology in deciding whether to approve nominees. From the earliest days of American history, this has been the case. The Senate rejected President George Washington's nomination of John Rutledge to be the second chief justice of the United States, even though it had previously confirmed Rutledge as an associate justice, because it disagreed with Rutledge's views about the United States being a neutral party in the war between England and France.

Through the nineteenth century, more than 20 percent of presidential nominees for the Supreme Court were rejected by the Senate, most on ideological grounds. In the twentieth century, there were many examples of this. In 1931, the Senate rejected President Herbert Hoover's nomination of federal court of appeals judge John Parker because it disagreed with Parker's anti-labor views. In 1969, the Senate rejected President Nixon's picks of Clement Haynsworth and Harold Carswell because of their anti-labor and anti–civil rights views. Most recently, in 1987, the Senate overwhelmingly rejected Robert Bork because of his restrictive views of constitutional liberties.

But increasingly the confirmation hearings have become what then senator Joseph Biden described as an exercise in "kabuki theater." Biden said this after the confirmation hearings of Samuel Alito. Alito had been a federal court of appeals judge for fifteen years before being nominated for the high court. His judicial record was consistently very conservative. He had been dubbed "Scalito," to reflect the similarity of his views to Scalia (and perhaps because of their common Italian heritage). President George W. Bush selected Judge Alito precisely because of his conservative views and conservatives were thrilled by the nomination. Since joining the Court, Alito has been everything that conservatives could have hoped for; there is no case so far in which he has not taken the conservative position on constitutional issues.

Yet the confirmation hearings were spent with the Republican senators denying that they knew what Alito would do as a justice and portraying him as an open-minded jurist without an ideology. Democratic senators spent the hearings trying to pin Alito into saying something that would show his conservatism in such a way as to make him unacceptable. The reverse, of course, occurred during the hearings for Sonia Sotomayor. Democrats presented her as an open-minded individual whose future votes on the Court could not be known, while Republicans tried to use their questions and her prior statements to show her to be an unacceptable liberal. The nominee in the hearings says as little as possible and utters platitudes like "judges are umpires" and "judges apply not make the law."

Such confirmation hearings serve little purpose beyond allowing the senators of both parties to use the televised hearings to appeal to their constituents. The lengthy hearings and intense questioning also give the public some sense of the person who will be serving on the high court for years to come. But not much beyond this is accomplished.

It should be acknowledged that the confirmation process seldom will be very meaningful when the president and the majority of the Senate are from the same political party. Rarely will the Senate reject a nominee from a president of the same political party. The only hope for the Democrats to block Alito was by a filibuster, and even with forty-two votes against him this was not something that they were willing to do. There were forty-eight votes against Clarence Thomas, but Democrats were unwilling to use a filibuster to stop his confirmation.

It is time to create a more meaningful confirmation process, one that starts from a recognition of what justices actually do. At their respective confirmation hearings, Chief Justice Roberts and Justices Alito and Sotomayor all refused to answer questions about their views on any issues that might come before them. Their reticence only makes sense, though, if their views don't matter.

The confirmation process is the most important check on the unelected judiciary. Given that a nominee's views will matter significantly in how he or she decides cases, those views should be explored by the senators responsible for confirming the nominee. The Senate should insist, as a condition for confirmation, that the nominee answer detailed questions about his or her views on important constitutional questions.

There are several possible reasons why nominees' ideologies are not explored more thoroughly, but none persuades. One possibility is that nominees simply don't have views on topics such as abortion, affirmative action, separation of church and state, and so on. At their confirmation hearings in 1990 and 1991 respectively, David Souter and Clarence Thomas both said that they had not thought about the abortion issue and had no views on it. This led Patricia Ireland, then president of the National Organization of Women, to quip that there are two adults in the country who did not have views about abortion and they are both on the Supreme Court. Thomas said this despite having written several articles arguing that *Roe v. Wade* was wrongly decided.

Another possible reason is that the harm of asking and knowing is greater than the benefits, that publicly airing potential justices' views destroys the appearance of judicial impartiality. But judges do not become more impartial by pretending that they don't have views. There can be little doubt as to how Justice Scalia or how Justice Ginsburg will rule the next time a party asks the Court to overrule *Roe v. Wade*, but no one would suggest that because we know this, they are disqualified. Nor would knowing a nominee's views create any greater problems. As a lawyer, I would much rather know the judge's views than pretend that the judge is a blank slate.

Because an individual's beliefs influence how he or she will decide cases, it is appropriate—indeed essential—for the appointing and confirming authorities to consider ideology. It is appropriate and necessary for the Senate to insist that the nominee answer questions concerning his or her views about issues, even those that will come before the Court, so long as the nominee is not asked how he or she will vote in a specific case. That obviously would depend on the record of the case, the briefs, the arguments, and the deliberations. Yale law professors Robert Post and Reva Siegel propose an elegant solution: insist that the nominee answer how he or she would have voted in cases already decided. It is possible that the same issues might again come before the Court, but the views would have been known if the person already had been on the bench at the time of the prior case.

The Senate can make clear that it will not confirm nominees who do not answer such questions. This procedure can be used by conservatives to block liberal nominees, as well as the other way around. But once we get past the myth of discretion-free judging, it is essential that there be a confirmation process that focuses on the ideology and values of the nominee to determine what he or she will do on the bench.

I have heard some say that this is inappropriate because it is not really possible to predict what someone will do as a justice. There are examples of justices changing over time: Felix Frankfurter, a liberal law professor, became a conservative justice; Harry Blackmun, a conservative in his first several years as a justice, became the Court's most liberal member by the time he retired. But such conversions are exceedingly rare. Few individuals have major ideological conversions in their fifties and sixties. Antonin Scalia and Clarence Thomas have not changed in their time on the Court; neither has Ruth Bader Ginsburg or Stephen Breyer.

There is another important benefit to exposing the myth of neutral, value-free judging: changing how judicial opinions are written. The myth distorts judicial opinions. Rather than justify and debate their value choices, judges act as if their results are dictated by the Constitution's text or the tradition surrounding the document. Many cases, though, such as the Supreme Court's recent decisions greatly expanding sovereign immunity (discussed in Chapter 6), cannot be justified based on the text of the Constitution or the intent of the framers. There is no provision concerning whether states can be sued in their own state courts; it is something that was never discussed by the framers. The real question is how the costs of potential state liability for money damages should be balanced against the benefits of holding state governments accountable. This balance should be the focus of judicial opinions dealing with sovereign immunity, but it is only briefly treated in the relevant cases.

Without the myth of discretion-free judging, judges would have to articulate and defend their value choices; they would have to explain, in terms of the text, framers' intent, traditions, precedent, and policy why they hold their view. Other judges would have to respond in kind. This essential discussion is forfeited when judges can pretend that they are not making choices at all.

A reasonable response to all of this is to ask: If justices are making value choices in constitutional interpretation, why not leave such decision making entirely to elected officials? Judicial review has an antidemocratic quality in that unelected judges are invalidating the choice of popularly elected officials. The answer to this question goes to the heart of the Constitution and the purpose of judicial review. It also points to the central flaw in the conservative assault on the Constitution as well as what must be done to reclaim the Constitution.

I begin every constitutional law class I teach by asking my students how the Constitution is different from all other laws. The answer, of course, is that the Constitution is much more difficult to change. Any statute or ordinance can be revised or repealed by a majority of the appropriate legislative body, but amending the Constitution requires approval by two-thirds of both houses of Congress and then ratification by three-fourths of the states. There have been only twenty-seven amendments to the Constitution since 1787 and only seventeen since the Bill of Rights was adopted in 1791.

The question then is why would a nation that sees itself as a democracy want to be governed by a document that no one alive today approved. The framers of the Constitution were deeply distrustful of majorities and wanted to make sure that the nation's most important commitments—such as separation of powers to achieve checks and balances, and individual liberties—were placed in a document difficult to alter. They knew from historical experience of the tendency to centralize power in a crisis and of the danger of persecution of the politically unpopular. The Constitution was meant to make it difficult for society to abandon its most precious commitments, such as those found in the structure of government and in individual freedoms.

I liken this for my students to a story from Homer's *Odyssey* about Ulysses and the sirens. The sirens' beautiful song lured sailors to their deaths on the rocky shoals. Ulysses had himself tied to the mast and then had the sailors plug their ears with wax so that he could hear the sirens' song, but no one would be endangered. The Constitution, I suggest, is the way that society tries to tie its own hands to avoid the sirens' song of tyranny that has tempted many other nations over time. Harvard law professor Laurence Tribe has described the Constitution as an elaborate edifice to make sure that our short-term values do not cause us to lose sight of our long-term commitments.

The Constitution is thus profoundly antidemocratic in that it limits what the majority at any moment can do. In fact, much of the government that the Constitution creates was based on the framers' distrust of majorities. Of the four governmental institutions created in the Constitution, only one is directly elected by the people. The president, as we were all reminded in 2000, is chosen by the electoral college, not by the popular vote. For the first 125 years of American history, senators were selected by state legislatures; popular election of senators did not occur until the Seventeenth Amendment was adopted in 1913. Federal judges are appointed by the president and confirmed by the Senate. Only members of the House of Representatives are elected directly by the people. It is far too simplistic to define democracy in the United States as "majority rule."

The Constitution is designed to restrict what the majority can do. Judicial review, the power of courts to review the constitutionality of laws and executive acts, is crucial to enforce the limits contained within the Constitution. In *Marbury v. Madison,* in 1803, Chief Justice John Marshall, writing for the Supreme Court, gave exactly this explanation for why the courts must review the constitutionality of executive and legislative acts. Without judicial review, compliance with the limits created in the Constitution would be left to the elected branches of government. Sometimes, maybe even often, the desire of elected officials to please their constituents' immediate preferences will cause them to ignore the Constitution's dictates.

To take a single example: legislatures and elected judges in the South would not have ended legally mandated segregation in the 1950s or '60s or maybe even later. Nor would Congress have acted to do this; southern senators successfully filibustered any civil rights legislation for years. Only the Supreme Court and the federal judiciary could enforce equal protection of the law and end Jim Crow.

On many occasions, the first assignment in my constitutional class has been for students to read a copy of the Stalin-era Soviet Constitution and the United States Constitution. My students are always surprised to see that the Soviet Constitution has a far more elaborate statement of rights than the American Constitution. I also assign them to read a description of life in the gulags. I ask how can it be that a country with such detailed statements of rights in its constitution could have such horrible abuses.

The answer is that in the Soviet Union no court had the power to strike down any government action. Judicial review, as it has existed since *Marbury v. Madison,* is at the core of enforcing the Constitution and of ensuring our freedom.

In 1992, not long after the fall of the Soviet Union, I was asked to go to Belarus along with three other Americans to help write a new constitution. Over the course of our week in Minsk, increasingly we focused on one thing: the importance of their creating an independent judiciary with the authority to invalidate actions, especially by the executive, that violated their constitution. We were convinced that without such judicial review the rest of the document would become irrelevant. Unfortunately, not long after adopting its constitution, Belarus was the first state of the former Soviet Union to revert to communism and totalitarianism. It is doubtful that any constitutional language would have prevented this; in fact, the omissions in the Belarussian constitution reflected the same impulses that led to the abandonment of democratic rule.

There are many implications to this defense of judicial review. First, throughout American history there have been some who have argued that judicial review should be eliminated. Pulitzer Prize–winning author and Williams College professor James Mac-Gregor Burns argued for this in a recently published book and Harvard law professor Mark Tushnet did so in a book published a decade ago. I think that their argument, which thankfully has little chance of being adopted, is fundamentally misguided because it places total trust in elected officials to comply with the Constitution and eliminates the crucial check of courts invalidating unconstitutional government actions. History provides little reason to believe that legislatures would protect the rights of prisoners or criminal defendants or speech by the politically unpopular.

Second, recognizing that the Constitution is itself antimajoritarian lessens the concern that judicial review is antidemocratic. The conservative argument for wanting judges to follow the Constitution's original meaning always starts with the claim that judicial review is inherently antidemocratic, so it must be limited. But this argument ignores the fact that the Constitution itself is antidemocratic; any enforcement of the Constitution to strike down what a political majority wants also will be antidemocratic. Any judicial review that invalidates government actions, whether based on the original understanding or not, is antimajoritarian. The criticism of judicial review as being antidemocratic because it strikes down majoritarian decisions is based on a simplistic definition of democracy. American democracy is not and never has been a simple matter of majority rule. The United States is a *constitutional* democracy, not a pure democracy. Enforcement of the commitments in the Constitution thus furthers this type of democracy even when the actions of elected officials are invalidated.

Finally and very importantly, the antimajoritarian nature of the Constitution protects minorities of all sorts. The majority rarely needs the Constitution to protect it; usually the majority can rely on its power in the political process. The framers' greatest concern was protecting political minorities. Judicial review exists to protect the minority that wants the Constitution enforced and the minority whose rights will suffer without this enforcement. As discussed in Chapter 4, when Congress at President Bush's urging eliminated habeas corpus for noncitizens held as enemy combatants, the Court enforced the Constitution and declared this action unconstitutional.

The First Amendment protects the ability of religious minorities to practice their faith and of political minorities to speak. Majority religions don't need the Constitution and judicial review to protect them. The constitutional guarantee of free speech isn't needed for speech that expresses popular positions; the government would allow that anyway. The assurance of equal protection exists above all to protect minorities that suffer discrimination and who by their numbers cannot protect themselves through the political process. In a famous footnote in a 1938 decision, the Supreme Court explained that aggressive judicial review was needed especially to protect "discrete and insular minorities," groups that by their numbers and social status are unlikely to succeed politically.

This basic account of the Constitution exposes what is wrong with the conservative vision and what is vital to reclaiming the Constitution. The conservative assault on the Constitution has led to a Court that has lost sight of the preeminent role of the Constitution and judicial review in protecting the rights of minorities. In Chapter 1, I explained how over the last few decades, the Court has abandoned the effort at equalizing schools and the result has been separate and unequal education, to the tremendous detriment of African-American and Latino children. Ironically, the focus of the Court has been far more on limiting affirmative action and protecting whites than remedying discrimination and advancing equality for racial minorities. The Court has failed to realize that there is a world of difference between the government using race to subordinate minorities and using race to benefit minorities and advance equality. Reclaiming the Constitution requires a renewed commitment to protecting minorities and ending the racial separation and inequalities in American public education.

A conservative philosophy of executive power that cannot be reviewed by the courts (or checked by Congress) began with Richard Nixon, expanded with Ronald Reagan, and reached its zenith (or nadir) with George W. Bush. Some of these abuses already have been repudiated, such as the use of torture in interrogation, warrantless electronic eavesdropping, and the use of military tribunals that violate international and domestic law. Others, such as the detentions at Guantanamo, are in the process of ending. But it is essential that the Obama administration and the Supreme Court reject unconstitutional notions of unchecked executive authority.

In Chapter 3, I described how the increasingly conservative Supreme Court has been undermining the rights of religious minorities. The Court has narrowly interpreted the protection of free exercise of religion in the First Amendment and has said that religious minorities must rely on the majority through the democratic process for protection of their religious freedom. The conservative majority on the Court is on the verge of largely leaving the limits on the establishment of religion to the political process. The court is jeopardizing the central vision of the religion clauses in the First Amendment that protect religious minorities in their free exercise of religion and assure a separation of church and state.

The Court's assault on the rights of criminal defendants is another example of political conservatism undermining constitutional protections. The political process cannot and will not safeguard the rights of those accused of crimes. Politicians compete with one another to see who can be tougher on crime; no politician wants to do something to aid criminals and thus give an opponent a sound bite for the next election. Since the Nixon campaign for the presidency, the conservative assault on the Constitution has steadily eroded the constitutional protections of criminal defendants. Reclaiming the Constitution requires that there be greater enforcement of these constitutional protections: a more robust assurance of effective counsel for all accused of crime and especially those facing death sentences, greater assurances that prosecutors meet their constitutional duty of turning over potentially exculpatory evidence to criminal defendants, a revival and reinvigoration of the exclusionary rule for illegally obtained evidence, and a reversal of the limits on the great writ of habeas corpus that have made it so difficult for federal courts to provide relief to those held in violation of the Constitution, including innocent individuals.

Conservative judges have limited individual liberties over the last few decades. Basic rights such as freedom of speech and privacy have been weakened. In other areas, the Court has failed to recognize vital rights, such as a right to an education, a right to protection from harm, and a right to assisted death. In all of these areas, the Court must play a preeminent role in advancing individual liberty. But it also is possible for Congress and state legislatures and state courts interpreting state constitutions to step in and provide this protection where the Supreme Court has failed. Statutes—federal and state—and state constitutions always can provide more rights than the United States Constitution.

The Supreme Court has increasingly closed the courthouse doors to those with constitutional claims by limiting when federal officers can be sued, restricting who has standing to sue in federal court, increasing the facts that must be pled to get into federal court, expanding sovereign immunity that keeps state governments from being held accountable, shifting contested matters to arbitration and away from juries, and limiting punitive damages. Constitutional rights can be nullified if no one can go to court to enforce them. Some of these changes, such as the pleading rules and the shift to arbitration, can be solved by federal legislation. Other limits on access to the courts require that the Supreme Court develop a jurisprudence that emphasizes that those with constitutional claims and other injuries should have their days in court.

My vision for reclaiming the Constitution is not radical; it is a vision that the Warren Court embodied and pursued. The central notion is that society is best off having an institution—the Supreme Court and the federal judiciary—largely insulated from majoritarian politics to enforce the Constitution and give it meaning. Most governing decisions—whether to send troops to Afghanistan, whether and what kind of health-care reform to adopt, whether to bail out banks, what disaster relief to give under what circumstances—are left entirely to the elected branches of government. But where the Constitution is involved, it is the judiciary that gives meaning to the Constitution and determines how it applies to modern issues. In doing so, the Court should be guided by the Constitution's underlying goal of creating a more perfect union, of upholding the decency of every individual, and of advancing liberty and equality in society. It is this vision that has been lost or at least compromised in the forty-year conservative assault on the Constitution and this vision that must be reclaimed.

I am not naïve and I realize that this is not likely to happen soon. Five justices appointed by Presidents Reagan, Bush, and Bush are likely to remain on the bench for the next decade. Just when the conservative hold on the Supreme Court lessens depends entirely on who leaves the bench and who picks their replacements. If Al Gore or John Kerry, rather than George W. Bush, had replaced William Rehnquist and Sandra Day O'Connor, the Supreme Court would be vastly different today and many of the decisions from the last few years described in this book would have come out differently. If John McCain rather than Barack Obama had replaced David Souter, I am certain that there would be five votes on the Court today to overrule *Roe v. Wade*.

Although the conservative majority on the Supreme Court will not end anytime soon, it is important nonetheless to realize how much the conservative assault on the Constitution has succeeded in remaking constitutional law and to begin to articulate an alternative vision. That has been my goal in this book. I am confident that it is a vision that will ultimately triumph.

The sweep of American history shows a tremendous expansion of equality and increase in individual liberties. The nation has gone from slavery to mandated segregation to prohibiting race discrimination to affirmative action. It has progressed from women being literally chattel, property of their husbands, to their having the right to vote, to having gender equality protected by statute and by the Constitution. In my lifetime, gays and lesbians have gone from being criminals when they engage in sex to having a constitutional right to private consensual sexual activities to being able to marry in some states (and, I hope, soon in the entire country). Individual liberties protected in the Bill of Rights have gone from applying only to the federal government to applying to state and local governments as well. Rights such as freedom of association and aspects of privacy—including the right to marry, the right to procreate, the right to custody of one's children, the right to control the upbringing of children, the right to purchase and use contraceptives, the right to abortion, and the right to refuse medical care—have been recognized and protected.

Thus I am confident that someday this period, the era of the conservative assault on the Constitution, will be looked back on as an aberration, an unfortunate time of retrenchment. The advancement of freedom and equality by the Supreme Court will resume. The Constitution will again be seen as a means to liberty and justice for all.

ACKNOWLEDGMENTS

Students sometimes ask me how long it takes to write a book about law. I am never quite sure how to answer. In one sense, this book is the result of more than thirty years of teaching, writing, and litigating about constitutional law. It reflects ideas that I have gleaned from teaching thousands of students and from countless conversations with colleagues.

I am especially grateful for the conversations with Bill Marshall, Neil Siegel, Stephan Siegel, and Larry Simon, which very much influenced my thinking on constitutional law. The cases that I describe litigating in this book were litigated together with other attorneys. I am particularly grateful to Paul Hoffman and Mark Rosenbaum, who were my co-counsel in several of the cases discussed (such as *Lockyer v. Andrade* and *Van Orden v. Perry*), and who are the best lawyers I have ever met.

In a more immediate sense, work on this book began in early 2007 when I was on the faculty at Duke Law School. Dean Kate Bartlett was very encouraging and generous in providing research support. Completion of the book was delayed by my moving to be the founding dean of the law school at the University of California, Irvine. Chancellor Michael Drake and Executive Vice Chancellor/Provost Michael Gottfredson have been tremendously supportive of my work and the law school in every way.

I have been assisted by very talented research assistants, especially Anet Castro, Kara Kapp, Kimberly Kisabeth, Nicholas Linder, Lori Speak, Tracey Steele, and Jonathan Tam. My superb assistant, Brandy Stewart, helped in so many ways.

I am very grateful to several individuals for reading drafts of the manuscript and providing me invaluable suggestions. Joan Biskupic, the wonderful journalist and the author of biographies of Justices O'Connor and Scalia, read a draft of every chapter and offered me terrific comments. Jeff Chemerinsky's brilliant insights and impressive editing made the manuscript much better. Catherine Fisk, as always, was tireless in her willingness to talk through the ideas on these pages and to read them and offer great suggestions. Jim Newton, also a terrific journalist and author, interrupted his busy schedule as a newspaper editor, an author, and a teacher to offer wonderful comments and suggestions. Marcy Strauss painstakingly read every word and offered countless excellent ideas. I feel so blessed to have such dear friends and family members. I cannot possibly thank them enough for their assistance. The errors in the book are all mine and I know that the manuscript would have been better if I had followed their advice even more.

Most of all, I am grateful to my editor at Simon & Schuster, Bob Bender. He believed in me and in this book from the beginning. He was patient as I was delayed in my writing by all of the other responsibilities in my life over the last few years.

Finally, I want to thank my family: Jeff, Adam, Alex, Mara, and my soon-to-be daughter-in-law, Kim. No words ever can express my love and appreciation for them. I dedicate this book to Catherine with thanks and love more than words can ever express.

NOTES

INTRODUCTION: THE CONSTITUTION TOUCHES EVERYONE

1 *My former client:* The story of my arguing Lockyer v. Andrade in the Supreme Court is told in Joe Domanick, *Cruel Justice: Three Strikes and the Politics of Crime in America's Golden State* (Berkeley: University of California Press, 2004), at 1–9.

1 *No one in the history:* Ewing v. California, 538 U.S. 11, 48 (2002) (Breyer, J., dissenting).

1 *Chief Justice Rehnquist and Justices Antonin Scalia and Clarence Thomas:* Harmelin v. Michigan, 501 U.S. 957 (1991).

1 *I was confident that I would get the votes:* Durden v. California, 531 U.S. 284 (2001) (cert. denied) (Souter and Breyer, JJ., dissenting); Riggs v. California, 525 U.S. 1114 (1999) (cert. denied) (Stevens, Souter, and Ginsburg dissenting).

2 *Almost seven years to the day:* The facts of the Andrade case are recited by the United States Supreme Court as well as the United States Court of Appeals for the Ninth Circuit. Lockyer v. Andrade, 538 U.S. 63 (2002); Andrade v. Attorney General, 270 F.3d 43 (9th Cir. 2001).

2 *Petty theft is defined as:* California Penal Code Ann. §490 (West Supp. 1998).

3 *Petty theft with a prior in California:* California Penal Code Ann. §666.

3 *in 1994 California voters:* California's "three-strikes" law was initially adopted by the California legislature as a statute, Stats. 1994, ch. 12, §1, and then approved by the voters as an initiative. Proposition 184, §1, approved by voters, Gen. Elec. (Nov. 8, 1994).

4 *At the time I argued his case:* Joanna M. Shepherd, "Fear of the First Strike: The Full Deterrent Effect of California's Two- and Three-Strikes Legislation," 31 *Journal of Legal Studies* 159, 164

(2002) (based on California Department of Corrections statistics of offenses for which individuals were sentenced under the three-strikes law).

5   *After Andrade was convicted:* People v. Andrade, 85 Cal.App.4th 579, 102 Cal.Rptr.2d 254 (2002).

6   *About a year earlier:* Durden v. California, 531 U.S. 284 (2001).

7   *Soon after the court decided:* Brown v. Mayle, 283 F.3d 1119 (2001).

8   *Almost a century earlier:* Weeks v. United States, 217 U.S. 349, 367 (1910).

8   *In 1983, the Court held that it was grossly disproportionate:* Solem v. Helm, 463 U.S. 277 (1983).

9   *In this and other cases:* Solem v. Hekn, 483 U.S. 287 (1982); Harmelin v. Michigan, 501 U.S. 957 (1991).

9   *As for the sentences imposed:* Andrade v. Attorney General, 270 F.3d 743, 762 (9th Cir. 2001).

9   *"Andrade's indeterminate sentence":* Ibid.

9   *Justice Stevens noted:* Riggs v. California, 525 U.S. 1114 (1999) (Stevens, J., dissenting from the denial of certiorari).

9   *As Justice Breyer observed:* Ewing v. California, 538 U.S. 11, 48 (2002) (Breyer, J., dissenting).

10 *One empirical study:* Linda S. Beres and Thomas D. Griffith. "Did 'Three Strikes' Cause the Recent Drop in California Crime? An Analysis of the California Attorney General's Report," 32 *Loyola of Los Angeles Law Review* 101, 102 (1998).

10 *The most extensive study:* Franklin E. Zimring, Gordon Hawkins, and Sam Kamin, *Punishment and Democracy: Three Strikes and You're Out in California* (New York: Oxford University Press, 2001), 101.

10 *This conclusion is supported:* Mike Males and Dan Macallair, "Striking Out: The Failure of California's 'Three Strikes and You're Out' Law,'" 11 *Stanford Law and Policy Review* 65, 66–67 (1999).

10 *Analysts at RAND:* Susan Turner, Peter Greenwood, Elsa Chen, and Terry Fain, "The Impact of Truth-in-Sentencing and Three Strikes Legislation: Prison Populations, State Budgets, and Crime Rates," 11 *Stanford Law and Policy Review* 11, 75 (1999).

15 *In* Ewing v. California: Ewing v. California, 538 U.S. 11 (2001); Lockyer v. Andrade, 538 U.S. 63 (2002)

16 *In 1968, Richard Nixon:* Thomas M. Keck, *The Most Activist Supreme Court in History: The Road to Modern Judicial Conservatism* (Chicago: University of Chicago Press, 2004), 107–12 (quoting Richard Nixon: "I want men on the Supreme Court who are strict constructionists, men that interpret the law and don't try to make the law").

16   *The Warren Court is perhaps:* Brown v. Board of Education, 347 U.S. 483 (1954).

16   *But it also ruled:* Mapp v. Ohio, 367 U.S. 643 (1961).

16   *In one of the most famous:* Miranda v. Arizona, 384 U.S. 436 (1966).

17   *Nixon promised:* Keck, *The Most Activist Supreme Court in History,* pp. 107–12.

17   *For example, they were two:* New York Times v. United States, 403 U.S. 713 (1971).

17   *Over time, though:* Linda Greenhouse, *Becoming Mr. Justice Blackmun: Harry Blackmun's Supreme Court Journey* (New York: Times Books, 2005).

17   *In addition to authoring:* Roe v. Wade, 410 U.S. 113 (1973).

17   *In powerful language:* Callins v. Collins, 510 U.S. 1141 (1994) (Blackmun, J., dissenting).

18   *For instance, the new Burger Court:* Harris v. New York, 401 U.S. 222 (1971) (allowing confessions gained without Miranda warnings to be used for impeachment purposes).

18   *They imposed significant new:* Stone v. Powell, 428 U.S. 465 (1976); Wainwright v. Sykes, 433 U.S. 72 (1977) (limiting the availability of habeas corpus).

18   *In other areas:* San Antonio Independent School District v. Rodriguez, 411 U.S. 1 (1973); Milliken v. Bradley, 418 U.S. 717 (1974) (both cases on schools are discussed in detail in Chapter 1).

18   *But I faced a Court:* For an excellent description of how these members came to be chosen, see Jeffrey Toobin, *The Nine: Inside the Secret World of the Supreme Court* (New York: Doubleday, 2007).

18   *Some of these conservatives were disappointed:* Joan Biskupic, *Sandra Day O'Connor: How the First Woman on the Supreme Court Became Its Most Influential Justice* (New York: Ecco, 2005), at 70–98.

19   *While a law clerk for Justice Robert Jackson:* Richard Kluger, *Simple Justice* (New York: Vintage, 1975) (quoting the Rehnquist memo and telling its story).

20   *For example, Bork opposed:* Robert Bork, *The Tempting of America* (New York: Free Press, 1989).

22   *For example, in 1990:* Metro Broadcasting v. F.C.C., 497 U.S. 547 (1991).

22   *After the Senate completed its hearings:* Jane Mayer and Jill Abramson, *Strange Justice: The Selling of Justice Clarence Thomas* (Boston: Houghton Mifflin, 1994).

24 *It turns out that the Bush administration:* Jan Crawford Greenberg, *Supreme Conflict: The Inside Story of the Struggle for Control of the Supreme Court* (New York: Penguin, 2007).

25 *For example, Breyer cast:* Board of Education of Independent School District No. 92 of Pottowotamie County v. Earls, 536 U.S. 822 (2002) (approving drug testing for students participating in extra-curricular activities); Hamdi v. Rumsfeld, 542 U.S. 507 (2004) (approving detaining an American citizen as an ememy combatant); Van Orden v. Perry, 545 U.S. 677 (2005) (approving Ten Commandments monument).

25 *It is, of course, the Court:* Bush v. Gore, 532 U.S. 98 (2000) (discussed in detail in the concluding chapter).

26 *Since then, the Supreme Court:* The story of the Roberts and Alito selections and confirmations are told in Greenberg, *Supreme Conflict.*

28 *in October Term 2008, for example:* These statistics can be found in "Supreme Court Review," *National Law Journal,* August 4, 2009, at 23.

1. SEPARATE AND UNEQUAL SCHOOLS

35 *The case attracted:* Alabama Coalition of Equity v. Hunt, 1993 WL 204083 (Ala.Cir. 1993.)

35 *For example, the Mountain Brook:* Ibid. at 6.

35 *The problem for their lawsuit:* San Antonio Independent School District v. Rodriguez, 411 U.S. 1 (1973).

36 *A number of states:* See, e.g., Serrano v. Priest, 557 P.2d 929 (Calif. 1977); Abbott v. Burke, 575 A.2d 359 (N.J. 1990); Tennessee Small School Systems v. McWherter, 851 S.W.2d 139 (Tenn. 1993); McDuffy v. Secretary of Education, 615 N.E.2d 516 (Mass. 1993); Rose v. Council for Better Education, 790 S.W.2d 186 (Ky. 1989); Edgewood Indep. School Dist. v. Kirby, 777 S.W.2d 391 (Tex. 1989).

36 *Alabama had amended:* "Alabama Coalition of Equity." Encyclopedia of Alabama, www.encyclopediaofalabama.org.face/Article (last checked February 7, 2010).

36 *The Alabama provision:* Washington v. Davis, 426 U.S. 229 (1976) (showing racially discriminatory impact is not enough to prove a racial classification; for a law that is facially race neutral there also must be proof of racially discriminatory purpose).

37 *After some initial successes:* James v. Alabama Coalition of Equity, 713 So.2d 937 (Ala. 1997).

37   *In 2002, the same court:* Ex parte James, 836 So.2d 813 (Ala. 2002).

37   *Harvard professor Gary Orfield's study:* Gary Orfield, *Schools More Separate: Consequences of a Decade of Resegregation* (Cambridge, Mass.: Harvard University Press, 2001), at 39.

37   *In 1954, at the time of:* Ibid. at 29.

38   *In 1986, 62.9 percent:* Ibid. at 31.

38   *Orfield's research:* Gary Orfield, *Reviving the Goal of Integrated Society: A 21st Century Challenge* (Los Angeles: Civil Rights Project of UCLA, 2009).

38   *The percentage of Latino students:* Orfield, *Schools More Separate,* at 2.

38   *Orfield notes:* Ibid.

38   *The overall statistics:* Jonathan Kozol, *The Shame of the Nation: The Restoration of Apartheid Schooling in America* (New York: Crown, 2005), at 8 (providing the statistics in this paragraph).

39   *Wealthy suburban school districts:* Orfield, *Reviving the Goal,* at 14.

39   *According to the most recent national statistics:* Ibid. at 9.

39   *I believe that both of these:* Kozol, *The Shame of the Nation;* Jonathan Kozol, *Savage Inequalities* (New York: Crown, 2001).

39   *More than a half century ago:* Brown v. Board of Education, 347 U.S. 483 (1954).

39   *Chief Justice Earl Warren:* Ibid. at 494.

39   *Justice Breyer, in a recent opinion:* Parents Involved in Community Schools v. Seattle School Dist. No. 1, 551 U.S. 701, 838 (2007) (Breyer, J., dissenting).

40   *Again, Justice Breyer, in his recent opinion:* Ibid.

40   *Former federal court of appeals judge Nathaniel Jones:* Nathaniel R. Jones, "The Desegregation of Urban Schools Thirty Years After Brown," 55 *University of Colorado Law Review* 515, 553 (1984).

41   *In 2006:* Orfield, *Reviving the Goal,* at 5–6.

42   *The only major:* Ibid. at 5.

42   *Kevin Phillips devised:* Ibid.

42   *During the 1968 campaign, Nixon strongly opposed:* Ibid.

43   *In August, 1971, he declared:* Richard M. Nixon, Statement About the Busing of School Children, August 3, 1971.

43   *In the spring of 1971:* Swann v. Charlotte-Mecklenburg Board of Education, 402 U.S. 1 (1971).

43   *In March 1972, he proposed legislation:* Richard M. Nixon, Address to the Nation on Equal Educational Opportunity, March 13, 1972.

43   *President Nixon explained his proposal:* Ibid.

43 *In addition to proposing this legislation:* McAndrew, "The Politics of Principle."

44 *William Bradford Reynolds:* "Reynolds's inquisition," *National Review* (July 12, 1985) (discussing opposition to Reynolds's promotion to associate attorney general).

44 *It reversed the position that the Carter:* Washington v. Seattle School Dist. No., 458 U.S. 457 (1982).

44 *It proposed to "shift control":* Quoted in Donald K. Sharpes, *Education and the U.S. Government* (Beckenham, England: Croom House, 1987), 80–82.

45 *From* Plessy v. Ferguson: Plessy v. Ferguson, 169 U.S. 537 (1896).

45 *As mentioned above:* Orfield, *Schools More Separate*, at 29.

45 *After* Brown, *southern states used:* Michael J. Klarman, *From Jim Crow to Civil Rights* (New York: Oxford University Press, 2004) (describing massive resistance to desegregation in the South).

45 *In the South, just 1.2 percent of black schoolchildren:* James T. Patterson, *Brown v. Board of Education: A Civil Rights Milestone and Its Troubled Legacy* (New York: Oxford University Press, 2001), at 113.

45 *In South Carolina, Alabama, and Mississippi:* Ibid.

46 *By 1968, the integration rate rose to 32 percent:* Orfield, *Schools More Separate*, at 29.

46 *In* Brown, *in 1954:* Brown v. Board of Education, 347 U.S. 483 (1954).

46 *A year later in* Brown II: Brown v. Board of Education, 349 U.S. 294, 301 (1955).

46 *In 1958, the Supreme Court ruled:* Cooper v. Aaron, 358 U.S. 1 (1958).

46 *until 1964:* Griffith v. County School Board of Prince Edward County, 377 U.S. 218, 229 (1964).

47 *It was not until 1971:* Swann v. Charlotte-Mecklenburg Board of Education, 402 U.S. 1 (1971).

48 *For example, by 1980, whites constituted:* Erwin Chemerinsky, "Lost Opportunity: The Burger Court and the Failure to Achieve Equal Educational Opportunity," 45 *Mercer Law Review, 999*, 1005 (1994).

48 *The Court considered this:* Milliken v. Bradley, 418 U.S. 717 (1974).

48 *For example, of the fourteen schools that opened in Detroit:* Ibid. at 726 (providing all of the statistics in these paragraphs).

49 *Nonetheless, the Supreme Court:* Ibid. at 744.

49 *Duke professor Charles Clotfelter:* Charles T. Clofelter, *After Brown: The Rise and Retreat of School Desegregation* (Princeton, N.J.: Princeton University Press, 2004).

49 *Chicago public schools are now:* Kozol, *The Shame of the Nation,* at 8.

50 *In 1972 sociologist and education expert Christopher Jencks:* Christopher Jencks, *Inequality: A Reassessment of the Effect of Formal Schooling in America* (New York: Basic Books, 1972), at 28.

50 *For example, in the early 1970s:* Kozol, *Savage Inequalities,* at 85–86 (providing the statistics in this paragraph).

51 *The Court had the opportunity:* San Antonio Independent School District v. Rodriguez, 411 U.S. 1 (1973) (the information presented about the San Antonio schools is drawn from the Court's opinion).

52 *"It is not the province of this Court":* Ibid. at 33.

52 Kadrmas v. Dickinson Public Schools: Kadrmas v. Dickinson Public Schools, 467 U.S. 450 (1988).

53 *Chief Justice Warren:* Brown v. Board of Education, 347 U.S. at 493.

53 *In virtually every major city:* Kozol, *The Shame of the Nation,* at 323–24 (statistics in this paragraph are from the charts on these pages and are from 2002–2003).

54 *In* Board of Education of Oklahoma City v. Dowell: Board of Education of Oklahoma City Public Schools v. Dowell, 498 U.S. 237 (1991).

55 *Ending the federal court's remedy:* Gary Orfield, *Dismantling Desegregation: The Quiet Reversal of Brown v. Board of Education* (New York: New Press, 1996).

55 *The Court reaffirmed:* Freeman v. Pitts, 503 U.S. 467 (1992).

56 *Finally, in* Missouri v. Jenkins: Missouri v. Jenkins, 550 U.S. 70 (1995).

57 *For example, the United States Court of Appeals for the Fourth Circuit:* Belk v. Capacchione, 274 F.3d 814 (4th Cir. 2001).

57 *Harvard professor Gary Orfield:* Orfield, *Schools More Separate,* at 29–32.

57 *Similarly, the United States Court of Appeals for the Eleventh Circuit:* Manning ex rel. Manning v. School Board of Hillsborough County, Florida, 244 F.3d 927 (11th Cir. 2001).

57 *During the Vietnam War, Senator George Aiken:* Albin Krebs, "George Aiken, Longtime Senator and G.O.P. Maverick, Dies at 92," *New York Times,* Nov. 20, 1984, at B-10.

58 *The Supreme Court's decision in 2007:* Parents Involved in Community Schools v. Seattle School Dist., No. 1, 551 U.S. 701 (2007).

59 *Roberts was emphatic:* Ibid. at 732.

60 *Chief Justice Roberts concluded:* Ibid. at 747.

60 *Roberts then asked:* Ibid. at 747.

60 *He ended his opinion by declaring:* Ibid. at 747–48.

61   *The Congress that ratified:* Stephen A. Siegel, "The Federal Government's Power to Adopt Color Conscious Laws," 92 *Northwestern University Law Review* 477 (1998) (describing the actions of the Congress that ratified the Fourteenth Amendment).

61   *In* Grutter v. Bollinger: Grutter v. Bollinger, 539 U.S. 982 (2003).

62   *To take law schools:* Data from the Law School Admissions Council (2009).

64   *As I mentioned:* Alabama Coalition of Equity v. Hunt, 1993 WL 204083 (Ala.Cir. 1993.)

64   *Four years later, the Alabama Supreme Court:* James v. Alabama Coalition of Equity, 713 So.2d 937 (Ala. 1997).

65   *The litigation languished:* Ex parte James, 836 So.2d 813 (Ala. 2002).

65   *"[W]e deal here":* Milliken v. Bradley, 418 U.S. at 782 (Marshall, J., dissenting).

2. THE IMPERIOUS PRESIDENCY

68   *A federal statute allows:* 28 U.S.C. §2242 (a habeas petition may be brought "on behalf" of another).

68   *Yagman put together a coalition:* Coalition of Clergy, Lawyers, and Professors v. Bush, 310 F.3d 1153 (9th Cir. 2002).

69   *During the Vietnam War:* Jane Mayer, *The Dark Side* (New York: Doubleday, 2008), at 121.

70   *The next day, Judge Matz released:* Coalition of Clergy, Lawyers, and Professors v. Bush, 189 F.Supp.2d 1036 (C.D. Cal. 2002).

71   *In November 2002, the court of appeals unanimously affirmed:* Coalition of Clergy, Lawyers, and Professors v. Bush, 310 F.3d 1153 (9th Cir. 2002).

72   *In December, it held in our favor:* Gherebi v. Bush, 352 F.3d 1278 (9th Cir. 2003).

72   *The United States Court of Appeals for the District of Columbia Circuit:* Al-Odah v. Bush, 321 F.3d 1134 (D.C. Cir. 2003).

72   *In June 2004, the Supreme Court reversed:* Rasul v. Bush, 542 U.S. 466 (2004).

72   *The Bush administration then successfully pushed the Republican-controlled Congress:* Detainee Treatment Act of 2005, Tit. X, 119 Stat. 2739.

72   *In response, in the fall of 2006:* Military Commission Act of 2006, 28 U.S.C. §2241(e) (2007 Supp.).

72   *On June 12, 2008:* Boumediene v. Bush, 533 U.S. 733 (2008).

74 *In 1798, Congress enacted the Alien and Sedition Act:* Sedition Act of 1798, 1 Stat. 596.

75 *In 1964, the Supreme Court said:* New York Times v. Sullivan, 376 U.S. 254, 276 (1964).

75 *During the Civil War, President Abraham Lincoln:* Geoffrey Stone, *Perilous Times: Free Speech in Wartime* (New York: Norton, 2004).

75 *During World War I:* Ibid.

75 *In one famous case:* Schenck v. United States, 249 U.S. 47 (1919).

75 *In another case, the famous socialist Eugene Debs:* Debs v. United States, 249 U.S. 211 (1919).

75 *During World War II:* William Manchester, *The Glory and the Dream* (Boston: Little, Brown, 1974), at 300.

76 *Tragically, in 1944, the Supreme Court upheld:* Korematsu v. United States, 321 U.S. 760 (1944).

76 *In the leading case decided by the Supreme Court:* Dennis v. United States, 341 U.S. 494 (1951).

76 *University of Chicago law professor Geoffrey Stone:* Stone, *Perilous Times.*

77 *Over thirty years ago:* Arthur M. Schlesinger, *The Imperial Presidency* (New York: Houghton Mifflin, 1973).

77 *Nixon's efforts to impound funds:* Impoundment Control Act of 1974, 31 U.S.C. § 1403.

78 *Dick Cheney, for example, has taken this position:* Vice President Richard B. Cheney, Remarks to the Traveling Press about Air Force Two en route Muscat, Oman (Dec. 20, 2005), available at http://www.whitehouse.gov.news/releases/2005/12/20051220–9.

78 *In 1972, the United States Supreme Court unanimously ruled:* United States v. United States District Court, 407 U.S. 297 (1972).

78 *The late Rutgers law professor Arthur Kinoy:* Arthur Kinoy, *Rights on Trial: The Odyssey of a People's Lawyer* (Cambridge, Mass.: Harvard University Press, 1983).

79 *The Boland Amendment:* Department of Defense Appropriations Act for Fiscal Year 1985, Pub. L. No. 98–473, §8066(a), 98 Stat. 1837, 1935 (1984). See generally United States: Legislation Relating to Nicaragua, 26 I.L.M. 433 (1987) (outlining all legislative restrictions on Nicaragua funding from 1980 to 1987, with reprints of relevant texts).

79 *The Republican Minority Report to the House committee:* Minority Report, in Report of the Congressional Committees Investigating the Iran-Contra Affair, H.R. Rep. No. 100–433, S. Rep. No. 100–216, at 431, 469 (1987).

80 *"If you want reference to an obscure text":* Lou Dubose and Jake Bernstein, *Vice: Dick Cheney and the Hijacking of the American Presidency* (New York: Random House, 2006), p. 83.

80 *Cheney has repeatedly taken the position:* Charlie Savage, "Hail to the Chief: Dick Cheney's Mission to Expand—or 'Restore'—the Powers of the Presidency," *Boston Globe,* November 26, 2007; Charlie Savage, *Takeover: The Return of the Imperial Presidency and the Subversion of American Democracy* (New York: Little, Brown, 2007).

80 *James Madison wrote in* The Federalist Papers: James Madison, "Number XLVII," *The Federalist 1787–88* (Norwalk, Conn.: Easton, 1973), at 322.

81 *In cases like* Youngstown Sheet: Youngstown Sheet & Tube Co. v. Sawyer, 343 U.S. 579 (1952); United States v. Nixon, 418 U.S. 683 (1974).

82 *In December 2005, the* New York Times *revealed:* See James Risen and Eric Lichtblau, "Bush Lets U.S. Spy on Callers Without Courts," *New York Times,* Dec. 16, 2005, at A1.

82 New York Times *reporter Eric Lichtblau:* Eric Lichtblau, *Bush's Law: The Remaking of American Justice* (New York: Pantheon, 2008), at 192.

82 *The president told the publisher:* Ibid. at 208.

83 *It has been revealed:* Jack L. Goldsmith, *The Terror Presidency: Law and Judgment Inside the Bush Administration* (New York: Norton, 2007).

84 *The Supreme Court made this distinction clear:* Hamdan v. Rumsfeld, 548 U.S. 557 (2006).

84 *In an important footnote:* Ibid. at 593 n. 23

84 *Between 1978 and 1999:* See Susan Herman, "The USA PATRIOT Act and the U.S. Department of Justice: Losing Our Balances?" at http://jurist.law.pitt.edu/forum/forumnew40.htm (Dec. 3, 2001).

84 *A federal district court:* American Civil Liberties Union v. National Security Agency, 438 F.Supp.2d 754 (E.D. Mich. 2006).

85 *But the United States Court of Appeals for the Sixth Circuit:* American Civil Liberties Union v. National Security Agency, 493 F.3d 644 (6th Cir. 2007).

85 *In 2002, the Office of Legal Counsel:* The memos can be found in David Cole, ed., *The Torture Memos* (New York: Oneworld, 2009).

86 *In a memo dated August 1, 2002:* Ibid.

86 *But as Professor Neil Kinkopf:* Neil Kinkopf, "The Statutory Commander in Chief," 81 *Indiana Law Journal* 1169, 1171 (2006).

86 *Jane Mayer, in her deeply disturbing book:* Jane Mayer, *The Dark Side* (New York: Doubleday, 2008).

87 *After the revelation of torture:* Letter from General Colin L. Powell to Senator John McCain (Sept. 13, 2006). Among other things, Powell noted, "The world is beginning to doubt the moral basis of our fight against terrorism. To redefine Common Article 3 would add to those doubts. Furthermore, it would put our own troops at risk." Quoted in George J. Annas, "Human Rights Outlaws," 87 *Boston University Law Review* 427, 461 n.148 (2007).

87 *The Red Cross issued a report:* Mark Danner, "The Red Cross Torture Report: What It Means," *New York Review of Books,* April 30, 2009.

87 *Two Suspected Al Qaeda leaders:* Scott Shaw, "Waterboarding used 266 Times on 2 suspects," *New York Times,* April 20, 2009, p. A1.

88 *Mayer tells the story of Khaled el-Masri:* Mayer, *The Dark Side,* at 282–87.

88 *Mayer describes his release:* Ibid. at 287.

88 *The federal courts agreed:* El-Masri v. United States, 479 F.3d 296, 302 (4th Cir. 2007).

89 *Jose Padilla is an American citizen:* See Rumsfeld v. Padilla, 542 U.S. 426 (2004).

89 *The Supreme Court, in a 5–4 decision:* Ibid.

90 *Nonetheless, the United States Court of Appeals for the Fourth Circuit:* Padilla v. Hanft, 423 F.3d 386 (4th Cir. 2005).

90 *Yaser Hamdi is an American citizen:* Hamdi v. Rumsfeld, 542 U.S. 507 (2004).

90 *Although the Court, in a 5–4 vote:* Ibid.

91 *Similarly, Ali Al-Marri was held by the Bush administration:* Al-Marri v. Pucciarelli, 534 F.3d 213 (4th Cir. 2008) (en banc).

92 *The federal court of appeals in a recent decision:* Al-Kidd v. Ashcroft, 580 F.3d 949, 952 (9th Cir. 2009).

93 *As the federal court of appeals says:* Ibid. at p. 952.

93 *In an opinion written by Judge Milan Smith:* Ibid. at p. 970.

94 *The case that came to the Supreme Court in 2004:* Rasul v. Bush, 542 U.S. 466 (2004).

94 *In March 2003, the United States Court of Appeals:* Al-Odah v. Bush, 321 F.3d 1134 (D.C. Cir. 2003).

94 *On June 12, 2008, the Supreme Court in a 5–4 decision:* Boumediene v. Bush, 533 U.S. 733 (2008).

95 *Jane Mayer noted that "the number of renditions":* Mayer, *The Dark Side,* at 115.

96 *A federal court of appeals declared:* Detroit Free Press v. Ashcroft, 303 F.3d 681 (6th Cir. 2002).

96 *Judge Damon Keith eloquently wrote:* Ibid. at p. 683.

96 *Another federal court of appeals:* New Jersey Media Group, Inc. v. Ashcroft, 308 F.3d 98 (3rd Cir. 2002).

97 *The Supreme Court declared illegal:* Hamdan v. Rumsfeld, 548 U.S. 557 (2006).

97 *A federal district court judge in New York:* Doe v. Gonzales, 500 F.Supp.2d 379 (S.D.N.Y. 2007).

98 *Ann L. Aiken, a federal judge in Oregon:* Mayfield v. United States, 504 F.Supp.2d 1023, 1042–43 (D.Ore. 2007).

99 A Justice Department report found that you and Bybee used flawed reasoning but did not commit a crime in the torture memos. Eric Lichtblau and Scott Shane, "Report Faults 2 Authors of Bush Terror Memos," *New York Times,* Feb. 19, 2010, p. A-1.

99 *Those who defend their actions:* Terminiello v. Chicago, 337 U.S. 1, 37 (1949) (Jackson, J., dissenting)

99 *Justice Louis Brandeis wrote:* Olmstead v. United States, 277 U.S. 438, 573 (1928) (Brandeis, J., dissenting).

3. Dismantling the Wall Separating Church and State

101 *I read the decision:* Van Orden v. Perry, 351 F.3d 143 (5th Cir. 2004).

101 *The monument is six feet:* The facts are presented in the court of appeals decision, ibid. and the United States Supreme Court decision, Van Orden v. Perry, 545 U.S. 677 (2005).

104 *In 1947, the Supreme Court held:* Everson v. Board of Education, 330 U.S. 1 (1947).

104 *James Madison, another of the founders:* In an 1803 letter objecting to the use of government land for churches, he wrote, "The purpose of separation of church and state is to keep forever from these shores the ceaseless strife that has soaked the soil of Europe in blood for centuries." http://www.faithofourfathers.net/madison .html.

105 *Jefferson's famous statement:* A Bill for Establishing Religious Freedom, in P. Kurland and R. Lerner, eds., *The Founders' Constitution,* no. 37, at 77 (Chicago: University of Chicago Press, 1987).

105 *The Supreme Court has described Jefferson's belief:* Rosenberger v. Rectors of the University of Virginia, 515 U.S. 819, 823 (1995).

105 *Madison said:* Madison's Memorial and Remonstrance ¶3, reprinted in Everson v. Board of Education, 330 U.S. 1, 65–66 (1947).

106   *Justice O'Connor has explained:* Wallace v. Jaffree, 472 U.S. 38, 69 (1985) (O'Connor, J., concurring).

106   *It is worth noting that under Justice Clarence Thomas's view:* Elk Grove Unified School District v. Newdow, 542 U.S. 1, 46 (2004) (Thomas, J., concurring).

106   *His view, expressed in many opinions:* Ibid.; Van Orden v. Perry, 545 U.S. 677, 692 (2005) (Thomas, J., concurring); Zelman v. Simmons-Harris, 536 U.S. 639, 677 (2002) (Thomas, J., concurring).

107   *Justice William Brennan observed:* School Dist. of Abbington Township v. Schempp, 374 U.S. 203, 240 (1963) (Brennan, J., concurring).

108   *Also, very importantly, there is not one version:* Steven Lubet, "The Ten Commandments in Alabama," 15 *Constitutional Commentary* 471, 474 (1998). The Protestant version of the Ten Commandments can be found in *The Heidelberg Catechism, Question and Answer 92,* in *Psalter Hymnal* (Grand Rapids, Mich.: CRC Publications 1987), at 903–4. The Catholic version can be found in United States Catholic Conference, Inc., *Catechism of the Catholic Faith* (1991), at 561. The Lutheran version can be found in *Luther's Catechism: The Small Catechism of Dir. Martin Luther and an Exposition for Children and Adults Written in Contemporary English* (1982), at 55. The Jewish version can be found in Alan M. Dershowitz, *The Genesis of Justice: The Stories of Biblical Injustice That Led to the Ten Commandments and Modern Law* (New York: Warner Books, 2000), at 247.

110   *Roger Williams, founder:* Mark Howe, *The Garden and the Wilderness* (Chicago: University of Chicago Press, 1965), (noting Roger Williams's view that "worldly corruptions . . . might consume the churches if sturdy fences against the wilderness were not maintained").

110   *Justice Souter also expressed:* Mitchell v. Helms, 530 U.S. 793, 871 (2000) (Souter, J., dissenting).

110   *One of President George W. Bush's first acts:* Exec. Order No. 13198, 3 CFR 750 (2001 Comp.); Exec. Order No. 13280, 3 CFR 262 (2002 Comp.); Exec. Order No. 13342, 3 CFR 180 (2004 Comp.); Exec. Order No. 13397, 71 Fed.Reg. 12275 (2006).

110   *For example, across the country:* Rachel F. Calabro, "Comment, Correction through Coercion: Do State Mandated Alcohol and Drug Treatment Programs in Prisons Violate the Establishment Clause?" 47 *DePaul Law Review* 565 (1998).

110   *In recent years, the federal government:* White House, Fact Sheet: Providing Help to Heal Americans Struggling with Addiction

(2003). ("In his State of the Union Address, President Bush announced a three-year, $600 million federal treatment initiative to help addicted Americans find needed treatment from the most effective programs, including faith-based and community-based organizations.")

111   *Often the criminal defendant:* National Center on Addiction and Substance Abuse at Columbia University, *So Help Me God: Substance, Abuse, Religion and Spirituality* (New York: Columbia University Press, 2001), at 24. ("Twelve-Step programs such as Alcoholics Anonymous (AA) or Narcotics Anonymous (NA) rely on spiritual concepts and methods to support individuals seeking to abstain from substance abuse.... The spiritual basis of a 12-Step program is apparent in its tenets which begin with an acknowledgment of God or a higher power.")

111   *In one recent case:* Americans United for Separation of Church and State v. Prison Fellowship Ministries, 509 F.3d 406 (8th Cir. 2007).

113   *Four justices:* County of Allegheny v. American Civil Liberties Union, Greater Pittsburgh Chapter, 492 U.S. 573 (1989).

114   *In a series of opinions:* Lynch v. Donnelly, 465 U.S. 668, 687 (1984) (O'Connor, J., concurring); Capitol Square Review Advisory Board and Commission v. Pinette, 515 U.S. 753, 772 (1995) (O'Connor, J., concurring).

114   *Justice Breyer also:* Capitol Square Review Advisory Board and Commission v. Pinette, 515 U.S. 753, 772 (1995) (O'Connor, J., concurring) (joining Justice O'Connor's opinion).

114   *The Barry Goldwater campaign for president:* Tali Mendelberg, *The Race Card: Campaign Strategy, Implicit Messages, and the Norm of Racial Equality* (Princeton, N.J.: Princeton University Press, 2001), at 85–86.

114   *Paul Weyrich:* William Martin, *With God on Our Side: The Rise of the Religious Right in America* (New York: Broadway, 2000), at 171–72.

115   *In 1979 Weyrich coined the term:* Sara Diamond, *Not by Politics Alone: The Enduring Influence of the Christian Right* (New York: Guilford, 1998), at 66.

115   *He said, "We are talking":* Quoted in S. I. Strong, "Christian Constitutions: Do They Protect Internationally Recognized Human Rights and Minimize the Potential for Violence Within a Society?," 29 *Case Western Reserve Journal of International Law* 1, 2 (1997).

115   *Thousands of fundamentalist preachers:* John C. Jeffries, Jr., and James Ryan, "A Political History of the Establishment Clause," 100 *Michigan Law Review* 279, 340 (2001).

115 *Their goal was to register:* Theocracy Watch, "The Rise of the Religious Right in the Republican Party," http://www.theocracywatch .org/taking_over.htm. ("Thousands of fundamentalist preachers participated in political training seminars that year, and by June, more than two million voters had been registered Republican. Their goal was to register 5 million by November.")

115 *In the 1980 elections:* Ibid. ("In the 1980 elections, the newly politicized Religious Right succeeded in unseating five of the most liberal Democrat incumbents in the U.S. Senate, and provided the margin that helped Ronald Reagan defeat Jimmy Carter. The year 1980 was the year that a sleeping giant was awakened, and the political landscape of the United States was dramatically altered.")

115 *The Reverend Timothy LaHaye:* See, e.g., Robert Dreyfuss, "Reverend Doomsday: According to Tim LaHaye Apocalypse is Now," *Rolling Stone* (Jan. 28, 2004).

115 *In 1979, LaHaye and his wife:* Ibid.

115 *Nixon was the first president:* Gary Wills, *Head and Heart: American Christianities* (New York: Penguin, 2007), at 490.

115 *According to historian Gary Wills:* Ibid.

116 *He said that in drafting the First Amendment:* Ronald Reagan, U.S. President, Remarks to the National Association of Evangelicals (March 8, 1983), at 361. 1983 Pub. Papers 359, 361.

116 *Reagan urged:* Ronald Reagan, U.S. President, Remarks at a White House Ceremony in Observation of National Day of Prayer (May 6, 1982), at 574.

116 *Reagan repeatedly criticized:* Ibid.

116 *On May 17, 1982, President Reagan proposed:* Ronald Reagan, U.S. President, Message to the Congress Transmitting a Proposed Constitutional Amendment on Prayer in School (May 17, 1982).

116 *It read:* Ibid.

116 *In 1989, the Court heard a case:* County of Allegheny v. American Civil Liberties Union, Greater Pittsburgh Chapter, 492 U.S. 573 (1989).

117 *Earlier the Supreme Court:* Lynch v Donnell, 465 U.S. 451 668 (1984).

118 *The closest they came:* Lee v. Weisman, 505 U.S. 577 (1992).

119 *In 1962,* in the famous "school prayer" case: Engel v. Vitale, 370 U.S. 421 (1962).

119 *A year later, in* Abbington: School Dist. of Abbington Township v. Schempp, 374 U.S. 203 (1963).

121 *This was initially evident:* Mitchell v. Helms, 530 U.S. 793 (2000).

122 *The other case:* McCreary County, Kentucky v. American Civil Liberties Union of Kentucky, 545 U.S. 844 (2005).

127 *As deputy solicitor general:* Lee v. Weisman, 505 U.S. 577 (1992) (Brief of the United States).

128 *In addition to* Lee v. Weisman: Santa Fe Independent School District v. Doe, 530 U.S. 290 (2000).

129 *For several decades:* Sherbert v. Verner, 374 U.S. 398 (1963).

129 *A decision from 1963:* Ibid.

130 *The case was* Employment Division v. Smith: Employment Division v. Smith, 474 U.S. 892 (1990).

131 *Herman Resnick is an Orthodox Jew:* Resnick v. Adams, 348 U.S. 763 (9th Cir. 2003).

132 *In 1997, in* City of Boerne v. Flores: City of Boerne v. Flores, 521 U.S. 507 (1997).

4. The Vanishing Rights of Criminal Defendants

135 *My client Phillip Wilkinson:* The case is Wilkinson v. Polk, 227 Fed. Appx. 210 (4th Cir. 2007).

135 *In* Brady v. Maryland: Brady v. Maryland, 373 U.S. 383 (1963).

136 *The code of ethics for lawyers:* American Bar Association, Model Rules of Professional Conduct, Rule 3.8. John S. Dzienkowski, ed., *Professional Responsibility: Standards, Rules and Statutes, 2009–2010, Abridged Edition* (Minneapolis: West, 2009), at 70.

136 *The Supreme Court has said:* Kyles v. Whitley, 514 U.S. 419 (1995).

138 *But the court declared:* Wilkinson v. Polk, 227 Fed.Appx. 210, 216 (4th Cir. 2007).

140 *The court of appeals, though, ruled:* Ibid. at 213.

141 *"unreasonable":* Ibid. at 220.

141 *"[W]e cannot say":* Ibid. at 220 (emphasis in original).

141 *In 1994, about six months before he retired:* Callins v. Collins, 540 U.S. 1131, 1144 (1994).

142 *He then said that no longer:* Ibid. at 1145.

142 *In 1976, the Supreme Court reversed itself:* Gregg v. Georgia, 428 U.S. 153 (1976).

142 *Justice Ruth Bader Ginsburg, in a speech:* Associate Justice Ruth Bader Ginsburg, Joseph L. Rauh Lecture at the University of the District of Columbia School of Law: In Pursuit of the Public Good: Lawyers Who Care (April 9, 2001) (transcript available at www .supremecourtus.gov/publicinfo/speeches/sp_04–09–01a.html).

142 *A study that was done in Florida:* Galia Benson-Amram, "Protecting the Integrity of the Court: Trial Court Responsibility for Preventing

Ineffective Assistance of Counsel in Criminal Cases," 29 *New York University Review of Law and Social Change* 425, 431 (2004).

142 *Another study in Georgia:* David C. Baldus, et al., *Equal Justice and the Death Penalty: A Legal and Empirical Analysis* (Boston: Northeastern University Press, 1990), at 158.

142 *A study done of 131 individuals:* Steve Mills et al., "Flawed Trials Lead to Death Chamber: Bush Confident in System Rife with Problems," *Chicago Tribune,* June 11, 2000, at 1.

142 *Justice Thurgood Marshall lamented:* Thurgood Marshall, "Remarks Made on the Death Penalty Made at the Judicial Conference of the Second Circuit," 86 *Columbia Law Review* 1, 1–2 (1986).

143 *In a famous case in Texas:* Burdine v. Johnson: Burdine v. Johnson, 231 F.3d 950, 964 (5th Cir. 2000), *vacated,* 262 F.3d 336, 357, 402 (5th Cir. 2001) (en banc).

143 *Thankfully, the entire Fifth Circuit reversed:* Burdine v. Johnson, 262 F.3d 336, 357, 402 (5th Cir. 2001) (en banc).

143 *Leading death penalty attorney Stephen Bright:* Stephen Bright, "Symposium: *Gideon*—A Generation Later," 58 *Maryland Law Review* 1333, 1375 (1999); Stephen B. Bright, "Counsel for the Poor: The Death Sentence Not for the Worst Crime but for the Worst Lawyer," 103 *Yale Law Journal* 1835 (1994).

143 *But that's better than Mississippi:* Ibid.; see also Miss. Code Ann. §99-15-17 (1972) (limiting compensation for appointed counsel to $1,000 per case and, in capital cases, in which two attorneys may be appointed, $2,000).

143 *In a 1984 decision:* Strickland v. Washington, 466 U.S. 668 (1984).

144 *Justice Marshall explained exactly this problem:* Ibid. at 710 (Marshall, J., dissenting).

144 *I can identify only two cases:* Wiggins v. Smith, 539 U.S. 510 (2003); Rompilla v. Beard, 545 U.S. 374 (2005).

144 *The second of these, in 2005:* Rompilla v. Horn, 355 F.3d 233 (3d Cir. 2003).

144 *"Habeas corpus" was derived from English law:* I review the history of habeas corpus in Erwin Chemerinsky, *Federal Jurisdiction,* 5th ed. (New York: Aspen, 2007), at 896.

145 *For example, during this latter time:* Stone v. Powell, 428 U.S. 465 (1976).

145 *The Court, in a direct reversal of Warren Court decisions:* Wainwright v. Sykes, 433 U.S. 72 (1977), effectively overruling Fay v. Noia, 372 U.S. 391 (1963).

145 *In a crucial 1989 case:* Murray v. Giarratano, 499 U.S. 1 (1989).

146   *John Grisham, in his powerful nonfiction book:* John Grisham, *An Innocent Man* (New York: Dell, 2006).

146   *The work of Innocence Projects:* Barry Scheck, Peter Neufeld, and Jim Dwyer, *Actual Innocence: Five Days to Execution and Other Dispatches from the Wrongly Convicted* (New York: Penguin, 2000) (describing the work of the Innocence Projects).

146   *In Illinois alone:* Robert E. Pierre and Kari Lyderson, "Illinois Death Row Emptied," *Washington Post,* Jan. 12, 2003, at A1 (reporting Governor George Ryan's commutation of 167 Illinois death sentences).

146   *The leading study on the execution of wrongly convicted individuals:* Hugo Adam Bedau and Michael L. Radelet, "Miscarriages of Justice in Potentially Capital Cases," 40 *Stanford Law Review* 21, 25 (1987); Michael L. Radelet, *In Spite of Innocence: Erroneous Convictions in Capital Cases* (Boston: Northeastern University Press, 1992).

146   *For example, there has been compelling evidence:* David Grann, "Trial by Fire: Did Texas Execute an Innocent Man?," *New Yorker,* Sept. 7, 2009.

147   *Recently Frank Sterling:* "Innocent But in Prison, "*Los Angeles Times,* May 31, 2010, at A24.

147   *There are instances of police fabricating evidence:* Erwin Chemerinsky, "An Independent Analysis of the Los Angeles Police Department's Board of Inquiry Report on the Rampart Scandal," 34 *Loyola Los Angeles Law Review* 545 (2001) (describing police fabricating evidence as part of Rampart scandal).

147   *Sometimes faulty eyewitness identifications:* Mark S. Brodin, "Behavioral Science Evidence in the Age of *Daubert:* Reflections of a Skeptic," 73 *University of Cincinnati Law Review* 867, 890 n.112 (2005).

147   *But studies such as those by:* Elizabeth F. Loftus, *Eyewitness Testimony* (Cambridge, Mass.: Harvard University Press, 1979).

147   *In* Herrera v. Collins. Herrera v. Collins, 506 U.S. 390, 400 (1993).

147   *But as recently as the summer of 2009:* In re Davis, 130 S.Ct. 1, 3 (2009).

148   *The conservative majority of the Supreme Court:* McCleskey v. Kemp, 481 U.S. 279 (1987).

148   *A study done in Memphis, Tennessee:* James J. Fyfe, "Blind Justice: Police Shootings in Memphis," 73 *Criminal Law & Criminology* 707, 718–20 (1982).

148   *A study in Minnesota:* Minnesota Supreme Court, Task Force on Racial Bias in the Courts, Final Report app. D (Hennepin County Misdemeanor Processing Analysis) (1993), available at http://www

.courts.state.mn.us/documents/CIO/pubsAndReports/Race_Bias_ Report_Complete.pdf. For assault charges, white defendants with prior convictions were released without bail in 13 percent of cases, compared with only 8 percent of black defendants without prior convictions; for prostitution charges, white defendants with prior convictions were released without bail in 25 percent of cases, compared with only 16 percent of black defendants without prior convictions; for theft charges, white defendants with prior convictions were released without bail in 46 percent of cases, compared with only 40 percent of black defendants without prior convictions.

148 *A study of sentencing in the United States:* Charles Ogletree, "Does Race Matter in Criminal Prosecutions?," *Champion,* July 1991, at 14; see also Samuel Gross and Robert Mauro, *Death and Discrimination* (Boston: Northeastern University Press, 1989), at 35–94.

148 *The National Sentencing Commission:* United States v. Prestemon, 929 F.2d 1275, 1279 n.4 (1991) (noting the findings of the Nationwide Sentencing Commission).

148 *In January 2010, the United States Court of Appeals:* Farrakhan v. Gregoire, 2010 WL 10969 (9th Cir. Jan. 5, 2010).

149 *A study by David Baldus at the University of Iowa:* David C. Baldus et al., "Comparative Review of Death Sentences: An Empirical Study of the Georgia Experience," 74 *Journal of Criminal Law and Criminology* 661 (1983).

150 *However, in* McCleskey v. Kemp: McCleskey v. Kemp, 481 U.S. 279 (1987).

150 *At the heart of his claim:* Baldus et al., "Comparative Review of Death Sentences."

151 *a memorandum from Justice Scalia:* The memorandum is quoted in Danielle Ward Mason, "Racism on Our Juries: The Impossibility of Impartiality in Capital Cases," 12 *Jones Law Review* 169 fn. 123 (2008).

152 *In one Florida case:* Peek v. Florida, 488 So. 2d 52, 56 (Fla. 1986).

152 *In a Georgia case:* Dobbs v. Zant, 720 F. Supp. 1566, 1578 (N.D. Ga. 1989).

153 *For example, in his speech:* Richard Nixon, Nomination Acceptance Address (Aug. 8, 1968), available at http://www.presidential rhetoric.com/historicspeeches/nixon/nominationacceptance1968 .html.

153 *Many perceived Nixon's appeal:* Francis Barry McCarthy, "Counterfeit Interpretations of State Constitutions in Criminal Procedure," 58 *Syracuse Law Review* 79, 84 (2007).

154   *The Supreme Court quickly created exceptions:* Miranda v. Arizona, 384 U.S. 436 (1966).

154   *In 1971, in* Harris v. New York: Harris v. New York, 401 U.S. 222 (1971).

154   *Similarly, in a series of decisions:* See, e.g., Michigan Mosley, 423 U.S. 96 (1975); North Carolina v. Butler, 441 U.S. 369 (1979).

154   *Ronald Reagan continued the Nixon attacks:* See, e.g., Ronald Reagan, Radio Address to the Nation on Crime and Criminal Justice Reform, September 11, 1982, http://presidency.ucsb.edu/ws/index .php.

154   *In a weekly radio address:* Ibid.

155   *The Bail Reform Act:* 18 U.S.C. §§3141–3156; Francois Quintard-Morenas, "The Presumption of Innocence in the French and Anglo-American Legal Traditions," 58 *American Journal of Comparative Law* 107 n.355 (2010). ("The Bail Reform Act of 1984 now allows federal courts to order the preventive detention of suspects deemed dangerous or likely to flee.")

155   *In 1984, the Sentencing Reform Act:* Pub. L. No. 98–473 §212, 98 Stat. 1987 (1984).

155   *In 2003, the number of people:* Fox Butterfield, "Prison Rates Among Blacks Reach a Peak, Report Finds," *New York Times,* April 7, 2003, at A12.

156   *An estimated 12 percent:* Ibid.

156   *"By contrast":* Ibid.

156   *There are over one million African-American prisoners:* As of 2006 there were 836,800 African-American men in state or federal prison or local jail, composing 41 percent of the two million men in custody. Bureau of Justice Statistics, U.S. Department of Justice, "Prison and Jail Inmates at Midyear 2006," at 9. This figure does not include those in jails, bringing the figure over one million.

156   *Nationally, five times more prisoners:* Dorothy E. Roberts, "The Social and Moral Cost of Mass Incarceration in African American Communities," 56 *Stanford Law Review* 1271, 1272 (2004).

156   *"Between 1991 and 1999":* Office of the Governor, Arnold Schwarzenegger, Comprehensive Prison Reform (2006), http://gov.ca.gov/ index.php?/fact-sheet/4966.

157   *At 7 A.M. on February 3, 1998:* Muehler v. Mena, 544 U.S. 93 (2005).

157   *In late April 2005:* Tory v. Cochran, 544 U.S. 734 (2005).

158   *The Supreme Court has held:* Stone v. Powell, 428 U.S. 465 (1976).

159   *In one case, the Court found, 5–4:* Illinois v. Wardlow, 528 U.S. 119 (2000).

159　*The case was* Whren v. United States: Whren v. United States, 517 U.S. 806 (1996).

160　*In 1914, in* Weeks v. United States: Weeks v. United States, 232 U.S. 383 (1914).

160　*One comprehensive study found:* Thomas Y. Davies, "A Hard Look at What We Know (and Still Need to Learn) About the 'Costs' of the Exclusionary Rule: The NIJ Study and Other Studies of 'Lost' Arrests," 1983 *American Bar Foundation Research Journal* 611.

161　*A study by the General Accounting Office: Report of the Comptroller General of the United States, Impact of the Exclusionary Rule on Federal Criminal Prosecutions: Report of the Comptroller General of the United States* (Washington, D.C.: U.S. Government Printing Office, 1979).

161　*One study found that "illegal search problems":* Davies, "A Hard Look."

161　*Another study found:* Steven Yarosh, "Operation Clean Sweep: Is the Chicago Housing Authority 'Sweeping' Away the Fourth Amendment?," 86 *Northwestern University Law Review* 1103, 1128 n. 184 (1992) (observing that "[f]ewer than 1% of Chicago defendants accused of violent crimes have their cases thrown out because the evidence was illegally obtained," that "[t]he exclusionary rule plays a significant role only in drug cases where violence is not involved," and that "[t]he rule has little impact on other kinds of cases"; quoting Joseph Tybor and Mark Eissman, "Illegal Evidence Destroys Few Cases: Justice in Chicago," *Chicago Tribune,* Jan. 5, 1986, at 1).

161　*Boston University law professor Tracey Maclin:* Tracey Maclin, "When the Cure for the Fourth Amendment Is Worse Than the Disease," 68 *Southern California Law Review* 1, 43 (1994).

161　*The Court initially signaled:* Hudson v. Michigan, 547 U.S. 586 (2006).

161　*For many years, the Court has held:* Wilson v. Arkansas, 514 U.S. 927 (1995); Richards v. Wisconsin, 520 U.S. 385 (1997).

162　*In 2000, after the Rampart scandal was exposed:* Erwin Chemerinsky, "An Independent Analysis of the Los Angeles Police Department's Board of Inquiry Report on the Rampart Scandal," 34 *Loyola Los Angeles Law Review* 545 (2001).

163　*In a separate opinion, Justice Kennedy said:* Hudson v. Michigan, 547 U.S. 586, 603 (2006) (Kennedy, J., concurring and concurring in the judgment).

163　*The case,* Herring v. United States: Herring v. United States, 129 S.Ct. 695 (2009).

164 *He concluded that:* Ibid. at 702.

164 *As Justice Ginsburg noted in her dissent:* Ibid. at 707 (Ginsburg, J., dissenting).

165 *As Justice Ginsburg explains:* Ibid.

5. The Erosion of Individual Liberties

168 *the law is clear:* Cruzan v. Director, Missouri Department of Health, 497 U.S. 261 (1990) (competent adults have the right to refuse life-saving medical treatment).

168 *For decades the Supreme Court:* See, e.g., Griswold v. Connecticut, 381 U.S. 479 (1965).

168 *Three years after my father died:* Compassion in Dying v. State of Washington, 79 F.3d 790 (9th Cir. 1996) (en banc).

168 *Almost simultaneously, the United States Court of Appeals:* Quill v. Vacco, 80 F.3d 716 (2d Cir. 1996).

169 *A year later, in 1997, the Supreme Court reversed:* Washington v. Glucksberg, 521 U.S. 702 (1997); Vacco v. Quill, 521 U.S. 793 (1997).

169 *since* Roe v. Wade *was decided in 1973:* Roe v. Wade, 410 U.S. 113 (1973).

169 *In fact, the major areas:* District of Columbia v. Heller, 128 S.Ct. 2783 (2008) (protecting individual right to have firearms under Second Amendment); Citizens United v. Federal Election Commission, 130 S.Ct. 876 (2010) (protecting right of corporations to spend money in election campaigns).

170 *The most famous critique:* John Hart Ely, "The Wages of Crying Wolf: A Comment on Roe. v. Wade," 82 *Yale Law Journal* 920, 947 (1973).

170 *Since early in the twentieth century:* Meyer v. Nebraska, 262 U.S. 390 (1923); Pierce v. Society of Sisters, 268 U.S. 510 (1925).

170 *In* Griswold v. Connecticut: Griswold v. Connecticut, 381 U.S. 479 (1965).

170 *In* Eisenstadt v. Baird: Eisenstadt v. Baird, 405 U.S. 438 (1972).

171 *In the 1920s:* Meyer v. Nebraska, 262 U.S. 390 (1923); Pierce v. Society of Sisters, 268 U.S. 510 (1925).

171 *In the 1940s:* Skinner v. Oklahoma, 316 U.S. 535 (1942).

171 *In the 1960s:* Loving v. Virginia, 388 U.S. 1 (1967).

171 *Professor Cass Sunstein has explained:* Cass R. Sunstein, *Radicals in Robes: Why Extreme Right-Wing Courts Are Wrong for America* (New York: Basic Books, 2005), 81–82.

172   *in the words of* Eisenstadt v. Baird: Eisenstadt v. Baird, 405 U.S. 438 (1972).

172   *Justice Blackmun expressed:* Roe v. Wade, 410 U.S. 113, 153 (1973).

172   *Justice Blackmun, writing for the majority:* Ibid at 163.

173   *"We need not resolve":* Ibid at 159.

173   *Harvard law professor Laurence Tribe:* Laurence H. Tribe, "Foreword: Toward a Model of Roles in the Due Process of Life and Law," 87 *Harvard Law Review* 1, 11 (1973).

173   *Professor Tribe wrote:* Ibid. at 21.

174   *About 15 to 20 percent of known pregnancies:* See Babycenter, "Understanding Miscarriage," http://www.babycenter.com/0_understanding-miscarriage_252.bc (last updated December 2005).

174   *Studies indicate that:* Dr. Spock, "What is Infertility?," http://www.drspock.com/article/0,1510,6262,00.html (Aug. 30, 2001).

174   *Almost two decades after* Roe: Planned Parenthood of Southeastern Pennsylvania v. Casey, 505 U.S. 833 (1992).

175   *Richard Nixon, for example, declared:* Richard M. Nixon, U.S. President, Statement About Policy on Abortions at Military Base Hospitals in the United States (April 3, 1971).

175   *Ronald Reagan was even stronger:* Ronald Reagan, U.S. President, 1988 Legislative and Administrative Message: A Union of Individuals (Jan. 25, 1988), at 120.

175   *In a typical speech he said:* Ronald Reagan, U.S. President, Remarks to the National Association of Evangelicals (March 8, 1983), 1983 Pub. Papers, at 361.

175   *In the first weekly radio address:* "Remarks to Participants in the March for Life Rally," Jan. 23, 1989, United States: National Archives and Records Service, *Public Papers of the Presidents of the United States: Book One: January 20–June 30, 1989: George Bush* (Washington, D.C.: U.S. Government Printing Office, 1990), at 12.

175   *President George W. Bush spoke repeatedly:* "Telephone Remarks to Participants in the March for Life," Jan. 22, 2002, United States: National Archives and Records Service, *Public Papers of the Presidents of the United States: Book One: January 1–June 30, 2002: George W. Bush* (Washington, D.C.: U.S. Government Printing Office, 2004), at 96.

176   *Three years earlier, in a case involving a Missouri law:* Webster v. Reproductive Health Services, 492 U.S. 490 (1992).

177   *We know now, thanks:* Linda Greenhouse, *Becoming Mr. Justice Blackmun* (New York: Times Books, 2005); David Savage, *Turning Right: The Making of the Rehnquist Supreme Court* (New York: Wiley, 1993).

178　*In Casey, though, the joint opinion:* Planned Parenthood of Southeastern Pennsylvania v. Casey, 505 U.S. 833, 876 (1992).

179　*In 2000, in* Stenberg v. Carhart: Stenberg v. Carhart, 530 U.S. 914 (2000).

179　"I am pleased": "Statement on the Supreme Court Decision on Partial Birth Abortion," June 28, 2000, United States: National Archives and Records Service, *Public Papers of the Presidents of the United States: Book Two: June 27–October 11, 2000: William J. Clinton* (Washington, D.C.: U.S. Government Printing Office, 2001), at 1335.

180　*He declared, for example:* "Statement on Senate Action on Legislation to Ban Partial-Birth Abortion," March 13, 2003, United States: National Archives and Records Service, *Public Papers of the Presidents of the United States: Book One: January 1–June 30, 2003: George W. Bush* (Washington, D.C.: U.S. Government Printing Office, 2001), at 263.

180　*Nonetheless, the Court in* Gonzales v. Carhart: Gonzales v. Carhart, 550 U.S. 124 (2007).

180　*Justice Kennedy said that the federal law:* Ibid. at 167–68.

181　*Justice Kennedy's majority opinion repeatedly referred:* Ibid. at 134, 151.

181　*He wrote, "[r]espect":* Ibid. at 159.

182　*A 1989 decision:* DeShaney v. Winnebago County Department of Social Services, 489 U.S. 189 (1989).

183　*The Supreme Court summarized:* Ibid. at 193.

183　*The Court declared:* Ibid. at 195.

184　*Justice Blackmun wrote a powerful dissent:* Ibid. at 213 (Blackmun, J., dissenting).

184　*On the evening of March 10, 1989:* Pinder v. Johnson, 54 F.3d 1169 (4th Cir. 1995) (en banc).

185　*One more recent example:* Town of Castle Rock, Colorado v. Gonzales 545 U.S. 748 (2005).

186　*As explained earlier, in 1997:* in Washington v. Glucksberg, 521 U.S. 702 (1997).

187　*For example, laws prohibiting interracial marriage:* Loving v. Virginia, 388 U.S. 1 (1967) (declaring unconstitutional state laws prohibiting interracial marriage).

187　*Judge Stephen Reinhardt:* Compassion in Dying v. State of Washington, 79 F.3d 790, 839 (9th Cir. 1996) (en banc).

188　*Judge Reinhardt wrote:* Ibid. at 839.

189　*In* Lawrence v. Texas: Lawrence v. Texas, 539 U.S. 558 (2003).

189　*In 1986, in* Bowers v. Hardwick: Bowers v. Hardwick, 478 U.S. 186 (1986).

189 *But seventeen years later, in* Lawrence v. Texas: Lawrence v. Texas, 539 U.S. 558 (2003).

190 *Justice Kennedy wrote eloquently:* Ibid. at 567.

191 *A federal court of appeals upheld an Alabama law:* Williams v. Attorney General of Alabama, 378 F.3d 1232 (11th Cir. 2004).

191 *The same federal court of appeals upheld a Florida law:* Lofton v. Secretary of Department of Children and Family Services, 377 F.3d 1275 (11th Cir. 2004).

191 *The Ohio Supreme Court:* State v. Lowe, 112 Ohio St.3d 507, 861 N.E.2d 512, 200 (2007).

192 *But that is the social reality:* District of Columbia v. Heller, 128 S.Ct. 2783 (2008).

192 *He stated:* Ibid. at 2817 n.27.

193 *The privacy decision, from 1989:* Michael H. v. Gerald D., 491 U.S. 110 (1989).

194 *A case that involved narrowing:* Garcetti v. Ceballos, 547 U.S. 410 (2006).

195 *The majority opinion by Justice Anthony Kennedy:* Ibid. at 421.

195 *The Court said that "[t]he inherent":* First National Bank of Boston v. Bellotti, 435 U.S. 765, 777 (1978).

196 *Several years ago, when I did a study:* Erwin Chemerinsky, "An Independent Analysis of the Los Angeles Police Department's Board of Inquiry Report on the Rampart Scandal," 34 *Loyola Los Angeles Law Review* 545 (2001).

197 *In a 1990 decision:* Austin v. Michigan Chamber of Commerce, 494 U.S. 652 (1990).

197 *In 2003, the Court reaffirmed:* McConnell v. Federal Election Commission, 540 U.S. 93 (2003).

197 *But on January 21, 2010, in* Citizens United: Citizens United v. Federal Election Commission, 130 S.Ct. 876 (2010).

6. CLOSING THE COURTHOUSE DOORS

201 *Vice President Dick Cheney:* The facts of this case are set out in Wilson v. Libby, 535 F.3d 697 (D.C. Cir. 2008), and 498 F.Supp.2d 74 (D.D.C. 2007). Also, they are recited in the Plaintiffs' Second Amended Complaint filed in Wilson v. Libby in the United States District Court for the District of Columbia.

202 *My attempt to gain Supreme Court review:* Certiorari denied, 129 S.Ct. 2825 (2009).

206 *titled her autobiography:* Valerie Plame Wilson, *Fair Game: My Life as a Spy, My Betrayal by the White House* (New York: Simon & Schuster, 2007).

207   *In 1971, in* Bivens v. Six Unknown: Bivens v. Six Unknown Named
      Federal Agents of Federal Bureau of Narcotics, 403 U.S. 388
      (1971).

208   *In the last two decades:* Schweiker v. Chilicky, 487 U.S. 412 (1988);
      Bush v. Lucas, 462 U.S. 367 (1983) (limiting *Bivens* suits).

208   *One of the most egregious examples:* United States v. Stanley, 483
      U.S. 669 (1987).

209   *After he dismissed our case:* Wilson v. Libby, 498 F.Supp.2d 74
      (D.D.C. 2007).

209   *Predictably, we lost 2–1:* Wilson v. Libby, 535 F.3d 697 (D.C. Cir.
      2008).

210   *Unfortunately, on June 22, 2009:* Wilson v. Libby, 129 S.Ct. 2825
      (2009).

211   *For example, in* Flast v. Cohen: Flast v. Cohen, 392 U.S. 83 (1968).

211   *In* Schlesinger: Schlesinger v. Reservists Committee to Stop the
      War, 418 U.S. 208 (1974).

212   *In another case, decided the same day:* United States v. Richardson,
      418 U.S. 166 (1974).

212   *Long ago, in 1803:* Marbury v. Madison 5 U.S. (1 Cranch) 137
      (1803).

212   *Just a few years ago, in* Hein: Hein v. Freedom from Religion Foun-
      dation, 551 U.S. 587 (1987).

213   *One of the most disturbing:* City of Los Angeles v. Lyons, 461 U.S. 95
      (1982).

214   *When asked why:* Quoted in James J. Fyfe, "The Los Angeles Choke-
      hold Controversy," 19 *Criminal Law Bulletin* 61, 63–64 (1983).

215   *For example, two federal district courts:* Jones v. Bowman, 664
      F.Supp. 433 (N.D. Ind. 1987); John Does 1–100 v. Boyd, 613 F.Supp.
      1514 (D.Minn. 1985).

216   *In 1957, the Supreme Court explained:* Conley v. Gibson, 355 U.S. 41
      (1957).

216   *The key case was* Ashcroft v. Iqbal: Ashcroft v. Iqbal, 129 S.Ct. 1937
      (2009).

217   *Senator Arlen Specter has introduced a bill:* Notice Pleading Restora-
      tion Act of 2009, S. 1504, 111th Cong. (2009) (as introduced in the
      Senate by Senator Specter, July 22, 2009).

218   *Michael Hason is a graduate:* Hason v. Medical Board of California,
      279 F.3d 1167 (9th Cir. 2002) (summarizing facts of the case).

219   *In 1996, in* Seminole Tribe of Florida v. Florida: 517 U.S. 44 (1996).

219   *In 1999, in* Florida Prepaid Postsecondary Education Board: Florida
      Prepaid Postsecondary Education Board v. College Savings Bank,
      527 U.S. 627 (1999).

220 *One of the most important decisions:* Alden v. Maine, 527 U.S. 706 (1999).

220 *In 2001, in* Kimel: Kimel v. Florida Board of Regents, 528 U.S. 62 (2000).

220 *A year later, in* Garrett: Board of Trustees of the University of Alabama v. Garrett, 531 U.S. 356 (2001).

220 *The principle of sovereign immunity:* See John V. Orth, *The Judicial Power of the United States: The Eleventh Amendment in American History* (New York: Oxford University Press, 1987), 195–97.

221 *Sovereign immunity undermines:* Marbury v. Madison, 5 U.S. (1 Cranch) 137 (1803).

222 *Yet, in* Alden v. Maine: Alden v. Maine, 527 U.S. 706 (1999).

222 *Justice Kennedy, writing for the majority, stated:* Ibid. at 728.

222 *In 1890, the Supreme Court:* Hans v. Louisiana, 134 U.S. 1 (1890).

223 *Justice Souter, after a detailed recounting:* Seminole Tribe of Florida v. Florida, 517 U.S. 44, 142–43 (1996) (Souter, J., dissenting).

224 *He wrote:* Alden v. Maine, 527 U.S. at 754–55.

224 *James Madison said: The Federalist*, No. 51 (James Madison) (New York: Buccaneer, 1992), at 262.

225 *I won Michael Hason's suit:* Hason v. Medical Board of California, 279 F.3d 1167 (9th Cir. 2002).

226 *In 2004, in* Tennessee: Tennessee v. Lane, 541 U.S. 509 (2004).

228 *Yale law professor Judith Resnik:* Judith Resnik, "Failing Faith: Adjudicatory Procedure in Decline," 53 *University of Chicago Law Review* 494 (1986); Judith Resnik, "Managerial Judges," 96 *Harvard Law Review* 374 (1982).

228 *Every study of the jury system:* See, e.g., Neil Vidmar and Valerie Hans, *American Juries: The Verdict* (New York: Prometheus, 2007) (comprehensively reviewing literature and studies).

228 *A key Supreme Court decision:* Circuit City Stores, Inc. v. Adams, 532 U.S. 105 (2001).

230 *In 2009, in* 14 Penn Plaza: 14 Penn Plaza LLC v. Pyett, 129 S.Ct. 1456 (2009).

231 *In the summer of 1992:* The facts are recited in Romo v. Ford Motor Co., 99 Cal.App.4th 1115, 122 Cal.Rptr.2d 139 (2002), and 113 Cal. App.4th 738, 6 Cal.Rptr.3d 793 (2003).

233 *In 1996, in* BMW v. Gore: BMW of North America v. Gore, 517 U.S. 559 (1996).

233 *After the jury:* State Farm Mut. Auto Ins. Co. v. Campbell, 538 U.S. 408 (2003).

235 *In its initial ruling:* Romo v. Ford Motor Co., 99 Cal.App.4th 1115, 122 Cal.Rptr.2d 139 (2002).

235   *Ten days after the oral argument:* Romo v. Ford Motor Co., 113 Cal. App.4th 738, 6 Cal.Rptr.3d 793 (2003).

235   *However, four years later:* Philip Morris USA v. Williams, 549 U.S. 346 (2007).

237   *Justice Souter, writing for the Court:* Exxon Shipping Co. v. Baker, 128 S.Ct. 2605 (2008).

238   *limiting the ability to sue federal officers:* Schweiker v. Chilicky, 487 U.S. 412 (1988); Bush v. Lucas, 462 U.S. 367 (1983) (limiting *Bivens* suits).

238   *The Court has also:* Buckhannon Board & Care Home, Inc. v. West Virginia Dept. of Health and Human Resources, 532 U.S. 598 (2001) (limiting attorneys fees); Alexander v. Sandoval, 532 U.S. 275 (2001) (limiting suits to enforce civil rights laws).

238   *The Prison Litigation Reform Act:* Prison Litigation Reform Act, 42 U.S.C. 1997(e).

238   *The Antiterrorism and Effective Death Penalty Act:* The Antiterrorism and Effective Death Penalty Act, Pub.L. No. 104–132, Title I, §104, 110 Stat. 1218.

CONCLUSION: RECLAIMING THE CONSTITUTION

241   *A few days later:* The decision of the trial court is unpublished, but is reviewed on appeal in Fladell v. Labarga, 775 So.2d 987 (2000).

241   *On the Monday after Thanksgiving:* For a detailed history of this litigation, see Jeffrey Toobin, *Too Close to Call: The Thirty-Six-Day Battle to Decide the 2000 Election* (New York: Random House, 2001).

243   *Justice Antonin Scalia released a short concurring opinion:* Bush v. Gore, 531 U.S. 1046 (2000).

244   *On Tuesday night, December 12:* Bush v. Gore, 531 U.S. 98 (2000).

245   *Justice Stevens stressed:* 531 U.S. at 126 (Stevens, J., dissenting).

247   *Justice Leander Shaw, in a concurring opinion:* Gore v. Harris, 773 So.2d 524, 538–29 (Fla. 2000).

248   Brown v. Board of Education: Brown v. Board of Education, 347 U.S. 483 (1954).

248   *After the federal courts refused:* DeLay issued a statement that "the time will come for the men responsible for this to answer for their behavior." See Mike Allen, "DeLay Wants Panel to Review Role of Courts: Democrats Criticize His Attack on Judges," *Washington Post,* April 2, 2005, at A9.

248   *At around the same time, Texas senator John Cornyn:* 151 Cong. Rec. S3113, 3126 (daily ed. April 4, 2005) (statement of Senator Cornyn).

249   *Nixon declared:* Thomas Keck, *The Most Activist Supreme Court in American History: The Road to Modern Judicial Conservatism* (Chicago: University of Chicago Press, 2004), at 107.

249   *"We've had too many":* "Reagan's Thoughts on Arms Talks, 'Star Wars,' " *Los Angeles Times,* June 24, 1986.

249   *When George H. W. Bush ran for president:* George H. W. Bush, Remarks Accepting the Presidential Nomination at the Republican National Convention in Houston, August 20, 1992.

249   *During a presidential debate:* Presidential debate at the University of California, Los Angeles, October 13, 1988, available at http://www.Presidency.ucsb.edu/we/print.php?pid=29412.

249   *In his acceptance speech at the 1992:* Bush, Remarks Accepting the Presidential Nomination.

249   *George W. Bush echoed the same themes:* Presidential debate in Boston, Massachusetts, October 3, 2000, available at http://www.presidency.ucsb.edu/ws/print.phhp?pid=29418.

249   *Bush said that:* Ibid.

249   *When President Bush nominated:* "President Announces Judge John Roberts as Supreme Court Nominee," *State Floor,* July 19, 2005.

249   *Similarly, in nominating Samuel Alito:* "President Nominates Judge Samuel A. Alito as Supreme Court Justice," *Cross Hall,* October 31, 2005.

249   *The 2008 Republican platform:* 2008 Republican Party Platform, http://www.gop.com/2008Platform.

250   *When John Roberts:* Confirmation Hearing on the Nomination of John G. Roberts, Jr., to be Chief Justice of the United States: Hearing Before Senate Committee on the Judiciary, 109th Cong. 55 (2005) (statement of John G. Roberts).

250   *The power of this conservative rhetoric:* "Sotomayor Pledges Fidelity to Law," CNN.com (July 13, 2009), http://www.cnn.com/2009/POLITICS/07/13/sotomayor.hearing/in dex.html.

250   *For example, as discussed in Chapter 5:* District of Columbia v. Heller, 128 S.Ct. 2783 (2008).

251   *Two quite conservative:* J. Harvie Wilkinson III, "Of Guns, Abortions, and the Unraveling Rule of Law," 95 *Virginia Law Review* 253 (2009); Richard A. Posner, *In Defense of Looseness: The Supreme Cour and Gun Control, New Republic,* Aug. 27, 2008, at 32.

251   *Another stunning example:* Citizens United v. Federal Election Commission, 130 S.Ct. 876 (2010).

253   *The conservative justices, albeit in dissent:* Boumediene v. Bush, 128 S.Ct. 2228 (2008).

254 *In 1997, I ran for election:* The story of the Los Angeles Charter Reform experience, including my role in it, is told in Raphael J. Sonenshein, *The City at Stake: Secession, Reform, and the Battle for Los Angeles* (Princeton, N.J.: Princeton University Press, 2004).

255 *Ultimately, the California Court of Appeal:* Woo v. Superior Court, 83 Cal.App.4th 967, 100 Cal.Rptr.2d 156 (2000).

256 *The most persuasive historical analysis:* Charles Fairman, "Does the Fourteenth Amendment Incorporate the Bill of Rights?," 2 *Stanford Law Review* 5 (1949).

256 *A particularly powerful example:* Brown v. Board of Education, 347 U.S. 483 (1954).

258 *In deciding whether colleges and universities:* Grutter v. Bollinger, 539 U.S. 306 (2003) (holding that colleges and universities have a compelling interest in having a diverse student body).

259 *yet opinion polls show:* "Poll: Americans Back Abortion Limits, Oppose Ban," CNN.com, Nov. 27, 2005, http://www.cnn.com/2005/US/11/27/abortion.poll/index.html.

260 *Through the nineteenth century, more than 20 percent:* Laurence H. Tribe, *God Save This Honorable Court* (New York: Random House, 1985).

260 *But increasingly the confirmation hearings:* Confirmation Hearing on the Nomination of John Roberts to be Chief Justice of the United States Supreme Court: Hearing Before the Senate Committee on the Judiciary, 108th Cong. (2005) (statement of Senator Biden, member, Senate Committee on the Judiciary).

262 *Thomas said this:* Clarence Thomas, "The Higher Law Background of the Privileges or Immunities Clause of the Fourteenth Amendment," 12 *Harvard Journal of Law and Public Policy* 63, 62 n.2 (1989); Clarence Thomas, "Civil Rights as a Principle Versus Civil Rights as an Interest," in David Bone, ed. *Assessing the Reagan Years* (Washington, D.C.: Cato Institute, 1988) 398–99; Lewis E. Lehrman, "The Declaration of Independence and the Right to Life," *American Spectator*, April 1987, at 21.

263 *Yale law professors Robert Post and Reva Siegel:* Robert Post and Reva Siegel, "Questioning Justice: Law and Politics in Judicial Confirmation Hearings," *Yale Law Journal* (The Pocket Part), Jan. 2006.

265 *I liken this for my students:* Jon Elster, "Imperfect Rationality, Ulysses and the Sirens," in his *Ulysses and the Sirens: Studies in Rationality and Irrationality* (New York: Cambridge University Press, 1979) (telling the story of Ulysses and the Sirens and applying it to constitutional law).

265   *Harvard law professor Laurence Tribe:* Laurence Tribe, *American Constitutional Law*, 2nd ed. (Mineola, N.Y.: Foundation Press, 1988), 11–12.

266   *In* Marbury v. Madison, 5 U.S. (1 Cranch) 103 (1803).

267   *Pulitzer Prize–winning author:* James MacGregor Burns, *Packing the Court* (New York: Penguin, 2009); Mark Tushnet, *Taking the Constitution Away from the Courts* (Princeton, N.J.: Princeton University Press, 1999).

INDEX